Other books have made the point that presuppositional apologetics is compatible with the use of evidences but few have shown practical ways of bringing these together. *The Certainty of the Faith* presents an "integrated" apologetic that uses many of the traditional types of arguments, as they are appropriate to different practical situations, always honoring the biblical teachings about how we come to know God. The author, Richard Ramsay, is well informed about modern culture, science, and philosophy, as well as biblical theology. The book is an excellent study tool, with graphics and questions for review and reflection.

John M. Frame, AB, BD, MA, MPhil, DD
Trimble Chair of Systematic Theology and Philosophy
Reformed Theological Seminary (Orlando)

Skepticism about what we can know, the means by which we can know anything, and whether we can attain certainty in any of these matters seems a permanent fixture in postmodern culture. *The Certainty of the Faith* offers an accessible introduction to Christian apologetics to those who desire to defend their faith in this difficult context. It juxtaposes the certainty accompanying God-centered reasoning over against the inadequacy of reasoning without God. Ramsay surveys the fluctuation between skepticism and certainty among Western thinkers and probes some of the enduring questions Christians must be prepared to answer. In addition, he outlines a strategy by which Christians can enter into dialogue and effectively challenge non-Christians to rethink their unbelief.

Andrew Hoffecker, BA, MDiv, PhD
Professor of Church History
Reformed Theological Seminary (Orlando)

I am delighted to know there is an outstanding resource like *The Certainty of the Faith* available for those who not only want to understand the Christian faith better but to explain and defend it in the most effective way possible in every kind of situation. Moreover, the rich analysis of various apologists from Augustine to Chesterton to Lewis to Francis Schaeffer is very helpful. I wish this had been available years ago.

Luder G. Whitlock Jr. , BA, MDiv, DMin, LittD, DD
Executive Director
The Trinity Forum

Richard Ramsay has given us a solid, reliable, and practical outlook on Christian apologetics. He goes directly to the central issues facing Christians as they share their faith with others in our day. I believe that God will use this book in the lives of many followers of Christ around the world.

Richard L. Pratt Jr., BA, MDiv, ThD
President and Founder
Third Millennium Ministries

Rich Ramsay addresses the primary crucial issue facing the church today. In my seminary experience in the 1970s, more than one professor addressed "the authority of Scripture," also more than once. Rich Ramsay brings this up again for another generation and from several different directions in his book about the certainty of the faith. I recommend it and will recommend it in the future to my students and friends.

Ron Smith, BA, MDiv, ThD
School of Biblical Studies
Youth With A Mission

In *The Certainty of the Faith*, Richard Ramsay draws on decades of cross-cultural ministry and mentoring experience to provide a practical introduction to apologetics in service to the gospel. Ramsay shows that obstacles to faith are not only intellectual but also emotional and, most profoundly, spiritual; and he affirms that only God's Spirit can give life to the dead and faith to the unbelieving. He therefore proposes a multi-pronged apologetic-evangelistic strategy that blends humility (concerning ourselves), confidence (concerning our God and his Word), and gentle respect (concerning our unbelieving friends). Those who want to present Christ's truth and grace persuasively and winsomely will find help here.

Dennis E. Johnson, BA, MDiv, ThM, PhD
Academic Dean and Professor of Practical Theology
Westminster Seminary California

Richard Ramsay has provided college students and, specifically, those who minister to college students, a useful and practical manual giving "honest answers to honest questions." This book does not simply say, "here are the answers and I dare you to think." It actually engages the reader in a warm and relational way. Richard does an excellent job of reviewing questions that unbelievers wrestle with, as well as giving believers examples of good questions to ask unbelievers. It is obvious that he writes from the presupposition that relationships are important. His love for people is evident. Students will read *The Certainty of the Faith* and want to have coffee with this guy!

Rod Mays, BA, MEd, DMin
National Coordinator
Reformed University Ministries

Here is a timely, intelligent, and practical book on presuppositional evangelism that will be of great use in many kinds of venues. At a time when evangelical faith is being attacked, even by self-proclaimed evangelicals, as an outmoded and dated expression of modernity, this book reminds evangelicalism that its ultimate source of authority and knowledge is not our own reason but the revealed Word of God. As such, *The Certainty of the Faith* is well suited for evangelism in our postmodern world.

Peter Jones, BA, BD, ThM, PhD
Director, Christian Witness to a Pagan Planet
Scholar-in-Residence and Adjunct Professor
Westminster Seminary California

Richard Ramsay's new book on Christian apologetics has many features that commend it. First, he offers a solid defense for defending the faith, and in the spirit of *reformata semper reformanda* he proposes "an integrated apologetics" that includes but goes beyond traditional presuppositional and classical methods of the Reformed tradition. Second, his brief but informative survey of Greek and modern philosophy shows how the journey of human thought in both periods ranges from certainty to doubt to struggle to despair and why, for theological reasons, it is ultimately characterized by a pessimistic "uncertainty." Third, Ramsay's helpful survey of a diversity of Christian apologists and apologetic methods from Augustine to Frame accents the epistemic certainty of the Christian faith that stands out in marked contrast to its philosophic competitors. Fourth, Ramsay's "DEFEND" approach—*Demonstrate interest in the person, Explain your faith, Furnish answers, Expose the presuppositions of the non-Christian, Navigate through the inconsistencies, Direct him to Christ*—is a persuasive method that proves to be effective in dealing with some of the most serious apologetic issues facing Christians and the church today. Finally, I like the fact that Ramsay personalizes his book with aspects of his own story, that he introduces his readers to thinkers outside of the North American orbit, that he employs illustrations from popular and high culture, and that he maintains a practical focus throughout his work. Whether *The Certainty of the Faith* is read by pastors, professors, pupils, or parishioners, not only will it be a helpful apologetic *and* evangelistic resource, it also will enable spiritually serious believers to attain "to all the wealth that comes from the full assurance of understanding, resulting in a true knowledge of God's mystery, that is, Christ Himself" (Col. 2: 2).

David K. Naugle, BA, ThM, ThD, PhD
Professor of Philosophy
Dallas Baptist University
Author of Worldview: The History of a Concept

Richard Ramsay has compiled a practical and thoughtful primer not only for students of apologetics but also for those of us seeking to communicate the gospel to an ever-increasingly secular world. Balancing reason and mystery, Ramsay never settles for simple answers to the complex. However, what he does do is make the complex understandable. He correctly cajoles us to become first and foremost listeners and question-askers. And he asks great questions! This book made me think. It challenged both my mind and my faith, and enlarged both.

Frank Ivey, BA, MA
Regional Director
Young Life Florida

In *The Certainty of the Faith*, Ramsay gives an interesting historical description of the philosophical search for certainty about the big questions of life. After reviewing various apologetic approaches to these questions, he rightly calls us to a posture of humble certainty in our defense of the faith by showing how truth is not anchored to us but to the living God. His apologetic approach is clear, sensitive, adaptive, and bold. It is practically applied in detail and honesty to some of the toughest questions we face about our faith. Good discussion questions at the end of each chapter enhance individual and small group learning. I recommend this book as a terrific aid to our evangelistic endeavors on campus.

Chris Keidel, BA MDiv
Area Director
InterVarsity Metro Philadelphia/Delaware

From ancient Greek philosophy to the postmodern generation, Richard Ramsay does a masterful job of showing us the way that humanity through the ages has dealt with the large questions of life. Ramsay paints with broad strokes the philosophical underpinnings of the great, ancient heroes of our Western culture and especially our Christian history. His ultimate aim, however, is to have us develop our own apologetic and to bring those around us into the kingdom. This relatively small volume gives us a great toolbox to help us understand our faith in a reasonable way and to articulate it to our modern contemporaries.

In my ministry, I work with young adults who often are struggling to articulate their faith and worldview in a culture that is increasingly post-Christian. Often, they feel inadequate when their faith is challenged by professors and peers. The material presented by Ramsay is so accessible, so readable, and makes philosophy and theology enjoyable and understandable to the average reader. *The Certainty of the Faith* is a volume that I will buy (by the case lot) to give to these dedicated disciples who want to share the depth of their faith with this generation.

James Bjork, BA, MDiv
Area Director
Young Life Flathead Valley, Montana

THE CERTAINTY OF THE FAITH

Apologetics in an Uncertain World

Richard B. Ramsay

P&R
PUBLISHING
P.O. BOX 817 • PHILLIPSBURG • NEW JERSEY 08865-0817

Italics within Scripture quotations indicate emphasis added.

Page design by P&R Publishing
Typesetting by Bits & Bytes, Inc.
Edited by John J. Hughes

Printed in the United States of America

Library of Congress Cataloging-in-Publication Data

Ramsay, Richard B., 1948-
The certainty of the faith : apologetics in an uncertain world / Richard B. Ramsay.
p. cm.
Includes bibliographical references and index.
ISBN 978-1-59638-065-3 (pbk.)
1. Apologetics. I. Title.
BT1103.R36 2007
239--dc22

2007043473

Dedicated to Nicolas and Melany.

We are very proud of you both!
We couldn't ask for a better son and daughter!
May the Lord strengthen you and help you
defend your faith in the challenging world of the university.

Angie, thank you for encouraging me by sharing your love for literature, philosophy, books and movies, and thank you for helping me keep it all practical!

Contents

Abbreviations

NASB	New American Standard Bible
NCV	New Century Version
NIV	New International Version
NT	New Testament
OT	Old Testament
PBS	Public Broadcasting Service
WCF	Westminster Confession of Faith

Preface

People are like houses. They have windows and doors around the walls of their hearts. Although a non-Christian may try to protect his house against the gospel message, when the Holy Spirit begins to work in his heart, a way into the house is opened. Instead of continually knocking on the same door, we should take time to walk around the house and seek an appropriate place to enter. It might be an intellectual question, a sense of uncertainty, a moment of spiritual reflection, or a personal tragedy. We may gain a person's confidence in a conversation over coffee, because of a compassionate gesture in a moment of grief, or through a lasting friendship.

Because everyone is unique, I believe evangelism should not be limited to one type of presentation. I like the probing questions of Evangelism Explosion—"If you died today, do you believe you would go to heaven? If you went before God and he asked you why he should let you into heaven, what would you answer?" These questions were especially helpful to me while I worked as a missionary in Chile. Generally speaking, there is a common belief among the people there in God and the Bible, though many do not understand that salvation is by grace through faith alone. However, when I tried these questions on my neighbor in Santiago, they completely failed. He simply answered, "Well, those questions don't mean anything to me at all, because I don't believe in God, and I don't believe in life after death!" The only open door we had with these neighbors was the fact that they loved our children. Children often break down heavy barriers.

The same applies to apologetics—the theological study of how we should defend the gospel. People frequently argue about which is the "right" approach to apologetics. Some highlight the use of evidences, others emphasize logical reasoning. Some appeal mainly to common sense, others refer especially to history. Although the presuppositional approach (which will be explained later in this book) was quite helpful to me, I think there is much to learn from other approaches to apologetics.

I would like to propose an "integrated apologetics," where we use every form of revelation and the best of various apologetic strategies, depending on the person and situation. When we face the ultimate questions, I believe we must renounce the unbelievers' sinful attempt to be independent from God, and we must cling to the absolute sovereign authority of God and the Scriptures. However, I also believe we should take advantage of the abundant evidence that surrounds us (general revelation) and that is within us (we are made in God's image). I believe "all truth is God's truth"[1]—that absolutely anything we consider within creation will point to God and that any thought that tries to deny God will inevitably lead to self-contradiction and uncertainty. If someone believes in evolution, and this impedes his faith in God, why not show him the evidence against this theory? If someone believes the Bible is full of contradictions, why not show him the complete coherence of the Scriptures? When used properly—and this is not always easy—all truth and any evidence should help us defend the gospel.

1. The source of this quotation is not clear. It has been attributed to Augustine—"Quentin J. Schultze," http://www.calvin.edu/~schu/ (July 25, 2006)—and to John Calvin—John Stahl, "Truth," http://www.asa3.org/archive/asa/199907/0004.html (July 25, 2006).

The fall of humanity affected the four fundamental relationships all people have—with God, with other people, with creation, and with ourselves. Because salvation restores all four of these relationships, an integrated apologetics should focus on all of them. We need to proclaim to the non-Christian what God says, let him hear the testimony of other people, show him the evidence in creation, and help him look inside himself to see the image of God. These four dimensions suggest the wisdom of using a variety of apologetic approaches.

Because the Holy Spirit works especially through the Scriptures to reveal the gospel, we must appeal especially to the teachings of the Bible as our most effective tool in the defense of the faith. Furthermore, Jesus Christ must be the center of our message. But God speaks through all of creation, and we should point to any and every form of revelation that might help the non-Christian come to faith.

My personal testimony will provide some of the background for this book. I grew up in a committed Christian home and attended a small church that was a vital part of our life. However, when I went to college I began to doubt everything I had been taught. I hope that my story of recovering faith in God, Jesus, and the Bible will add a personal touch to this study of apologetics. When I experienced my turnaround, I told the Lord I wanted to help others who were going through the same kind of spiritual despair that I had suffered. That's why I entered the ministry, and that's why I am writing this book; it is a partial fulfillment of that promise.

This book is not a practical manual on evangelism. Neither is it a philosophical treatise on apologetics. It aims somewhere in between. I would like to enable Christians to defend their faith more effectively by giving them some theoretical tools. First, I offer a *simplified overview* of Western philosophy—a sort of "X-ray" of non-Christian thinking. This overview shows how reasoning leads to uncertainty when God is not recognized as the source of all truth. Next, I provide an analysis of key Scripture passages that explain man's real problem. After that, I review some examples of popular apologetic approaches and arguments, surveying authors such as Thomas Aquinas, John Calvin, C. S. Lewis, Francis Schaeffer, Norman Geisler, Cornelius Van Til, Antonio Cruz, R. C. Sproul, John Frame, and others. Finally, I suggest ways to develop an apologetic mind-set that is prepared to look for the "open window" and to customize the most appropriate defense of the faith for that unique person in that particular moment.

ACKNOWLEDGMENTS

First, I would like to thank my former students in various countries who dialogued with me over the years as I taught them apologetics. Born in my classes in Chile, this book matured through subsequent classes in Cuba, Miami, Columbia, Kazakhstan, and Mexico. Thanks also to the staff and faculty of Universidad FLET and Miami International Seminary for the privilege of teaching these courses, to Mission to the World for allowing me to work with these organizations, and to the churches and individuals who support my wife, Angelica, and me as missionaries.

I am indebted in my thinking to all the apologists mentioned in chapters five and six, especially to Francis Schaeffer, Cornelius Van Til, and John Frame. It was a great privilege to study under these last two theologians. I also wish to thank Dr. Frame for taking time to read the manuscript and make helpful suggestions. Thanks also to Bryce Craig and the P&R staff for giving me the opportunity to publish the book.

I am deeply grateful for the careful editing of John Hughes. Many things would have been easily misunderstood without his enormously helpful insights and suggestions. He gave me a lot of work to do, but it was worth it!

Finally, I especially want to thank Angelica for her support and encouragement, and especially for her patience during the last few years as I worked on this book in off hours. Please forgive me for those moments when you found me a bit distant, staring off somewhere, lost in thought, as I mulled over the contents of this volume!

I pray that *The Certainty of the Faith: Apologetics in an Uncertain World* will be helpful to many, and that Christ will be honored by it.

PART 1

UNCERTAINTY IN NON-CHRISTIAN THOUGHT

For even though they knew God, they did not honor Him as God or give thanks, but they became futile in their speculations, and their foolish heart was darkened.

Romans 1:21

1

Why Do We Need Apologetics?

Always being ready to make a defense to everyone who asks. . . .
1 Peter 3:15

My Story

I dared to take "Introduction to Philosophy" my first semester of college. The first day the professor began class by asking a question: "How many of you believe in God?" Of about two hundred of us, only half raised a hand. Then the professor declared his intention for the course: "I hope that by the end of the semester, all of you will see there is no reason to believe in God." As we studied the traditional arguments for the existence of God, I began to realize that all of them could be questioned, and my faith began to wobble. When I talked with my brother, who was in the same class, neither of us dared to say exactly what we were thinking, and we would usually end our conversations with a half-hearted attempt to cover up our doubts by saying, "Well, I guess you just believe by faith." I took walks to think about it all: Does God really exist, or did everything develop through an evolutionary process? I tried it backwards also: Suppose God doesn't exist? Can you prove that he doesn't? If he doesn't exist, why should I be good instead of bad? Why am I here, anyway? I began to view my life as a page of scribbled, disorderly class notes with no heading.

One night on campus, I decided to lie down on the grass and look at the stars. There were thousands of them, sparkling like diamonds, and I sensed the endlessness of the universe as well as my smallness. Suddenly, I knew God was there. I began to pray and said, "Lord, I can't prove it with arguments, but I know you are there. Do whatever it takes to get me back on the right road." I felt like a derailed train that had been given a supernatural shove to put it back on the tracks. I walked home that night with a sense of joy and peace that I had never felt before. Not only did I know God was there, I knew God!

During the next two years, I seemed to be doing fine and growing spiritually stronger. My pastor taught me to study the Bible and to share my faith. Then I went to Germany for a junior year abroad program. There I had little Christian fellowship and troubling conversations with Jehovah's Witnesses. They made me doubt the divinity of Jesus. Furthermore, my brother had never recovered from the struggles of the philosophy class. In his letters, he was challenging my faith in the Bible. When I returned to the United States for my last year of college, I told my pastor I still was a Christian but that I wasn't sure about the Bible or the divinity of Jesus. He would read from the Bible to show that it was inspired, but I told him he was using a circular argument. How could he use the Bible to prove the Bible?

I knew that I was heading down a dark alley with no escape, and it was frightening. I was using Descartes' method of only accepting what I could not doubt. I still believed in God and would say to myself, "OK, God exists. Now what other truth can I build on that foundation?" But I was getting nowhere! I couldn't put any new bricks on top of the first one. In my spiritual pilgrimage, I began to read books by C. S. Lewis and Francis Schaeffer, whose book *The God Who Is There* was especially helpful. It helped me realize there were intelligent Christians who were trying to answer questions like the ones I had. I liked what Schaeffer had—a complete and coherent system of truth that was based on the Bible. I decided that truth was not something to build, one piece at time, but a complete package of truths that stand or fall together. I wasn't totally convinced yet, but at least I *wanted* to believe in the Bible.

I decided to go to seminary. I couldn't go on without some important answers. I had seen some books by Cornelius Van Til, and I wanted to study where he was teaching. When I visited Westminster Theological Seminary in Philadelphia, one of the students told me that his studies with Van Til had made him so sure of his faith that he would be willing to talk to anyone about the gospel, even the most intelligent philosopher on earth! I thought to myself, "Wow! That's the way I want to feel!"

I confess that my first classes with Van Til were disappointing. He seemed old, and he repeated himself a lot. Every day he would draw two circles on the chalkboard—one to represent God and the other to represent the creation. Finally, I realized why he was repeating himself so much. It wasn't because he was so old but because we had to hear his basic points ten times to begin to understand them! His explanation of Adam and Eve in the garden of Eden definitely broke through my stubborn heart and mind. He said, here they were, mere creatures of the almighty Sovereign God, asking themselves, "I wonder . . . I wonder . . . I wonder if God is right, or if this serpent is right!" They had no right to question God! Who did they think they were! This was the beginning of the fall. It was their arrogant pretension that they could set themselves up as judges of the truth, even over God himself, that wrecked everything. "Wow! That's exactly what I am doing," I thought to myself. Who am I to wonder if God's Word is true? By what standard do I judge him? Again, instead of finding a clever argument to convince me, I needed a spiritual awakening. I needed to repent! I asked the Lord to forgive me, and I told him that I would accept whatever he told me. I remember thinking, "If God tells me the moon is green cheese, then the moon is green cheese! I'll just have to change my thinking about the moon, about the color green, and about cheese!" Of course, God will never make a statement that so clearly contradicts our normal use of language, reason, and observation, but this idea expressed my new attitude of absolute submission to him.

That insight and its accompanying experience were similar to a second conversion. Not only did my heart belong to God, now my mind did, too. I can't tell you how important this change was for me. I felt I had been pulled out of the quicksand in which I was sinking and set on a rock. As David said:

> He brought me up out of the pit of destruction, out of the miry clay;
> And He set my feet upon a rock making my footsteps firm. (Ps. 40:2)

What Is Apologetics?

I tell my story partly to make apologetics more practical and partly to show that our apologetic task is not simply to give the right logical argument. Our doubts are caused as much by spiritual issues as they are by intellectual ones. If this is so, why bother with another book on apologetics? Precisely because I want to clarify the relationship between these two struggles—the intellectual and the spiritual. I am going to propose an apologetic that integrates important aspects of our evangelistic approach, instead of focusing solely on the intellectual dimension.

The first thing we should recognize with regard to apologetics is that we cannot convince anyone to become a Christian by intellectual argument alone. If we simply argued people into agreeing with us about the postulates of the Christian faith, they would not necessarily be saved. In order to be saved, you must put your personal faith in Jesus Christ as Lord and Savior. This means trusting Jesus with your eternal life. Although it definitely must include intellectual assent to the truth, saving faith is much more than that; it is a *personal commitment*. After all, doesn't Satan "know," in a purely *intellectual* sense, the basic truths of the gospel (James 2:19)? But he is not saved because he lacks a *personal commitment* to Jesus Christ. In fact, he *hates* Jesus! Paul tells the Corinthians that he did not come to them with persuasive words of wisdom but that he preached Jesus Christ crucified. Why? So that their faith would not rest on the wisdom of men but on the power of God.

> And when I came to you, brethren, I did not come with superiority of speech or of wisdom, proclaiming to you the testimony of God. For I determined to know nothing among you except Jesus Christ, and Him crucified. I was with you in weakness and in fear and in much trembling, and my message and my preaching were not in persuasive words of wisdom, but in demonstration of the Spirit and of power, so that your faith would not rest on the wisdom of men, but on the power of God. (1 Cor. 2:1–5)

Man's most basic problem is spiritual, not intellectual. Nevertheless, this does not mean that intellectual reasoning has no place in apologetics. The non-Christian has built up defensive walls that include arguments and reasoning. Part of our job is to break down these barriers. As long as we keep our feet firmly planted in the Scriptures, we should be willing to dialogue about anything with the non-Christian in order to help him see the truth. Without compromising our position, we can try to understand his thinking, try to persuade him of his error, and try to show the beauty and consistency of the gospel. Paul used the Scriptures to "reason" with the Jews about the resurrection.

> And according to Paul's custom, he went to them, and for three Sabbaths reasoned with them from the Scriptures, explaining and giving evidence that the Christ had to suffer and rise again from the dead, and saying, "This Jesus whom I am proclaiming to you is the Christ." (Acts 17:2–3. See also Acts 17:17.)

Peter exhorts us to be ready to give a "defense" or an "answer" (NIV) to everyone who asks us why we believe. The Greek word is *apologia*, from which we get our term *apologetics*.

> But sanctify Christ as Lord in your hearts, always being ready to make a defense to everyone who asks you to give an account for the hope that is in you, yet with gentleness and reverence. (1 Peter 3:15)

Some people need a heavy dose of apologetic arguments to help bring them to Christ. For example, author Nancy Pearcey tells that her conversion came only after having "all her own ideas shot down." She says, "The only step that remained was to acknowledge that I had been persuaded—and then to give my life to the Lord of Truth."[1]

We can define apologetics as the "defense of the faith," as long as we realize that a good "defense" of the gospel also includes a good "offense." That is, we also need to show the non-Christian the errors and inconsistencies in his or her thinking. Our goal is to take "captive" every thought for Christ. As Paul says:

> We are destroying speculations and every lofty thing raised up against the knowledge of God, and we are taking every thought captive to the obedience of Christ. (2 Cor. 10:5)

1. Nancy R. Pearcey, *Total Truth: Liberating Christianity from its Cultural Captivity* (Wheaton, IL: Crossway Books, 2005), 55.

Becoming a Christian is primarily a matter of spiritual renewal—giving our hearts to Christ, but it also includes surrendering our minds to the Lord. It is the Holy Spirit who sovereignly brings about this change in both areas. The spiritual change involves intellectual change, and the intellectual change demands spiritual change. The two are inseparable.

> And do not be conformed to this world, but be transformed by the renewing of your mind, so that you may prove what the will of God is, that which is good and acceptable and perfect. (Rom. 12:2)

We should never separate apologetics from the gospel. In fact, apologetics is an essential aspect of evangelism.

We have a big task at hand. We need to understand non-Christian thinking; we need to discover scriptural principles about apologetics; we need to learn the best ways to present and defend the gospel; and we need to discern the unique shape of our message for each individual. That's apologetics.

The Present Opportunity

Although our postmodern age is challenging, it presents a unique opportunity. People are facing an uneasy life—often without hope in an absolute truth and often disoriented about right and wrong. Although people may seem reluctant to make a commitment, they have a sincere interest in spiritual things, and both ethical issues and personal relationships are very important to them.

The songs of a popular group called "System of a Down," as well as the comments of their fans, may help us understand the current mind-set of many people.[2] Some of their lyrics are

2. The lyrics and comments made about System of a Down by their fans (which differ greatly in their interpretations) can be found at: http://www.songfacts.com/search_fact.php?artistsearch=System%20Of%20A%20Down.

angry shouts of protest against social problems, such as war and genocide. They especially want to remind the world of the Armenian genocide that occurred between 1915 and 1923, since their grandparents had to witness the death of many of their own family members at the hand of the Turks.[3]

We detect a typical postmodern disillusion with technology and a growing interest in spiritual things in songs like "Science."

> Science fails to recognize the single most
> Potent element of human existence
> Letting the reins go to the unfolding
> Is faith, faith, faith, faith.
> Science, has failed, our world
> Science has failed our Mother Earth.
> Spirit-moves-through-all-things
> Spirit-moves-through-all-things.

According to one observer, the title of the song "Chop Suey" describes the group's musical style, because it has "lots of stuff thrown together." It is hard to make sense of some lyrics. Try to decipher the message of one of their most popular songs, "Toxicity."

> Conversion, software version 7.0,
> Looking at life through the eyes of a tire hub,
> Eating seeds as a past time activity,
> The toxicity of our city, of our city,
> Now, what do you own the world?
> How do you own disorder, disorder,
> Now, somewhere between the sacred silence,
> Sacred silence and sleep,
> Somewhere, between the sacred silence and sleep,
> Disorder, disorder, disorder. . . .

The individual phrases make sense. They seem to be focusing on some kind of corruption or pollution, but to me, the over-

3. System of a Down helped produce a video about this called "Screamers," first broadcast in January 1, 2006. I saw it on the SCINE channel, September 24, 2007.

all structure appears fragmented. According to one fan, group member Daron Malakian stated that the song was about ADD (Attention Deficit Disorder).[4] It is risky to try to interpret someone else's song, but I wonder if they are expressing their sense of disorder (either as seen in the cruel atrocities their family members witnessed, in the corruption of the drug world, in life in general, or as a person with ADD might perceive things) by making the very structure of the song itself disorderly.

According to some comments they appear to have made, System of a Down is quite tolerant about how people interpret their songs. Group member Serj Tankian is quoted as saying, "I've had people come up to me with the strangest interpretations of what lyrics might mean, and I'm like, 'You go! I never thought of that, but that works.' . . . I think true art is a universal reflection, and true artists are just messengers of that reflection—or, at best, skilled presenters."[5]

It is not always easy to communicate our message to this present generation, because many people may not give a high priority to coherency and absolute truth. However, deep down they must sense there is order and meaning to life. Furthermore, many really care about what happens to the world, and they have an unusual interest in spiritual things. We need to listen to them with respect, develop sincere friendships with them, help them struggle with social problems, and share our hope with them.

4. See: http://en.wikipedia.org/wiki/Toxicity_%28song%29 (September 19, 2007).

5. See: http://thinkexist.com/quotes/serj_tankian/ (September 21, 2007). According to several fans, Malakian has commented that the song "Aerials" is about "nothing." Another fan claims that the same member confessed that none of the group had any idea what the song "Vicinity of Obscenity" meant, that they were just "having fun." See http://en.wikipedia.org/wiki/Toxicity_%28song%29 (September 19, 2007). Apparently, the name of the group was chosen because of how it sounds, rather than because of some special meaning. See http://en.wikipedia.org/wiki/System_of_a_Down (September 19, 2007).

One of the most terrifying paintings I have seen is called *Head VI* by Francis Bacon (1909–92), painted in 1949.[6] I refer to it all the time because it graphically reflects postmodern despair.

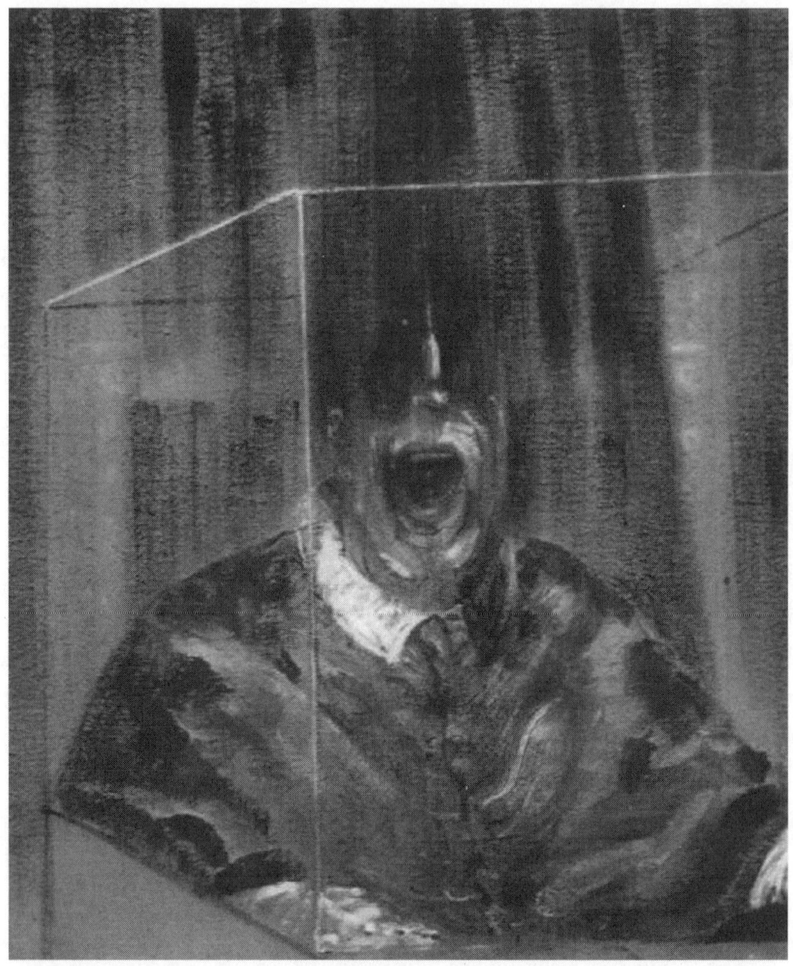

It shows a man dressed in religious garb, sitting as if he were being exhibited in a glass box. His head is disappearing, and there is hardly anything above his nose, except for the eye cavities and black smears. The only part of his head you can see clearly is his

6. http://www.francis-bacon.cx/figures/headvi.html (May 19, 2005).

mouth, which is open in a chilling scream. I cannot pretend to know what the artist himself meant to communicate with this painting, but to me it represents the feelings of fear, being boxed in, and losing your mind.[7] Bacon himself once wrote, "Man is aware that he is an accident, that he is a completely futile being, and that he must finish the game without reason."[8] Don't you think people like Francis Bacon would be willing to listen to our encouraging message that we are not really just an accident?

Hard Questions People Ask

Here are some of the most common questions I hear people ask. When I teach classes on apologetics, I ask the students what hard questions people throw at them. They usually mention the same ones. Keep these questions in mind. We will come back to them, and later in the book I will suggest ways to answer them.

- How can you prove God exists?
- How can you be sure the Bible is true? What about the apparent contradictions and errors?
- What about other religions? How can you be sure they are not legitimate, too?
- What about the theory of evolution? Doesn't it prove the Bible is wrong?
- How can a good God condemn people?
- If God is good and all-powerful, why does he allow evil?

7. Tate Gallery, London, wrote the following comments about this picture for an exhibition in 1962: "The earliest of Bacon's paintings of Popes, this combines a number of themes which were to recur in many of his later works: the framework around the figure, like a glass box; the tassel; the paraphrase of Valasquez's portrait of Pope Innocent X; and the screaming mouth derived from the close-up of the nurse from [the film] Battleship Potemkin." See http://www.francis-bacon.cx/figures/headvi.html (September 20, 2007).

8. H. R. Rookmaaker, *Modern Art and the Death of a Culture* (Downers Grove, IL: InterVarsity Press, 1970), 174.

I believe the toughest issue the apologist faces is the question of evil. Here our battle can become bloody; we need to be prepared.

Recently, I watched a fascinating program on television (PBS) called "The Question of God." Dr. Armond Nicoli, a Harvard professor, gathered a group of intellectuals with diverse beliefs to discuss the lives of C. S. Lewis and Sigmund Freud—one believed in God, one did not. The group was analyzing the way faith (or the lack of it) affected both men. One of the representatives did a great job of representing the Christian position, until he came to the question of suffering. At that point, he surrendered absolutely to the atheists, saying he had no answer and that the question troubled him deeply. Immediately, the representative from *Skeptic Magazine* jumped on the opportunity to ridicule him by saying he should become an atheist, because atheists don't have to struggle with this problem.

The web site "Losing My Religion,"[9] which is managed by people who say they used to be Christians, challenges Christians to debate difficult questions.[10] The harsh attitudes and weak responses of some Christians there have disappointed me; I would like to see us do a better job of apologetics.

If you can tolerate offensive language, read these lines from a dialogue between Darcy West of "Losing My Religion" and a Christian named Roger.[11] Darcy, while dealing with the subject of hell, tries to make God sound like a hateful and perverted father or a tyrant like Hitler.

> Darcy West: Roger, what would you think of a father who said to his child, "Love me by the time you are six, or I will bake

9. http://www.losingmyreligion.com/ (May 19, 2005).

10. I believe a person who truly has been born again never will totally lose his or her faith, though he or she may fall away for a time.

11. Darcy West, "Heaven and Hell: Interview One," http://www.losingmyreligion.com/ (May 19, 2005).

you in the oven."?

Roger: Darcy, God doesn't say that . . . he says, "Here's the way out of hell, PLEASE TAKE IT."

Darcy West: Are you suggesting that hell exists outside of God's control?

Roger: What do you think?

Darcy West: If hell is not a danger that exists outside of God's control, then the analogy you used does not work. In your analogy, you portray God as trying to protect his child against a danger over which he has no control. Yet, in the case of the biblegod, hell is a danger which he created. It would be as if a parent said, "Don't go into the street or you will be hit by a car." Then, when the child goes into the street, the parent jumps in a bus and runs the child over. If the parent then says, "Well, he made his choice," would you believe that the parent did the right thing?

Roger: Darcy, hell was created for Satan and his demons, not for humans.

Darcy West: Roger, the abusive parent bought the oven to bake cookies. However, if he uses it to bake his children, does that remove his guilt?

This dialogue ends with Roger giving in to Darcy's argument, admitting that it would be better not to bow down to such a tyrant. Darcy felt victorious:

Darcy West: Who do you feel is more worthy of respect. . . . a man who worships Hitler to avoid being sent to the ovens, or the man who refuses to bow to Hitler, regardless of the price.

Roger: Darcy, the man who refuses.

Darcy West: Roger, thank you very much.

Would you like to develop an apologetic understanding that would help you in situations like this? If so, I trust this book will not disappoint you.

GROUP EXERCISE

Look at the painting *Head VI*, by Francis Bacon (back a few pages in this chapter) and discuss what you see. Mention details and talk about what they mean. Discuss how this painting helps us understand people today.

REVIEW QUESTIONS

1. What is the illustration used to represent the non-Christian in the preface to this book?
2. In what ways should apologetics be "integrated"?
3. Which kind of revelation should have the priority in apologetics?
4. What was the author's "second conversion"?
5. Why is a person not saved when he has only intellectually accepted the postulates of the Christian faith?
6. What is man's greatest impediment to becoming a Christian?
7. Why does reasoning have a place in apologetics?
8. What is the origin of the term *apologetics*?
9. Write out 1 Peter 3:15.
10. How can we define *apologetics*?
11. What can we learn from the painting *Head VI,* by Francis Bacon?

QUESTIONS FOR REFLECTION

1. Why do you think it is important to study apologetics?
2. What were the most important factors leading to your own conversion?
3. Which of the six questions mentioned in this chapter do you frequently hear from non-Christians?
4. What is your opinion about the dialogue between Darcy

and Roger? What suggestions would you give Roger?

5. What do you think we can learn about contemporary people from the lyrics of the songs by System of a Down? What does this teach us about defending the gospel today? Do we face a greater challenge or a greater opportunity than previous generations?

2

THE LINE OF UNCERTAINTY IN GREEK PHILOSOPHY

INTRODUCTION

Why study philosophy? Because it gives us an X-ray of how non-Christians think. This study may seem unnecessary at first to some readers, but you will be surprised at how it will help you identify the underlying presuppositions of non-Christians. It is especially revealing and useful to discover the sources of uncertainty in non-Christian thought. If philosophy is not one of your favorite subjects, please be patient and try to follow these two chapters carefully. If you do, in the succeeding chapters you will see their practical importance as we draw conclusions about man and develop a solid defense of our faith.

Previously, I believed philosophers were certain of their beliefs. Now I realize it is their struggle with uncertainty that drives them to philosophize. In these two chapters, I present a *simplified overview* of Western philosophy that traces the general pattern of this struggle.

I believe we can locate philosophers somewhere along a *line of uncertainty*. This line follows a chronological order and describes the vacillation between believing you know something and being skeptical about knowledge.[1]

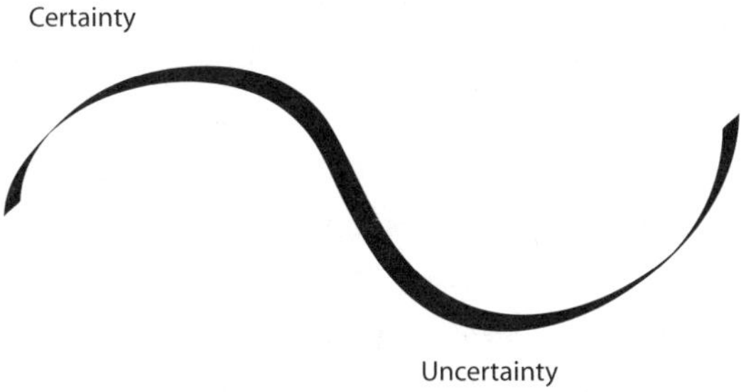

Human experience is more complex than this diagram. Beginning with certainty, philosophers experience doubt and end in a low of despair and uncertainty. However, it is too painful to live without meaning, so they struggle to escape; they seek a way to be sure of something. Finally, they seem to accept uncertainty and lose interest in the deeper questions of philosophy, while, curiously, beginning to concentrate on ethics.

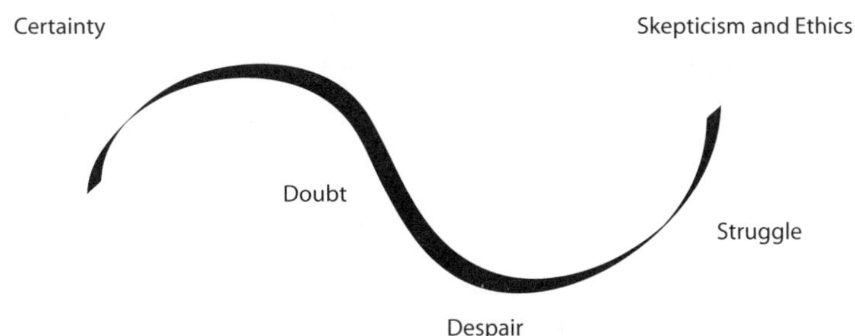

Philosophy is usually divided into three fields—ontology (the study of being, also known as "metaphysics"), epistemology (the study of knowing), and ethics (the study of right and wrong). Ontology asks: What is the nature of things? Epistemol-

1. Francis Schaeffer speaks of the "line of despair" in modern thought. See his *The God Who Is There* (Downers Grove, IL: InterVarsity Press, 1998). Although my "line of uncertainty" is quite different, I recognize that his concept helped me think of it and that I have been heavily influenced by him.

ogy asks: How do we know the truth? Ethics asks: How do we know what is right and wrong? These two chapters will focus on epistemology and ontology.

As we study philosophy, we find reflections of God's revealed truth, but we also see how his truth has been distorted. Frequently, the history of philosophy is taught as if knowledge developed through a positive process, as if the human race grew in its understanding over time. For example, someone might assume that early man did not believe in God, that he then developed the idea of many gods, then one God, and finally realized he did not need God, after all. This concept fits an evolutionary scheme. However, the Bible gives us a different picture. It teaches that the one and only true God has revealed himself from the very beginning and that man has borrowed and often distorted this revelation. Because of common grace,[2] many philosophers and religious leaders have discovered various aspects of God's truth—for example, a sense of morality, a sense of guilt, a sense of a supreme being, and a sense of eternity. However, their presuppositions and their observations are out of focus. As we examine the Greek philosophers, we will see residues of God's truth and how these philosophers twisted it.[3]

Three Problems in Knowing

Greek philosophy struggled with the problem of what constitutes reality (ontology), especially as this relates to knowing (epistemology). To illustrate the three main problems with knowing, let's analyze the problems related to our knowledge of an apple.

2. *Common grace* is a theological term that refers to God's kindness toward all people, even non-Christians. People do not simply discover truth on their own, and God graciously allows even non-Christians to understand some things properly.

3. This review of philosophy is greatly simplified for the purpose of helping Christians get a grasp of the main issues. For a more complete study of philosophy, I recommend the literature in the bibliography at the end of this book, especially by Frederick Copleston, Frank Thilly, Gordon Clark, and Colin Brown.

First, there are an infinite number of details related to an individual apple. We cannot possibly know them all, since our minds are limited. For example, what color is an apple? How does this particular apple I am holding differ from an orange? How are apples cultivated? What is an apple tree like? How tall do they get? Where do apple trees grow? When is apple season in these countries? Do the apples from Chile taste different from those in Washington State? We may not know the answers to all these questions, but we could find out, even if it took a long time. However, we can think of other apple-related questions that most likely we could not answer in a whole lifetime; for example, are there apples on some other planet? In fact, to make a *complete* description of the apple, we would have to explain how the apple is related to *everything* else that exists; for example, animals and insects that may eat the apple, sugar that comes from it, the biological process of how the apple tree grows, the sun, water, minerals, and so on. Once we think about it, we realize that we don't really know much about the apple, after all. Finally, there are other questions we simply cannot answer at all; for example, how many apples existed on earth in the year 4,000 BC? Consequently, we lose confidence regarding our knowledge of apples. How do I know there is not an unknown fact that makes my present understanding incorrect?

Second, everything changes, and this leaves me uncertain of what I can know.[4] How do I know what the apple will look like tomorrow? How can I know what it will taste like tomorrow? Will it even exist tomorrow? Will there still be apples on the earth two thousand years from now? What happens to the apple when I eat it? Does it still exist? When does it stop being an apple? These changes are disconcerting and force us to look

4. This is technically a subdivision of the first problem, since it presents us with one more vast ocean of things we don't know. But it deserves special attention, since it often comes up in the history of philosophy.

behind the particular items to find something universal that does not change.

I remember a disturbing physics class when I was a senior in high school. The teacher was talking about relativity, and I remember wondering: If the whole universe suddenly shrank to half its size, and yet everything kept its proportion, would we even notice it? It frightened me, because it made me feel uncertain. However, God quickly reminded me that he is there, and he would know if everything shrank. That thought comforted me immensely.

But if I do not have God in my world, I look for something else that is stable behind the changes. I look for something comprehensible behind the confusion of infinite details.

As I focus on the unity of all things, it leads to a third problem: If I take God out of the picture and if the universe is fundamentally impersonal and mechanistic, then man loses his freedom and his thoughts lose their significance. I become part of a huge impersonal organism or machine, and everything I do or say is determined by natural mechanisms. My thoughts mean no more than the ticking of a clock or the flow of a chemical reaction. I am trapped inside a box, like the terrified man in Bacon's painting. Without God, my thoughts are deterministic and meaningless: "The brain secretes thoughts as the liver secretes bile," as the French philosopher Cabanis said.[5]

5. Cabanis, quoted in James Sire, *The Universe Next Door* (Downers Grove, IL: InterVarsity Press, 1997), 98. However, Sire does not give the original source or the full name. He is probably quoting Pierre-Jean-George Cabanis, a French philosopher, from an article written in 1802, "Rapports du physique et du moral de l'homme" ("Relations of the Physical and the Moral in Man"). See "Cabanis, Pierre-Jean-George," *The New Encyclopædia Britannica*, 15th ed., vol. 2 (Chicago: Encyclopædia Britannica, Inc., 2003), s.v. See also L. G. Crocker, "Cabanis, Pierre-Jean-George," *Encyclopedia of Philosophy*, 2nd ed., ed. Donald M. Borchert (Detroit: Thomson Gale, 2006), vol. 2, s.v.

The Downward Spin in the Early Greeks

Thales (585–548)

Considered "the first philosopher of Greece,"[6] Thales sought the universal reality. He is known for his postulate that everything is *water*. How could he think something so ridiculous? We have to keep in mind the lack of scientific knowledge at the time. To be fair, when you consider that water can become vapor and that when heated enough everything can be melted and converted into gas, then you can understand why someone might think that all vapor is basically the same and that everything has one common essence—water.

Notice this: Thales thought he truly *knew* something. Other Greek philosophers believed that everything—the basic reality—was the atom, or numbers, or reason, or that there were four elements (air, water, earth, and fire). But at least they affirmed *something*. The main topic of discussion among these early Greek philosophers concerned what everything is made of, not how we can know anything with certainty.

Heraclitus (535–475)

According to Heraclitus, everything is in flux, and everything is one.

> You cannot step twice in the same river, for fresh waters are ever flowing in upon you.
>
> All things are one.
>
> Good and ill are one.

6. Frank Thilly, *A History of Philosophy* (New York: Henry Holt and Company, 1914), 23.

> To God all things are fair and good and right, but men hold some things wrong and some right.[7]

For Heraclitus, life is like a flowing river; everything changes from one moment to another. Apparent contrasts are really in harmony. Notice that even the distinction between right and wrong supposedly disappears in God's sight. Thus, Heraclitus opened the door to doubt and uncertainty.

Protagoras (500 or 480–420)

Agreeing with Heraclitus, Protagoras proposed that truth is relative, that every opinion is true. What is "cold" for one person may be "hot" for another. According to Protagoras:

> Man is the measure of all things.

In fact, you can agree with two contradictory statements. If I have one eye closed and another open, I can truthfully say both that "I see" and that "I do not see."[8] With this concept of relativity, we lose absolute truth and certainty of knowledge. When speaking of the gods, Protagoras admits:

> With regard to the gods, I cannot feel sure either that they are or that they are not, nor what they are like in figure; for there are many things that hinder sure knowledge.[9]

Gorgias (483–375)

Gorgias concluded that knowledge is impossible. His thoughts are summarized as follows:

7. "The Heraclitus Fragments," http://members.aol.com/cyberstoic/Heracliteans/heraclitus.html (July 25, 2006). See also Herbert Granger, "Heraclitus of Ephesus," *Encyclopedia of Philosophy*, ed. Borchert, vol. 4, s.v.

8. Gordon Clark, *Thales to Dewey* (Boston: Houghton Mifflin Company, 1979, 61–70.

9. Frederick Copleston, *A History of Philosophy* (Garden City, NY: Image Books, 1962), 1.110.

1. Nothing exists.
2. If something did exist, it could not be known.
3. If something could be known, it could not be communicated.[10]

Cratylus

The belief that knowledge and communication are impossible leads to despair and destroys the desire to even try. A disciple of Heraclitus named Cratylus decided to live consistently with this conclusion, and so he stopped talking![11]

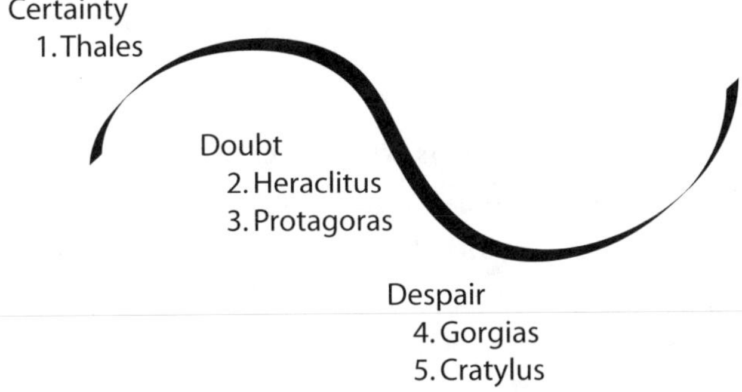

The Greek Giants

We come now to three of the greatest Greek philosophers: Socrates, Plato, and Aristotle. They all represented hope for true knowledge—one by means of dialogue, another through mystical experience, and the third by logic.

10. Rachel Barney, "Georgias of Leontini," *Encylopedia of Philosophy*, ed. Borchert, vol. 4, s.v.

11. G. B. Kerferd, "Cratylus," *Encyclopedia of Philosophy*, s.v. See also Humberto Giannini, *Esbozo para una Historia de la Filosofía* (Santiago, Chile: Talleres Vera y Giannini, 1981), 34. Cratylus was not totally consistent with his refusal to communicate, because he made signs with his hands.

Socrates (469–399)

One of the most famous sayings attributed to Socrates is "I only know that I know nothing."[12] For Socrates, the "wise" person is the one who knows he does not know. However, this is just the starting point of Socrates' reasoning, not its end. He believed man could discover truth in dialogue with others. As we recognize our ignorance, we clear our mind of incorrect notions, then test and rebuild our views on a firmer foundation.[13] He did not pretend to construct a system of philosophy. His goal was to motivate love for truth and virtue. He was more interested in practical moral issues than in speculation about metaphysics.[14]

Plato (429–347)

According to Plato, *ideas* are true reality, and they exist independently from the human mind. What we see and observe are only shadows of that reality. Man's soul, not his body, is his real essence. Plato believed our souls existed previously and inhabit our bodies at birth. As evidence for this, Plato focused on the soul's ability to "remember" ideas from its previous existence. For example, supposedly a person does not acquire the abstract notion of *equality* in this present life but is born with it. Thus learning is "recollecting."[15]

12. Some have questioned this quote, since it cannot be found in Plato's writings but only in later reports. See C. C. W. Taylor, "Socrates," *Encyclopedia of Philosophy*, ed. Borchert, vol. 9, s.v. However, the following sources confirm the quote. Richard Popkin, "Skepticism, History of," *Encyclopedia of Philosophy*, ed. Borchert, vol. 9, s.v.; Will Durant, *The Story of Philosophy* (New York: Simon and Schuster, 2005), 8; and *The Oxford Dictionary of Quotations*, 4th ed. (Oxford: Oxford University Press, 1992), 654.

13. Scholars discuss the difficulty of knowing what Socrates believed. He wrote nothing; we are dependent on the reports of others, especially Plato and Aristotle. In Plato's dialogues, it is not clear whether Plato put his own ideas in Socrates' mouth or whether he was expressing Socrates' ideas. See Copleston, *A History of Philosophy*, 1.1.120–24.

14. Thilly, *History of Philosophy*, 65–68.

15. This idea is attributed to Socrates in Plato's dialogues. See *Phaedo, Great Books of the Western World*, ed. Robert Maynard Hutchins (Chicago: Encyclopaedia Britannica, Inc., 1952) 7.182–83, 228.

Plato's "Allegory of the Cave" describes how we can know the truth by means of a mystical experience. In the story, he described how some men are chained in a cave, watching shadows on the wall. They think the shadows are reality because they know nothing else. However, when one leaves the dark cave and comes into the light, he realizes that the real world is outside, not in the cave.

> At first, when any of them is liberated and compelled suddenly to stand up and turn his neck round and walk and look towards the light, he will suffer sharp pains; the glare will distress him, and he will be unable to see the realities of which in his former state he had seen the shadows; and then conceive some one saying to him, that what he saw before was an illusion, but that now, when he is approaching nearer to being and his eye is turned towards more real existence, he has a clearer vision, what will be his reply? And you may further imagine that his instructor is pointing to the objects as they pass and requiring him to name them, will he not be perplexed? Will he not fancy that the shadows which he formerly saw are truer than the objects which are now shown to him?
>
> You will not misapprehend me if you interpret the journey upwards to be the ascent of the soul into the intellectual world according to my poor belief, which, at your desire, I have expressed whether rightly or wrongly God knows.[16]

We can detect a residue of truth in Plato's notion that there is something beyond the material world. However, this mystical concept of discovering truth does not provide certainty. Truth for Plato is more blinding than illuminating, and it cannot be communicated to others.

Aristotle (384–322)

Aristotle's philosophy is considered "the most comprehensive synthesis of knowledge ever achieved by the mind of man."[17]

16. Plato, "The Republic," *Great Books of the Western World*, 7:388–89.
17. Thilly, *History of Philosophy*, 118.

He wrote works on logic, natural sciences, psychology, metaphysics, ethics, politics, and rhetoric. Although he accepted Plato's distinction between ideas and matter, he believed both were real, inseparable, and eternal. Ideas only exist as they are expressed in concrete objects.

Aristotle grounded his hope for true knowledge in logic. He maintained there is objective knowledge, and he sought to refute the relativism of earlier philosophers. A statement is not true because you think it is. It is true and you are correct when you think it is true. Knowledge begins with perception of observable things. Then, by using inductive logic we arrive at "primary premises"—general conclusions that serve as the basis for further thought. Finally, by using deductive logic we can arrive at other conclusions. For example, we can observe many triangles and measure the sum of the degrees of their angles. They all add up to 180 degrees. Second, we conclude that all triangles have 180 degrees. Finally, we can deduce that any other triangle we find also will have 180 degrees.

Curiously, intuition is necessary in this process.[18] We cannot study every single triangle, but after observing many triangles, our intuition grasps the concept that all triangles have 180 degrees. It must be true!

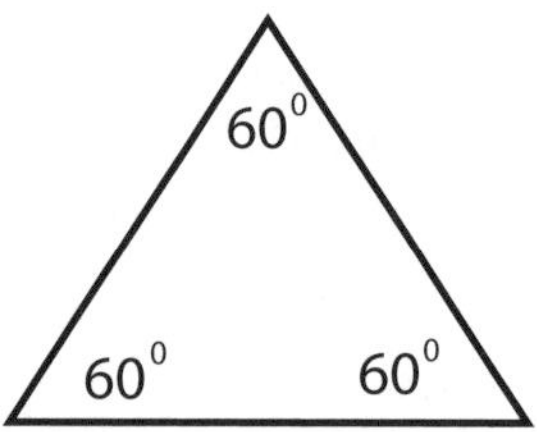

Aristotle formalized the logical law of non-contradiction. If x equals y, then it cannot be true that x does *not* equal y. If a tree is an apple tree, it cannot be true that it is *not* an apple tree.

18. See Julián Marías, *History of Philosophy*, trans. Stanley Appelbaum and Clarence C. Strowbridge (New York: Dover Publications, Inc., 1967), 63.

Aristotle also defined the syllogism:

1. Major premise: All triangles have 180 degrees.
2. Minor premise: This figure is a triangle.
3. Conclusion: This figure has 180 degrees.

Aristotle made a noble attempt to save knowledge. His explanation of the laws of logic is exemplary. Most Western people instinctively tend to think along logical lines. Logic, I believe, is a reflection of God's truth that he has allowed even non-Christians to discover. It is part of the image of God in man. However, logic must be submitted to God because it can be misused and lead us into error. God is infallible, but our use of logic is not.

Notice the subtle but important role that intuition plays in the learning process, according to Aristotle. It is curiously out of place in his otherwise completely logical scheme, thus betraying an innate sense that logic cannot explain everything.

There are additional problems in Aristotle's theory of knowledge. His emphasis on observation and logic leads to an overwhelming notion that there are an infinite number of things to know. How can we be certain that some new information will not destroy our present convictions? Finally, how can we be sure that logic may not sometimes mislead us?

Skepticism and Ethics after Aristotle (300 BC–529 AD)

Among the Greeks, there was a reaction against systematic philosophy after Aristotle. They preferred something more human and practical. They sought inner peace. Some were skeptical about finding true knowledge; others emphasized ethics.

The *Stoics* maintained that all reality is one living, rational, divine being. But their view of "god" was more fatalistic than personal and loving. In order to be happy, we must submit to the law of the universe, living in harmony with its overall design. True freedom comes from desiring what will necessarily occur.[19]

The Stoics despised material possessions and lived like hippies, with little clothing. Their name came from *Stoa*, which is the Greek word for *portico* and which represented the place they often met to talk.

The *Epicureans* wanted to live a serene life. They believed happiness is the ultimate goal of life and that it is not to be found in uninhibited, superficial pleasures but in moderation and internal tranquility.

> When, therefore, we maintain that pleasure is the end, we do not mean the pleasures of profligates and those that consist in sensuality, as is supposed by some who are either ignorant or disagree with us or do not understand, but freedom from pain in the body and from trouble in the mind.[20]

The Skeptics believed that to avoid disappointment it is better to admit your uncertainty, instead of being dogmatic. For some, such as Carneades, all knowledge was futile.[21] Common sayings among the Skeptics included, "I determine nothing," "Everything is inapprehensible," and "Opposed to every account there is an equal account."[22] According to Sextus Empiricus, these comments are not philosophical principles but simply explanations of how they feel. To be consistent, he is even skeptical about skeptical sayings! Sextus says,

19. Giannini, *Esbozo para una historia de la filosofía,* 74.

20. Epicurus, "On Pleasure," http://radicalacademy.com/adiphiloessay7.htm (January 5, 2006).

21. Frank Thilly, *History of Philosophy,* 143.

22. Sextus Empiricus, *Outlines of Scepticism*, ed. Julia Annas and Jonathan Barnes (Cambridge: Cambridge University Press, 2000), 49–51.

> In the case of all the sceptical phrases, you should understand that we do not affirm definitely that they are true. After all, we say that they can be destroyed by themselves, being cancelled along with what they are applied to, just as purgative drugs do not merely drain the humours from the body, but drive themselves out too along with the humours.[23]

This completes our survey of the "line of uncertainty." The Greeks moved from certainty, to doubt, to despair, to a struggle to save knowledge, and finally to a period that mixes skepticism with an emphasis on ethics. Although this review may not do justice to the complexities of Greek philosophy, I believe it properly reflects general tendencies and helps us understand the dilemma of man without God.

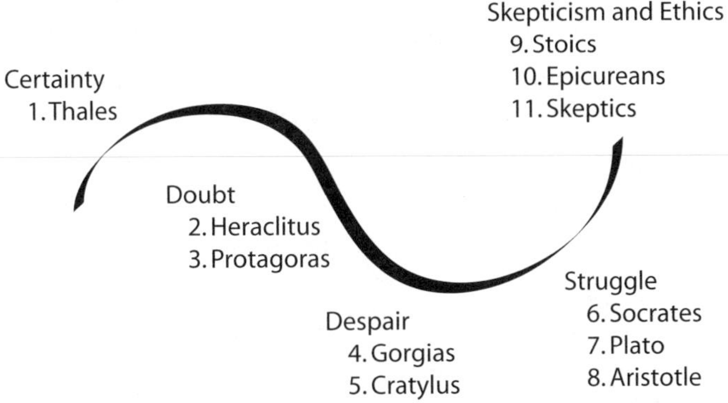

The line of uncertainty represents many of our own epistemological journeys. We begin by thinking we know something, then we doubt, and then we begin to lose hope of true knowledge. But we cannot live with total uncertainty, so we struggle to find meaning, even if we have to accept some inconsistency. Many of us never have the courage or capacity to face the consequences of life without meaning, so we skip over the bottom stage and move on to struggle for some kind of hope. Finally, if we don't turn to God and find the truth in his revelation, we learn to live with a

23. Sextus Empiricus, *Outlines of Scepticism*, 52.

degree of uncertainty and try not to think about it. However, we cannot avoid establishing some guidelines for living. After all, we have to make decisions about war, money, politics, sex, and abortion, for example. Because of the unavoidable ethical decisions we face, we continue to argue about what is right and wrong, even if we believe we have no basis for it! Ironically, sometimes the people who are most passionate about how we should live are the least certain about how we can know anything at all.

GROUP EXERCISE

Take an apple, or some other simple object, and start mentioning things you can know about it. Then play devil's advocate and ask yourself whether you can really be sure about the statements you made. Then think of questions you could ask about the apple that might be difficult to answer. Discuss how you can really be sure of anything about the apple without knowing everything about it.

REVIEW QUESTIONS

1. Identify the five stages of the "line of uncertainty."
2. What major problems do people face in knowing what is true?
3. Briefly describe the key thought of each philosopher:
    - Thales
    - Heraclitus
    - Protagoras
    - Gorgias
    - Cratylus
    - Socrates
    - Plato
    - Aristotle
    - The Stoics

- The Epicureans
- The Skeptics

4. Place each philosopher or school of philosophy from the previous question in the proper place on the "line of uncertainty."

Questions for Reflection

1. Have you passed through the same stages of the "line of uncertainty" as described in this chapter? Explain.
2. Do you understand the key thoughts of the philosophers studied in this lesson? If not, which one do you have trouble understanding?
3. Who do you think would have the most followers today, Plato or Aristotle? Why?

3

The Line of Uncertainty in Modern Philosophy

Although I like to watch World War II movies, sometimes the Nazis' cruelty leaves me angry and perplexed. How could they commit such atrocities? Why did they consider compassion a weakness? According to the movie *Downfall*, Hitler saw that Germany was losing the war. Not wanting to leave anything for the enemy, he commanded his officers to destroy German cities while Germans were still living in them! Hitler said the Germans deserved to be destroyed because if they could not win the war, they were weak.[1] Some might say Hitler was mentally ill. If so, how could so many people follow him? One concentration-camp survivor, Viktor Frankl, found the answer in philosophy. Frankl said:

> The gas chambers of Auschwitz were the ultimate consequence of the theory that man is nothing but the product of heredity and environment—or, as the Nazis liked to say, "of blood and soil." I am absolutely convinced that the gas chambers of Auschwitz, Treblinka, and Maidenek were ultimately prepared not in some ministry or other in

1. *Downfall*, directed by Oliver Hirschbiegel, distributed by Newmarket Film Group, 2005.

> Berlin, but rather at the desks and in lecture halls of nihilistic scientists and philosophers.[2]

In this chapter about modern philosophy, we will see the philosophical background the Nazis used to justify genocide. Modern philosophy follows a line of uncertainty similar to the Greeks.

The word *modern* can be misleading, especially in the field of philosophy. It does not mean "contemporary" but refers to the period that began with Sir Francis Bacon and René Descartes in the sixteenth century and that continued until the twentieth century. This period is called modern because the philosophers of the period broke with the culture and thought of the Middle Ages.

Before looking at the modern era, we will analyze its medieval background, when Christian theology dominated European thought.

The Medieval Background

Since Christian thinking prevailed in the Middle Ages, I call this study a "parenthesis" in our analysis of non-Christian thinking. In this period, knowledge was considered possible through faith in God's revelation. A key question for theologians such as Augustine, Anselm, and Aquinas was the relationship between faith and reason.[3]

Augustine (354–430) said, "I believe in order to understand" (*credo ut intelligam*). He insisted that even the most mundane knowledge requires faith. For example, we trust our family to tell us who our father is.[4]

2. Viktor Frankl, *The Doctor and the Soul* (New York: Knopf, 1982), xxi. Quoted by Ravi Zacharias in *Can Man Live Without God?* (Nashville: W. Publishing Group, 1994), 25.

3. We will talk more about the apologetic arguments of these theologians in chapter 5.

4. Gordon Clark, *Thales to Dewey* (Boston: Houghton Mifflin Co., 1957), 226.

Anselm (1033–1109) said something similar to Augustine, "For I do not seek to understand in order to believe, but I believe in order to understand. For this I believe, that 'unless I believe, I will not understand.' "[5] Anselm also affirmed that after initially obtaining truths through faith, reason can elaborate rational proofs for the same doctrines.

Aquinas (1225–74) assigned reason a greater importance than his two predecessors. G. K. Chesterton said Aquinas "reconciled religion with reason."[6] Aquinas admired Aristotle and even wrote commentaries on his works. According to Aquinas, we can study creation (general revelation) and use our reason to understand many things. For example, we can come to believe that God exists by studying arguments for his existence.[7] But this method of reasoning only helps us up to a certain point. After that we need special revelation and faith. For example, nature will not lead us to believe in the Trinity; we need faith for that.[8] According to Aquinas, from man's, not God's, perspective there are "two kinds of truth."

> The one kind of truth pertains to the investigation of reason, whereas the other wholly exceeds the reach of reason.[9]

Scholars disagree regarding Aquinas's view of the proper use of reason. However, it is safe to say that although he does *not* give reason priority over faith (understood as embracing special

5. *Proslogion*, chapter 1. See William C. Placher, *Readings in the History of Christian Theology, Volume 1: From its Beginnings to the Eve of the Reformation* (Philadelphia: Westminster Press, 1988), 145. Apparently, Anselm was referring to Isaiah 7:9, as quoted by Augustine in an old Latin version. See also Julián Marías, *History of Philosophy,* trans. Stanley Appelbaum and C. Clarence (Mineola, NY: Dover Publications, 1967), 144.

6. G. K. Chesterton, *Saint Thomas Aquinas: The Dumb Ox* (New York: Image Books, 1956), 32.

7. See chapter 5 for his five proofs for the existence of God.

8. *Summa Contra Gentiles*, 1.9. Ralph McInerny, ed., *Thomas Aquinas: Selected Writings* (London: Penguin Books, 1998), 244–45.

9. *Summa Contra Gentiles*, 1.9. *Selected Writings*, 244.

revelation) as our ultimate authority, he does place a high degree of trust in reason.

The Downward Spin in Early Modern Philosophy

Modern philosophy began with certainty and fell into skepticism. Thinking became secular. Special revelation in the Scriptures no longer was regarded as the primary source of truth. Man displaced God as the center of attention.

Modern philosophy centered on two great issues: Is truth objective or subjective, and is man free or determined? The first issue is about the location of truth and the means whereby we obtain it. Some modern philosophers believe truth is only in our minds (subjective) and that our reasoning can find it and understand it. Others believe truth is outside our minds (objective), that we begin by observing with our senses and then process our observations with our reason.

Sir Francis Bacon (1561–1626)

Bacon moved away from medieval faith in revelation and embraced the inductive method for finding truth. He preferred using his powers of observation to study nature. This method of discovering truth by using our five senses is called the *empirical* method, and the view that empirical knowledge is the most fundamental and authoritative kind of knowledge is called *empiricism*. Bacon had complete confidence in his ability to find true knowledge by using the empirical method. Bacon says:

> I have taken all knowledge to be my province.[10]

10. Francis Bacon, *The Advancement of Learning*, quoted in Will Durant, *The Story of Philosophy* (New York: Simon and Schuster, 2005), 94.

> My praise shall be dedicate [sic] to the mind itself. The mind is the man, and knowledge mind; a man is but what he knoweth.[11]

> The true method of experience first lights the candle, and then by means of the candle shows the way.[12]

> If we would rate things according to their real worth, the rational sciences are the keys to all the rest.[13]

René Descartes (1596–1650)

Closing himself up in a "stove-heated room" (in some sources in a large oven, a *poêle*) for a day of meditation, Descartes decided to follow the guideline that he would not accept anything as true if he could doubt it. His first conclusion was that since he perceived himself to be thinking, he could not doubt that he existed—an insight made famous in the Latin phrase *cogito ergo sum*, "I think, therefore I am."[14] From this basis, Descartes arrived at the conclusion that God existed. Descartes reasoned that his thoughts of God must come from outside himself, from a source greater than himself—from God. Descartes also concluded that the world exists externally outside himself and that he can trust his senses to observe the world. Why? Because God would not deceive us.

While his purpose was probably simply to keep warm, the image of Descartes meditating in a closed room graphically illustrates the new subjective tendency of modern philosophy. It has a new starting point—the self-conscience of the individual. His subjective logical methodology is called *rationalism*.

11. Francis Bacon, "The Praise of Knowledge," quoted in Durant, *Story of Philosophy*, 87.

12. Francis Bacon, *The New Organon*, quoted in Durant, *Story of Philosophy*, 102.

13. Bacon, *The Advancement of Learning*, quoted in Durant, *Story of Philosophy*, 99.

14. Descartes, *Discourse on Method, Part IV, Great Books of the Western World* (Chicago: Encyclopedia Britannica, 1994), 31.51.

John Locke (1632–1704)

Locke was more like Bacon than Descartes in that he emphasized empirical observation. He believed there are no innate ideas—no ideas previous to experience. Reality is outside the mind. The mind is a "tabula rasa"—a blank writing board—that receives sensations from without that are caused by the qualities of the things (empiricism). Through reflection on what it observes, the mind develops complex ideas.

Rationalism

Like Descartes and Bacon, Locke believed in the possibility of knowledge. Together, these three began a new cycle of certainty and uncertainty in Western philosophy.

David Hume (1711–76)

Hume was a skeptical empiricist. He believed knowledge came through observation, but he questioned the existence of things. He concluded that only perceptions exist. He also insisted we cannot predict with certainty anything based on previous experience (such as the sunrise in the mornings). That is, even though we perceive what we believe to be a series of causes and effects that suggest regular patterns, we cannot guarantee that these patterns will continue to be the same.

> That the sun will not rise tomorrow is no less intelligible a proposition, and implies no more contradiction, than the affirmation, that

> it will rise. We should in vain therefore, attempt to demonstrate its falsehood.
>
> May I not clearly and distinctly conceive that a body, falling from the clouds, and which, in all other respects, resembles snow, has yet the taste of salt or feeling of fire? [15]

My philosophy professor once asked, "What would Hume say if you asked him, 'If a tree falls in a forest but nobody is there to hear it, is there really a sound?' " The majority of the students wanted to show that they knew Hume was a skeptic, so they answered, "Hume would say 'No'. " But our teacher pushed us further: "No. Hume would say, 'What forest?' " In other words, since only perceptions exist, nothing exists that is not perceived by man.[16]

Once we start questioning our perceptions, it is easy to fall into a disconcerting skepticism. I remember the daughter of some missionary friends who once asked me when she was twelve years old, "How do I know if I see those trees as the same color you do?" I had to admit there was no way to be sure exactly how another person perceives things like that. Others might ask, "How do you know that you aren't just dreaming everything?"

Psychologists like to show pictures that can be interpreted in different ways, such as the following favorite on the next page. Some see an old woman; others see a young lady. The psychologists ask who is right, and the answer is supposedly both! It's a question of perception.

This is a valid point; we tend to perceive things differently. However, it becomes a problem when taken to the extreme of

15. David Hume, *An Enquiry Concerning Human Understanding: A Critical Edition*, ed. Tom L. Beauchamp (Oxford: Oxford University Press, 1999), 24, 31.

16. Previously, Berkeley proposed a similar view, but Hume took it even further. Berkeley believed objects do not cease to exist when no human is there to observe them, because God is always there to perceive them. See Colin Brown, *Philosophy and the Christian Faith* (Chicago, InterVarsity Press, 1969), 64–68.

denying absolute truth or the possibility of knowledge or communication. If we hold fast to God, we can resolve this problem. Even if there is no person in the forest to hear the sound of a falling tree, God hears it. Scripture teaches that the creation actually exists. The world is not an illusion; what we perceive is not a dream. Although our perceptions may vary, we can trust God to enable us to perceive things with sufficient precision to live in this world and to communicate adequately among ourselves. God does not play with us as we might play with optical illusions. Nevertheless, if we take God out of the scheme, we lose all certainty. Thus modern philosophy fell into doubt . . . and despair.

The Valley of Despair

Skepticism leads to despair, and despair leads to moral degeneration. A life consistent with the denial of God and absolute truth turns into an abusive life centered on self. Let's look at two representatives of this aberration, Marquis de Sade and Friedrich Nietzsche.

Notice the slight chronological variation in the line of uncertainty among modern philosophers, in comparison with the Greeks. Although the Greek philosophers who fall under the category of despair (Gorgias and Cratylus) came before those who were struggling to save truth (Socrates, Plato, and Aristotle), the order is different among modern philosophers. Marquis de Sade was a contemporary of the first modern philosophers in this stage of the struggle (Kant and Hegel), but Nietzsche came one hundred years later, born during the lifetime of Kierkegaard. It is as though Kant, Hegel, and Kierkegaard were jumping ahead to avoid the despair, but Nietzsche dared to go back and look into the dark abyss.

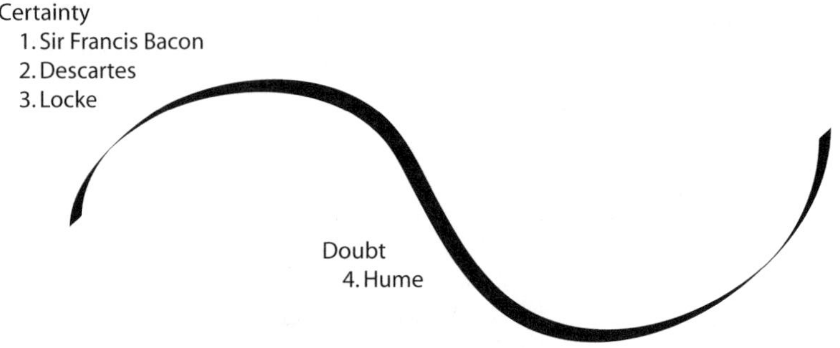

Marquis de Sade (1740–1814)

Although he is not normally considered a "philosopher," I include the Marquis de Sade because he was an influential writer who represented the dark underside of agnostic despair. Marquis de Sade lived between the time of Kant and Hegel. He was known for moral libertinism and for receiving pleasure from sexual cruelty, from which the term *sadism* is derived. Cynical and dedicated to his vices, he was not concerned about the consequences of his actions. He wrote from prison:

> By Nature created, created with very keen tastes, with very strong passions; placed on this earth for the sole purpose of yielding to them and satisfying them . . . I am only sorry for the modest use I made of the faculties (criminal in your view, perfectly ordinary in mine) she gave me to serve her . . .

> Renounce the idea of another world; there is none, but do not renounce the pleasure of being happy and of making for happiness in this.[17]
>
> Does this shock you, o virtuous people? Does this burn those ears of yours, which from infancy have been assailed with the fables of the church? Well, go in peace; if those absurdities which you have been taught are true; if, as you have been told, there is a hell wherein shall be punished the perpetrators of vice, then, no doubt, we shall burn there. But, as Blangis might have put it, a hell inhabited by those of our stripe is, all its tortures notwithstanding, infinitely preferable to a heaven occupied by the monotonous creatures whom we find held up to us as examples of virtue.[18]

Friedrich Nietzsche (1844–1900)

Son of a Protestant pastor, Nietzsche is famous for declaring "God is dead." He denied God, who alone gives meaning to life and morality. He suggested that Christianity encourages weakness. Christian ethics come from the instinct to protect yourself, based on fear, not love. Nietzsche taught we should become like the *Übermensch* (superman), who has been freed from external ethical norms and can create his own values and impose his own will. Not only can the *Übermensch* suffer, he can make others suffer without feeling bad about it. Hitler, interpreting rightly or wrongly, nurtured his tyranny using Nietzsche's philosophy. According to Nietzsche, there was no longer any "up and down"; the world had become "cold." It is hard to find a more gripping expression of godless despair than the following:

> Haven't you heard of that madman who in the bright morning lit a lantern, and ran around the marketplace, crying incessantly: "I'm looking for God! I'm looking for God!"

17. Marquis de Sade, "Dialogue between a Priest and a Dying Man," *Justine, Philosophy in the Bedroom, and Other Writings*, trans. Austryn Wainhouse and Richard Seaver (Jackson, TN: Grove Press, 1994), 165–66, 174.

18. Marquis de Sade, Afterword to *120 Days of Sodom, The Complete Marquis de Sade*, trans. Paul J. Gillette (Los Angeles: Holloway House, 2005), 301.

> Since many of those who did not believe in God were standing around together just there, he caused great laughter. Has he been lost, then? asked one. Did he lose his way like a child? asked another. Or is he hiding? Is he afraid of us? Has he gone to sea? Emigrated? Thus they shouted and laughed, one interrupting the other. The madman jumped into their midst and pierced them with his eyes.
>
> "Where is God?" he cried. "I'll tell you. We have killed him—you and I. We are all his murderers. But how did we do this? How were we able to drink up the sea? Who gave us the sponge to wipe away the entire horizon? What were we doing when we unchained this earth from its sun? Where is it moving to now? Where are we moving to? Away from all suns? Are we not continually falling? And backwards, sidewards, forwards, in all directions? Is there still an up and a down? Aren't we straying as though through an infinite nothing? Isn't empty space breathing at us? Hasn't it got colder? Isn't night and more night coming again and again? Don't lanterns have to be lit in the morning? Do we still hear nothing of the noise of the grave-diggers who are burying God? Do we still smell nothing of the divine decomposition? Gods, too, decompose. God is dead! God remains dead! And we have killed him!"[19]

Nietzsche's philosophy has been called *nihilism.* (from *nihil*, nothing). While he pretended to avoid it, he inevitably empties life of its meaning and purpose.

In spite of Nietzsche's theoretical rejection of Christian ethics, thankfully he was not totally consistent with this view in his own actions. In fact, his last gesture before becoming mentally ill was to intervene on behalf of a horse that someone was beating. He threw his arms around the neck of the animal, then collapsed and was never the same again.[20]

19. Friedrich Nietzsche, *The Gay Science* (Cambridge: Cambridge University Press, 2001), 119–20.

20. Kathleen M. Higgins and Robert C. Solomon, *Introduction to Thus Spoke Zarathustra*, trans. Clancy Martin (New York: Barnes and Noble, 2005), vi.

The Struggle

Kant, Hegel, and Kierkegaard attempted to rescue knowledge from skepticism, as did Socrates, Plato, and Aristotle among the Greeks.

Immanuel Kant (1724–1804)

Kant believed he solved the subjective-objective, rationalist-empiricist debate by combining the two methods of arriving at the truth. He proposed that a thing does not exist in itself but only as it is perceived. You cannot separate the perceiving subject from the perceived object. Although things truly exist outside the mind, we cannot know them without the subjective influence of our own mental filter that processes the data.[21] "Perceptions without conceptions are blind."[22] Duncan Richter compares Kant's view of our minds to a radio that is bombarded by sound waves and converts them into coherent words and music.[23]

Kant also addressed the second major debate of modern philosophy—freedom versus determinism. He anticipated the problem that arises if only the material world exists—man loses his freedom. Everything in the physical realm obeys the laws of cause and effect. If man is an integral part of this impersonal process, how can he be free? However, man *appears* to be free *somehow* outside this deterministic sphere. To explain this, Kant makes a distinction between two realms, the realm of "noumena" (from the Greek word *nous*, meaning "mind" or "thought") and the realm of "phenomena"—between the metaphysical world and the physical world (a concept similar to that of Plato). "Pure reason" functions in the physical

21. Immanuel Kant, *Critique of Pure Reason*, trans. J. M. D. Meiklejohn (New York: Prometheus Books, 1990), 21–45.

22. Kant, *Critique of Pure Reason*, quoted in Durant, 206. Otherwise translated as, "intuitions without conceptions are blind." *Critique of Pure Reason*, 45.

23. Duncan John Richter, "Kant for Beginners," http://academics.vmi.edu/psy_dr/Kant%20for%20beginners.htm (April 18, 2007).

world; "practical reason" functions in the metaphysical. Science deals with "phenomena"; morality deals with "noumena."

Kant's distinction between the phenomenal and the noumenal is similar to Aquinas's separation between the use of reason and the use of faith. Kant's noumenal realm allowed him to preserve man's freedom, though he did not explain how this freedom logically fits into his whole system. If man is not free in the world of cause and effect, he still can be free in the noumenal world. Kant accepted this as an "antinomy," as something apparently incompatible with the observable world as we rationally analyze it but at the same time as something we must believe. It is like accepting the fact that the universe must be infinite but at the same time accepting that this is not logically comprehensible.

We can certainly see residues of God's truth in the way Kant struggles to explain the instinctive sense of man's freedom and his moral nature. The problem is that according to Kant, reason, as we normally think of it, does not apply to metaphysical issues. Therefore, things in the noumenal world are *unknowable*. They are in a "stormy ocean" covered by a "fog bank," surrounding the island of the world of pure reason.

> We have now not only traversed the region of the pure understanding, and carefully surveyed every part of it, but we have also measured it, and assigned to everything therein its proper place. But this land is an island, and inclosed by nature herself within unchangeable limits. It is the land of truth (an attractive word) surrounded by a wide and stormy ocean, the region of illusion, where many a fog bank, many an iceberg, seem to the mariner, on his voyage of discovery, a new country, and while constantly deluding him with vain hopes, engages him in dangerous adventures, from which he can never desist, and which yet he can never bring to a termination.[24]

24. Kant, *Critique of Pure Reason*, 93.

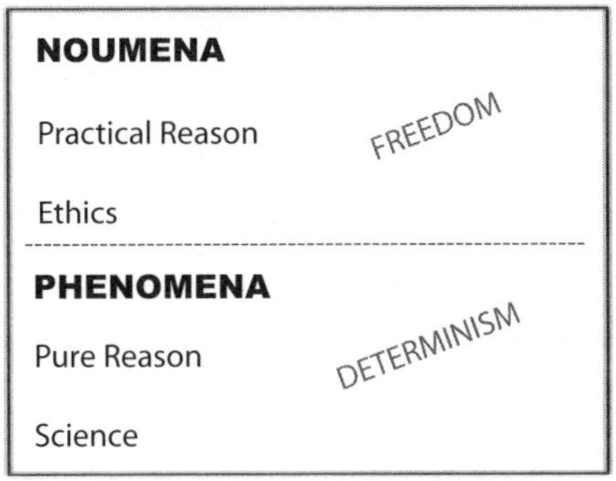

NOUMENA

Practical Reason — FREEDOM

Ethics

PHENOMENA

Pure Reason — DETERMINISM

Science

Although Kant tried to save freedom and ethics, unfortunately he destroyed any confidence that we can have true knowledge of the non-physical realm. Thus, Kant's noumenal realm begins to look more like "wishful thinking"[25] than reality. Like Plato's world of ideas, it cannot be explained rationally. In fact, it is now commonly accepted that something that can be proven scientifically is more credible than something related to spiritual things. This attitude fits Kant's perspective better than it does the Bible's.

Georg Wilhelm Friedrich Hegel (1770–1831)

Hegel wrought a colossal change in Western thinking. According to Hegel, reality is basically one, and it is not material but spiritual. Hegel calls this reality the *Geist* (spirit, mind, reason), the interior being of the world.[26] The *Geist* involves all of history, nature, and human thought.[27] Everything, even knowledge, is in a dynamic process of development.

25. Colin Brown, *Philosophy and the Christian Faith* (Downers Grove, IL: InterVarsity Press, 1969), 105.

26. G. W. F. Hegel, *The Phenomenology of Mind*, trans. J. B. Baillie (London: Swan Sonnenshein and Co., 1910, republished London: Routledge, 2004), 1.22. The title of this work is often translated *The Phenomenology of the Spirit*.

27. Frank Thilly and Ledger Wood, *A History of Philosophy* (New York: Henry Holt and Co., 1959), 478–84.

> The truth is the whole. The whole, however, is merely the essential nature reaching its completeness through the process of its own development.[28]

This process is a kind of spiritual evolution. Later, Marx would turn Hegel's idea upside down and propose that although reality is in a continual dynamic process, it is not spiritual but material.

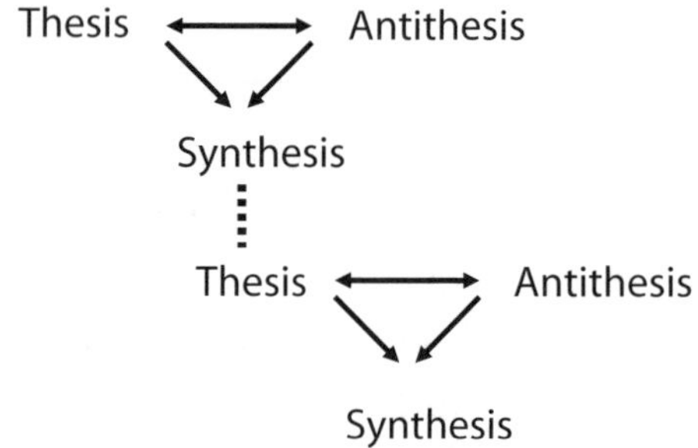

Hegel proposed the notion of *dialectic*—a dynamic in which conflicts merge into one another as the great spirit evolves. Instead of looking at two apparently contradictory positions (a thesis and its antithesis) as mutually exclusive choices, we should look at them as different aspects of a larger truth and expect them to merge into a synthesis. Each synthesis becomes a new thesis, which in turn merges with its antithesis to form another synthesis. This dialectic process continues on and on.

The religions of the world serve as an example. According to the dialectic, man has passed through different stages of belief, but none negates the previous stage. Each religion forms part of the process of the development of thought.

28. Hegel, *Phenomenology*, 17.

Truth is like a plant that grows and produces a bud, then a flower. Although the bud disappears, it still is present in the flower.

This reminds us of the philosophy of Heraclitus, where everything is united and constantly in flux. This reduces human beings to an insignificant part of an impersonal process; our decisions are not free, and they do not make a difference. Furthermore, it leads to a change in the normal way we use logic in our thinking. If Hegel is right about the *Geist* and the dialectic, then the truth is everything, and everything would eventually be true. Previously, most Western philosophers accepted the logical law of non-contradiction. If A was true, then you could not also say that A is not true. When you were presented with two contradictory statements (2+2=4 versus 2+2 ≠4 or 2+2=5), then at least one of these statements is false, and you would have to make a choice between them. Although there is much debate about whether Hegel really meant to deny the law of non-contradiction, the principle of dialectic can easily lead someone to abandon it.

Søren Kierkegaard (1813–55)

Although some existentialists seem pessimistic and agnostic, they can be included among those struggling to find truth. They balked at the unpalatable consequences of nihilism and tried to find meaning and maintain human freedom. Camus said,

> In the darkest depths of our Nihilism, I have sought only for the means to transcend Nihilism.[29]

Kierkegaard is considered the "grandfather" of key aspects of existentialism. Contrary to many others in this school of thought, Kierkegaard espoused the Christian faith.

29. Quoted from *L'Été* by James Sire, *The Universe Next Door: A Basic Worldview Catalogue* (Downers Grove, IL: InterVarsity Press, 1997), 95.

Kierkegaard resisted the consequences of a dynamic, impersonal universe. He sought to save man's freedom and leave space for faith in God. He especially reacted against Hegel and liked to make fun of him. Some of the titles of his books are meant to ridicule Hegel, for example, *Concluding Unscientific Postscript* and *Philosophical Fragments.* Kierkegaard believed Hegel's philosophy was too theoretical to be helpful as a guide for living. He found Hegel's pure thought akin to "having to travel in Denmark with a small map of Europe on which Denmark is no larger than a steel pen-point."[30] Kierkegaard wanted something more personal.

> . . . the thing is to find a truth which is true for me, to find the idea for which I can live and die.[31]

Kierkegaard rejected the logical conclusion of Hegel's dialectic that reduced our thoughts to the flow of history. Kierkegaard's way of escaping this determinism was to focus on man's subjective free choice. Kierkegaard introduced a moment of freedom within the otherwise irresistible flow of things. For him, this "moment" is actually eternal and infinite. It is as if time were suspended, breaking the inevitable process and allowing for individuality and faith. Faith may seem to contradict reason, but we must believe anyway. It is a "leap," a free act of the human will.

> Faith is the objective uncertainty along with the repulsion of the absurd held fast in the passion of inwardness.[32]

Kierkegaard did not say there is no objective truth. Rather, he means that truth seems paradoxical as it relates to us.[33] Faith

30. Søren Kierkegaard, *Concluding Unscientific Postscript,* quoted in Gordon Graham, *Eight Theories of Ethics* (London: Routledge, 2004), 72.

31. Søren Kierkegaard, *The Journals,* quoted in *A Kierkegaard Anthology,* ed. Robert Bretall (New York: Random House, 1946), 4–5.

32. Søren Kierkegaard, *Post-Scriptum,* quoted in Bretall, *Kierkegaard Anthology,* 255.

33. See Copleston, *A History of Philosophy,* 7.2.115–18.

is like love; you cannot explain it fully. It is a passion—a matter of the heart—more than the intellect.

We see again in Kierkegaard, as we did in Kant, an instinctive need to save freedom from the stranglehold of determinism. We can appreciate the fact that he is in the Christian camp and that he considers faith to be more than just an intellectual decision. However, he goes too far in his distrust of reason. His view leaves the gospel vulnerable, since it is difficult to defend, understand, or explain in a rational way.

Jean Paul Sartre (1905–80)

Later existentialists, such as Sartre, would leave God out of the picture and take subjectivity to an extreme. Life then seems absurd, and freedom becomes frightening. Man must make choices without objective norms and determine his own meaning.[34] Sartre described the struggle for identity in this seemingly absurd world in his novel called *Nausea*. Antoine Roquentin stares at himself in the mirror until he can no longer recognize himself. He sees only "insipid flesh blossoming and palpitating." His eyes look like fish scales, and his wrinkled face looks like an "embossed map.[35] I see an analogy between Sartre's perspective of life and the description of the music that Roquentin hears on the phonograph. Although life must have a recognizable "melody," at times events appear uncontrollable and without meaning, like the seemingly random jazz notes of the section of the song he hears:

> For the moment, the jazz is playing; there is no melody, only notes, a myriad of tiny jolts. They know no rest, an inflexible order gives birth to them and destroys them without even giving them time to recuperate and exist for themselves. They race, they press forward,

34. T. Z. Lavine, *From Socrates to Sartre: The Philosophic Quest* (New York: Bantam Books, 1984), 328–82.

35. Jean Paul Sartre, *Nausea* (New York: New Directions, 1964), 17.

> they strike me a sharp blow in passing and are obliterated. I would like to hold them back, but I know if I succeeded in stopping one it would remain between my fingers only as a raffish languishing sound. I must accept their death; I must even will it. I know few impressions stronger or more harsh.[36]

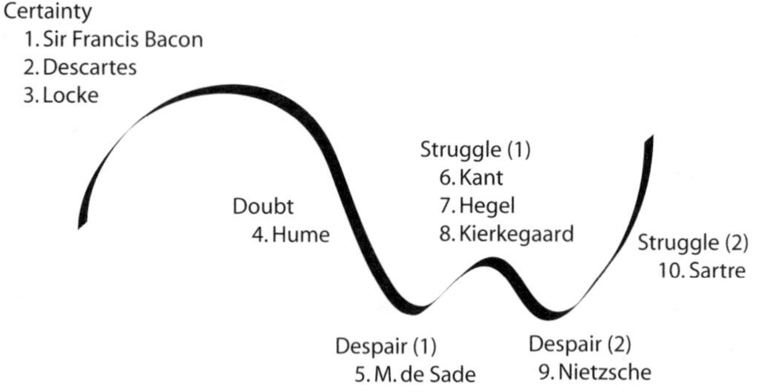

SKEPTICISM AND ETHICS

After a philosophy course in ethics, my classmates concluded that not even the greatest philosophers knew much about ethics. After discussing many options, one view seemed just as indefensible as another. Everyone has to decide what is right for himself, my classmates said. In the middle of this confusion, our professor told us a joke. I think the joke is funny only in a moment filled with the kind of frustration we were sensing in that class, but it does illustrate the inconsistency in the last stage on the line of uncertainty. He told us about two men riding through the desert on horseback. Suddenly, one man jumped off his horse onto a cactus. The other man was shocked to see him hanging on the cactus, bleeding. "Why did you do that?" he shouted. "I don't know, but it seemed like a good idea at the time!" replied the first. If there are no absolutes, and if there is no foundation for right and wrong, why not?

36. Sartre, *Nausea*, 21.

Just as it happened among the Greeks, modern philosophers struggle with uncertainty, but they have decided this will not keep them from continuing their lives. They simply resign themselves to the fact that life is that way and try to make the best they can of it. In fact, even more than the Greeks, many modern representatives consciously *combine* skepticism with ethics.

Liberal Theology and Liberation Theology

Liberal theology admits having a skeptical posture toward truth, while emphasizing ethics. Liberals abandoned the foundation of the inspired Scriptures and lost the notion of absolute truth.[37] Nevertheless, irrationally, they continued to defend ethical principles. They reduced Jesus to a moral example, rather than exalting him as a Savior. Although in one sense "liberals" are on the "Christian" side, their epistemology has more in common with non-Christians than with orthodox Christianity.

We will examine one liberal theologian, José Míguez Bonino, from Argentina. He represents a particular brand of liberal theology called "liberation theology," which is especially popular in Latin America. Liberation theology is an unusual combination of Marxism and liberal theology.

Bonino begins with a concern for poverty and injustice and then develops a distorted theological defense of political movements that are trying to overthrow capitalistic power structures. Behind the sociopolitical movement is a new "hermeneutic" that begins with praxis instead of with the Scriptures. By *praxis* he means life itself in the present historical context. To him, doing theology is not simply a cognitive reflection about abstract ideas.

Bonino believes truth is found in history, not in concepts. That is, to know the truth is to experience it, not merely to think it. Bonino accepts a theory of communication that eliminates all

37. Examples of theologians who are considered "liberal" include Friedrich Daniel Ernst Schleiermacher, Adolf von Harnack, Rudolf Bultmann, and Paul Tillich.

certainty. For him, the meaning of any communication between two people involves the complete situation: the tone of voice, gestures, the background of each person, and an infinite number of factors surrounding them. Since it is impossible to communicate an infinite number of factors, it is impossible to be sure about the validity of the message given and received.[38] This reminds us of Gorgias! For Bonino, this problem also affects the communication between God and man. It is impossible to be sure about our understanding of God's message to us.[39]

However, in spite of this epistemological skepticism, Bonino has no problem encouraging us to make a commitment to the Marxist revolutionary movement to help the poor and the oppressed. He admits that this Christian cooperation with the Marxist revolution is an "uneasy alliance and that liberation theology could be mistaken!"

> May nobody think, then, that I am proclaiming "liberation theology" as it has appeared in Latin America and in other places, as the theology for the new world, or as the precursor of a new Christianity. It is simply an initial and ambiguous answer and a tenuous perception of a new task and a new responsibility. It is destined to die. May God permit that its life and death be fruitful.[40]

Regardless of the tentative and temporary nature of his theology, Bonino has strong convictions about injustice, the causes of poverty, and ethics. He asks for a commitment to the possibility of using violence—something very radical considering the fragile basis of his convictions!

38. José Míguez Bonino, *La fe en busca de eficacia* (Salamanca: Ediciones Sígueme, 1977) 118, 119. English version: *Doing Theology in a Revolutionary Situation* (Philadelphia: Fortress, 1975, 1986).

39. An answer to this problem is suggested in chapter 7, in the section "The Christian Answer to Uncertainty."

40. José Míguez Bonino, "New Trends in Theology," *Duke Divinity School Review* 42 (Fall, 1997): 141,142.

Postmodernism

Obviously, *postmodernism* does not technically belong in a study of *modern* philosophy. Nevertheless, we must include it in our review, since it explains the situation we are currently experiencing. Postmodernism is not a philosophy in the normal sense of an organized system of thought; it is a term used to describe a whole set of cultural tendencies, including art, music, and moral and philosophical values (or lack of values!). The name suggests a reaction against modernism. Whereas modernism began with a trust in reason and science, postmodernism no longer trusts them. Unlike modernists, postmodernists do not care so much about what reality is like (ontology) or about how you can know the truth (epistemology). Gilles Lipovetsky, considered a representative of postmodern thought, says, "postmodern society is one in which the indifference of the masses reigns."[41]

Antonio Cruz explains:

> The postmodern individual . . . has been transformed into a vagabond of ideas. He doesn't hold on to anything sincerely. He has no absolute certainties. He doesn't seem to be surprised by anything, and of course, nothing keeps him awake at night. He changes his opinion today as easily as he changes his shirt.[42]

The best word to describe postmodernism is "eclectic"; anything and everything is acceptable. Richard Rorty said the key slogan for postmodernism is "Truth is made, not found."[43]

41. Quoted by Antonio Cruz in *Postmodernidad* (Barcelona: CLIE, 1996), 47 (translated by the author).

42. Cruz, *Postmodernidad*, 52. Other authors who represent postmodernism are Jean-Francois Lyotard, Michel Leiris, Bernard-Henri Lévy, and Jean Baudrillard. See Antonio Cruz, *Postmodernidad*, 18. See books by Michael Foucalt, *The Order of Things* (New York: Vintage Books, 1994) and *Madness and Civilization: A History of Insanity in the Age of Reason* (New York: Vintage Books, 1988).

43. Richard Rorty, *Contingency, Irony, and Solidarity* (Cambridge: Cambridge University Press, 1989), chapter 1. Quoted by Nancy Pearcey in *Total Truth*, 242.

Douglas Groothuis suggests that the tendency is pluralist, relativist, and nihilist. Postmodern art uses all kinds of styles and forms, "with no visible coherence."[44]

The song "Toxicity" that was quoted in the first chapter gives us a clear idea of the postmodern sense of ambiguity and confusion. Postmodernists feel like they are looking at life "through the eyes of a tire hub." Life seems to be "disorder, disorder, disorder."[45]

The following words from another current song reveal an attitude of giving up on right and wrong. The only thing left is to try to enjoy life.

> Don't you know the devil is in me and God she is too
> my Yin hits my Yang But what the heck ya gonna do
> I choose a rocky ass path but that's how I like it
> life's a bowl of punch go ahead and spike it.[46]

Yin and *Yang* are oriental words for apparent opposites that actually form part of the universal oneness, according to Taoism.

I can understand certain attitudes of postmodernists. I can see why they would be disillusioned with science and technology for not changing man in a more profound way, for not solving serious problems, for example, war, hatred, prejudice, and genocide. I understand why they rebel against the idea of being considered an animal, caged in a closed universe. I can see why they would want to avoid becoming like Thomas Gradgrind, the bor-

44. Douglas Groothuis, *Truth Decay* (Downers Grove, IL: InterVarsity Press, 2000), 239–62.

45. "Toxicity," by System of a Down.

46. 311, "Plain" (July 26, 2006) http://www.najical.com/311/03ahydro.htm.

ing schoolmaster of Dickens's *Hard Times*, who says: "Now what I want is, Facts. Teach these boys and girls nothing but Facts. . . . You can only form the minds of reasoning animals upon Facts: nothing else will ever be of any service to them."[47]

Now we can better appreciate Francis Bacon's painting mentioned in chapter one, *Head VI*. No wonder the man inside the box is screaming; he believes he is an "accident." We have come a long way from the other Bacon—Sir Francis Bacon, the philosopher from the seventeenth century who trusted in reason and the scientific method.

Postmodernism has certain characteristics in common with the last stage of Greek philosophy. First, postmodernists are skeptics. They tend to believe we cannot be sure of anything. Second, although they say they do not believe in ethical norms, primarily they seek their own happiness, much like the Epicureans. In that sense, they show a definite ethical emphasis, though not in the traditional manner. Third, they share with the Stoics a certain passive resignation to the injustices and evils of this world. Antonio Cruz calls it "conformism" and cites a postmodern poet, Fernando Pessoa:

> Injustice exists, as death exists.
> I would never take a step to alter
> that which is called injustice in this world.
> I accept injustice as I accept
> the fact that a rock is round,
> or that an acorn was not born a pine tree or
> an oak.[48]

How is postmodernism different from nihilism? What is the difference between this stage and the stage of despair? In both

47. Charles Dickens, *Hard Times* (New York: Barnes and Noble, 2004), 9. Originally published in 1854.

48. Fernando Pessoa, *Obra poética*, quoted in Antonio Cruz, *Postmodernidad*, 104 (translated by author).

cases, they admit the absence of an epistemological foundation. But on the one hand, in the case of Gorgias, Cratylus, Marquis de Sade, and Nietzsche, they lived more consistently with their beliefs. One stopped talking and others gave themselves over to their lower instincts. On the other hand, in the case of the Stoics, the Epicureans, liberals and postmodernists, they did not want to live that way. They preferred to overlook the profound uncertainty and "spike the punch" of life. In summary, the postmodern attitude is less consistent, but less negative, than the nihilistic attitude.

I observe some refreshingly positive elements among many young people today, elements that manifest the grace of God, in contrast with the negative aspects of postmodernism. For one thing, there often is a healthy emphasis on friendship and interpersonal loyalty. Furthermore, many young people are genuinely interested in spiritual things. Finally, I think we would have to agree with their concern to keep things practical. Without going to the extreme of eliminating important abstract theoretical thinking, we certainly need to make sure our road map is a helpful guide to living, as Kierkegaard reminded us.

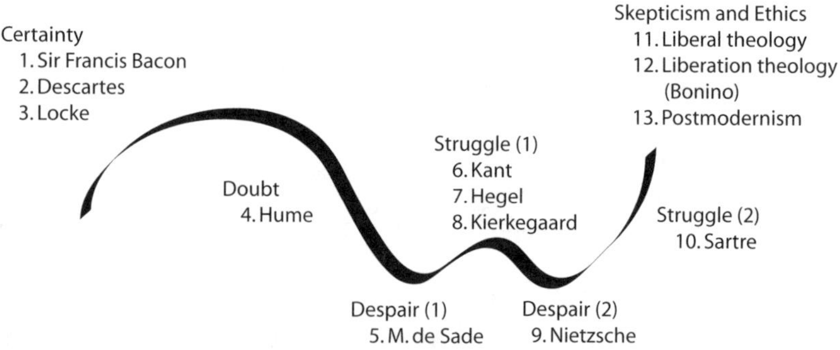

With these sketches of modern philosophy, we complete the line of uncertainty. Just as in our review of the Greeks, this summary has left many complexities aside. The purpose has been to show a general tendency, especially the struggle with uncertainty, and therefore it has been greatly simplified.

Group Exercise

Look at the picture of the young lady/old woman in this chapter. Can you see both? Help one another see them both. Now look at some other object, such as a desk or a tree outside. Discuss whether we can know how each other really perceives this object. When I say something is "green," do I see the same thing you do? How does this affect your sense of certainty in knowing things and in communicating what you know? Does it make you feel like everything is relative? What is the solution to this problem?

Review Questions

1. Explain the difference between the positions of Augustine, Anselm, and Aquinas regarding the relationship between faith and reason.
2. Explain the following debates in modern philosophy:
   - Rationalism versus empiricism
   - Freedom versus determinism
3. Briefly describe the key thoughts of each:
   - Sir Francis Bacon
   - René Descartes
   - John Locke
   - David Hume
   - Immanuel Kant
   - Friedrich Hegel
   - Marquis de Sade
   - Friedrich Nietzsche
   - Søren Kierkegaard
   - Jean Paul Sartre

- José Míguez Bonino

4. Briefly describe the essence of the following schools of thought:
    - Liberal theology
    - Liberation theology
    - Postmodernism
5. Locate each philosopher from question 3 and each school of thought from question 4 in their proper place on the "line of uncertainty."

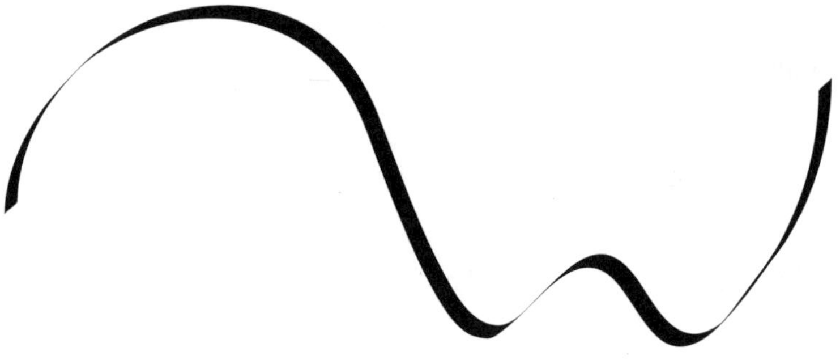

QUESTIONS FOR REFLECTION

1. How do you think faith is related to reason? What should their relationship be?
2. Do you have problems understanding any of the key thoughts of the philosophers studied in this lesson? If so, which one?
3. If you were not a Christian, which philosophy studied in this chapter would you possibly espouse? Why?
4. In what ways have you seen postmodernism expressed in your context? Give examples.

4

Conclusions About the Non-Christian

While writing this chapter, hurricane Katrina[1], one of the worst natural disasters in the history of the United States, hit the coast of the Gulf of Mexico. During the storm, we watched nervously, because most of the city of New Orleans is below sea level. Although retention walls surrounded the city and its canals, we wondered, with most of America, if these walls could resist Katrina's category-four strength. As we feared, the walls broke in three places, and the whole city was inundated. Actually, one break would have been sufficient to cause extensive flooding.

The non-Christian is like New Orleans. He has a sophisticated facade, but he is extremely vulnerable. His epistemology is his weakest spot; this is where his worldview collapses. He does not know how he can be sure of anything. If we persist in asking him why he believes something, he becomes aware of his problem. He realizes that his starting point is not solid, that he has no reliable foundation.

For apologetic purposes, if we had to use a single word to describe non-Christians it would be *uncertain*. The history

1. August 2005.

of Western philosophy is a repetitive struggle to overcome this epistemological problem of *uncertainty.*

If we had to use one phrase to describe *the root of man's problem* with regard to finding the truth, it would be that he *pretends to be the ultimate judge of truth.* This started in the garden of Eden with Adam and Eve, and it was the cause of the fall.

Notice that the temptation presented to Adam and Eve was precisely to eat of the tree of *knowledge.* Eating from this tree symbolized the attempt to obtain truth independently from God—an attempt to become autonomous like God. When Satan distorted the truth and challenged Adam and Eve to rebel against God, they began to weigh the choices. The fall began when they asked themselves, "I wonder who is right, God or the serpent?" At that point, they already had made themselves judges of truth, pretending to be independent of God.

When Jesus, who is "the way, the truth, and the life" (John 14:6), stood before Pilate, the Roman ruler asked him, "What is truth?" (John 18:38). Apparently, Pilate didn't expect an answer, because he went out to speak to the crowds. Then, ironically, instead of listening to the source of all truth, he had Jesus crucified. This illustrates man's most foolish mistake. With the truth before our very eyes, we refuse to accept it. Instead, we crucify it and set ourselves up as judges of what is and is not true.

UNCERTAINTY

Generally speaking, the Greeks followed a cycle of certainty, doubt, and desperation in their attempt to save knowledge but ended in skepticism and then chose to emphasize ethics. Modern philosophy has followed a similar pattern, and individuals often go through the same stages. Modern man thinks he knows something, then doubts, maybe despairs, then struggles to avoid total uncertainty, because he simply can't live that way, and ends up defending his ethical views, even though this is inconsistent with his skepticism.

Once you exclude God as the source and ground of truth, only four basic epistemological choices remain. Modern man may assume that truth is outside of himself or that truth is inside his head. Another alternative is to deny the possibility of truth altogether. Finally, modern man could say the opposite—everything is true.

If Truth Is Objective

If modern man thinks truth is objective—outside himself—and if he pretends to be the ultimate judge of the truth, he encounters the dilemma of needing to know everything in order to be sure of anything. The fact that everything keeps changing also is disconcerting.

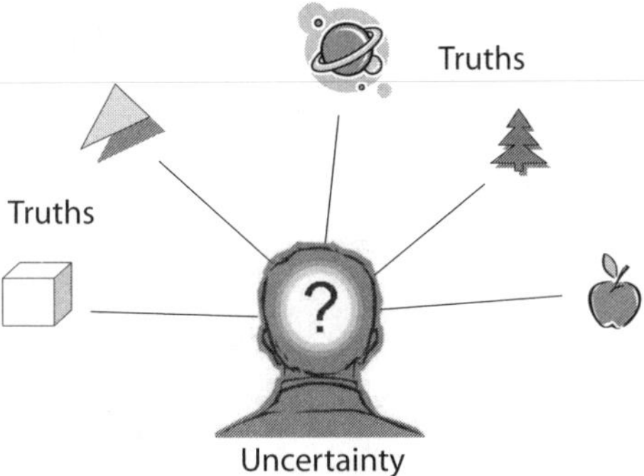

I ask a person who takes this position a question I know he cannot answer, for example, "Will there be human life on earth two thousand years from now?" I might also ask, "Is there a star a million light years directly north of the North Pole?" Or it may be something as simple as, "What color was the sweater of the girl who just walked behind you?" Although eventually he may be able to find answers to some of these questions, the fact that he does not know the answers now makes him feel uncertain. He realizes his present field of knowledge is quite limited. Furthermore, how can he be sure that what he perceives is not some kind of "virtual reality" show that does not really exist and that there is another parallel real world, like the one in the movie *The Matrix*? I then suggest that, since there are so many things he does not know, how can he be sure there are not important truths that if known could completely change his worldview. If he rejects Christianity out of hand, how can he be sure it is not true?

If Truth Is Subjective

If modern man thinks truth is subjective—a product of his own mind—and if he pretends to be the ultimate judge of the truth, he must admit that he cannot live consistently with this position. Thinking something is true does not make it so; belief does not create truth. This position ultimately reduces modern man to pretending he is God, which he knows he is not.

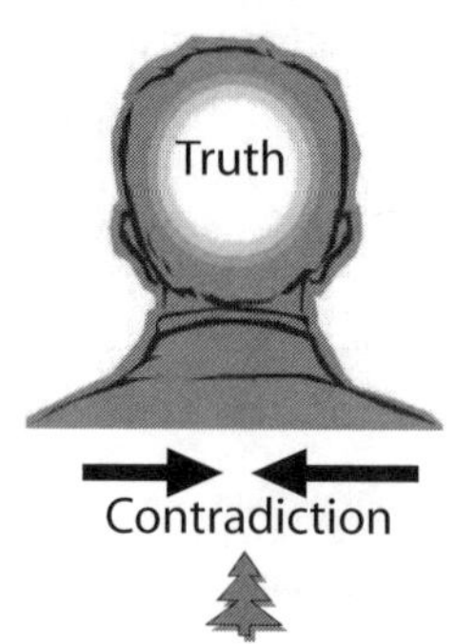

I ask people who take this position to imagine they are standing between the rails on a railroad track. Then I ask them what they would do if they saw a train coming. Would they simply decide the train is not coming? I guarantee they would not try this! They would jump off the tracks, as anyone in his or her right mind would do! What does this prove? Simply that people cannot live consistently with the idea that we create truth in our minds—that belief creates truth.

If Truth Is Impossible

Another alternative is to deny the possibility of knowledge. This position is even more problematic than the preceding ones. The moment one affirms that nothing can be affirmed, one has affirmed something and so has contradicted oneself. If I cannot be sure of anything, how can I be sure that I cannot be sure of anything? This is a self-refuting position. It is like saying, "Everything I say is a lie!" Again, we come back to Cratylus: It would be better to say nothing!

While I was studying in seminary, I worked as a night supervisor in a college library nearby to pay for my studies. Another student also worked there, and frequently we talked about my faith. She once said, "You can't be sure of anything." When I asked her how she could be sure of that, she became furious and stomped out. Several hours later, she returned and muttered, "I *think* you can't be sure of anything." Then she abruptly turned and walked away without waiting for an answer. At least she had become aware of her inconsistency!

If Everything Is True

Have you ever heard someone say, "What is true for you is true for you, and what is true for me is true for me"? In our day, it is popular to avoid conflict and in the name of tolerance to accept anything and everything as true. But if everything is true, then nothing is really true!

Truths contain within themselves the denial of other truths. For example, if we say there is *only one* straight line between two points, then we are denying that there are *two* straight lines between two points. We cannot consistently believe both. If we begin to say that A is true and A also is not true, then we are losing our mental sanity.

We would be like the young man who appeared before his church leaders to be examined for ordination as a pastor. When they asked him if he believed in the divinity of Jesus, he said, "I don't deny the divinity of Jesus; I don't deny the divinity of anybody!" The problem is, if everyone is divine, then divinity loses its meaning. The very concept of divinity includes being superior. If everyone is God, then no one is God.

THE SELF-CONTRADICTION OF IMPERSONAL MONISM

Although many impersonal worldviews postulate some kind of unity, the unavoidable conclusion is that man also is part of this impersonal unity. Therefore, he loses his freedom and identity as an individual. Without an external reference point and a personal God who is separate from the universe and who makes sense out of everything, man becomes lost in a deterministic, impersonal process. Therefore, even his own thoughts lose their significance for they, too, are determined by the impersonal universe.[2]

Freedom can have a wide variety of meanings. It can mean *total* freedom of thought, decision, and action, with absolutely no restraints.[3] Few people believe man has this kind of freedom. After all, who is "free" to jump to the moon? It also can mean freedom to *think* your own thoughts and make your own decisions, even though you might be limited in carrying out your will. Most peo-

2. In teaching classes on this section, some students have brought up the fact that we are one in Christ—that the church is one body with many parts, and that we do not lose our identity because of this. My answer is that there are essential differences between the unity of the Church and the philosophical concept of the unity of all things. In the Christian scheme, we are not part of an impersonal unity, we do have an external reference point, and God is a personal God outside of things, defining our identity.

3. Freedom from all causation is called "libertarianism". See John Frame, "Determinism, Chance, and Freedom," in W. C. Campbell-Jack, Gavin J. McGrath, and C. Stephen Evans, eds., *New Dictionary of Christian Apologetics* (Downers Grove, IL: InterVarsity Press, 2006), s.v.

ple innately sense they have this kind of freedom. Although the Bible teaches that God has sovereignly planned all things (Eph. 1:11), it also considers man responsible for his own thoughts and decisions.[4] The Westminster Confession of Faith says:

> God has endued the will of man with that natural liberty, that is neither forced, nor, by any absolute necessity of nature, determined good, or evil.[5]

Impersonal monism, as described in this book, would eliminate freedom of thought because it would mean that something outside ourselves causes our thoughts. For example, if deism is true and the universe is like a huge clock, why would our thoughts have any more meaning than the "tick tock" of the clock?

Ancient Greek philosophers understood this problem, and it led them into skepticism. Heraclitus maintained that the universe was in constant movement like a river.[6] Other Greek philosophers began to question whether knowledge and communication were possible.[7] Why? Because you cannot believe the universe is a great flowing river and also pretend you are standing on the riverbank, outside of it, observing the flow in an independent and objective way. You also must be part of the river. And if you are only a drop of water in the river, how can you pretend to give your opinion about the nature of the river? Cratylus was consistent with this scheme, and he decided to stop talking all together! At least this was an honest response. If communication and knowledge are impossible, why talk?

This dilemma also perplexed Kant, and it gave birth to modern existentialist philosophy. Kant proposed an unknowable

4. John Frame calls this "compatibilism." See Frame "Determinism, Chance, and Freedom," *New Dictionary of Christian Apologetics,* s.v.

5. WCF, 9.1.

6. Humberto Giannini, *Esbozo para una historia de la filosofía* (Santiago, Chile: Talleres Vera y Giannini, 1981), 17.

7. Giannini, *Esbozo,* 25.

world of "noumena," where man is free. Kierkegaard could only suggest that we must live with this tension; man is a part of the impersonal process, but somehow he also is free.

Think of the theory of evolution. If the world is nothing more than a product of an impersonal, evolutionary process, and if nothing exists except matter, then my thoughts also are nothing more than a movement of atoms, a silent chemical reaction. A crude way of saying this is, "The brain secretes thoughts in the same way that the liver secretes bile."[8] Therefore, why should we pretend that our thoughts are correct? Why would we think they mean anything? The very theory that I am proposing is just a chemical reaction. This is like sawing off the branch I am sitting on! At best, our thoughts are only animal-like responses. Darwin himself wrote in a letter:

> The horrendous doubt always arises whether the convictions of man's mind, which has developed from the mind of the lower animals, are of any value or at all trustworthy. Would anyone trust the conviction a monkey's mind, if there are any convictions in such a mind?[9]

C. S. Lewis quotes the succinct argument of J. B. S. Haldane against materialism:

> If my mental processes are determined wholly by the motions of atoms in my brain, I have no reason to suppose that my beliefs are true . . . and hence I have no reason for supposing my brain to be composed of atoms.[10]

8. Cabanis, quoted in James Sire, *The Universe Next Door*, (Downers Grove, IL: InterVarsity Press, 1997), 98.

9. Quoted in Sire, *Universe Next Door*, 83. Sire attributes the quote to a letter to W. Graham (July 3, 1881), quoted in *The Autobiography of Charles Darwin and Selected Letters* (New York: Dover, 1892, new printing, 1958).

10. J. B. S. Haldane, *Possible Worlds and Other Essays* (London: Chatto & Windus, 1937), quoted by C. S. Lewis in *Miracles*, 22.

Monism leads to a similar problem with regard to *ethics*. Monists tend to deny that there are ultimate distinctions between true and false and between good and evil, but they cannot live consistently with this denial. If I ask one of them if I can hit him in the nose, surely he will say, "No!" But if I ask him why not, what can he answer? If there is no distinction between right and wrong, it is equally right to hit him or not to hit him!

The point here is not just to win an argument with someone who believes in monism. The point is to help them see that they do not really believe in this system, at least not *consistently*. They know their thoughts really *do* have meaning—that some things *are* right and some things *are* wrong, and that they *are* somehow free. Therefore, they need to seek an alternative explanation of the universe that explains this.

The following illustration might help the non-Christian understand the problem of losing his identity in the oneness of everything. Imagine being alone in your house for a week, as I recently was when my wife was visiting her family in Chile. You would feel lonely, and you would desire the company of friends. This represents the desire for unity. Now imagine that you attend a huge conference with 15,000 people, like an InterVarsity Conference in Urbana, Illinois. In this context, you quickly sense a need to identify yourself as a unique individual. As you meet with others, you want to let them know your name, tell them where you are from, and provide details about yourself so they know who you are. Without this, you feel lost in the multitude. This represents the loss of identity in universal oneness. Of course, as Christians we have the solution in a personal relationship with God. We have his company when we are alone, and we have our identity in him when we are in a multitude. Philosophically speaking, he is our external point of reference who allows us to see how all things fit together, but without losing our significance.

KEY CHARACTERISTICS OF MAN, ACCORDING TO THE BIBLE

The Bible clearly describes who we are as human beings. There are several key passages and fundamental biblical truths that provide an important orientation for apologetics on this topic.

We Are the Image of God

This point is essential: Christians and non-Christians alike are the image of God, and we can appeal to this commonality in our apologetic outreach. The non-Christian is not beyond our reach; we can communicate the gospel to him because he, too, is God's image. What does the "image of God" include? To understand it, think of the differences between people and animals. Man is creative. He is the sovereign master over the rest of creation. He has social relations, a moral sense, the capacity to reason, the ability to communicate with language, a will, and emotions. When we wake up in the morning and force ourselves out of bed, we manifest our willpower. When we compose a song, paint a picture, or write a poem, we show our creativity. When we enjoy time with our family, we reveal our emotions and our need for personal relationships. When we talk to our friends on the phone, we demonstrate our linguistic capabilities. The image of God permeates everything we do.

> Then God said, "Let Us make man in Our image, according to Our likeness; and let them rule over the fish of the sea and over the birds of the sky and over the cattle and over all the earth, and over every creeping thing that creeps on the earth." God created man in His own image, in the image of God He created him; male and female He created them. God blessed them; and God said to them, "Be fruitful and multiply, and fill the earth, and subdue it; and rule over the fish of the sea and over the birds of the sky and over every living thing that moves on the earth." (Gen. 1:26–28)

Most scholars consider "in our image" and "in our likeness" to be synonymous phrases in verse 26, especially in light of the typical Hebrew style of parallelism. However, scholars are not in such agreement about what aspects of man are included in the image of God. Luther regarded the image only as man's original righteousness before the fall and thus concluded that man no longer is the image of God.[11] I agree with Calvin who included in the image those things in general that distinguish man from the animals. For Calvin, the image of God is found in the non-physical aspects of man, but even our physical characteristics reflect God's glory.

> I retain the principle which I lately laid down, that the image of God extends to everything in which the nature of man surpasses that of all other species of animals. Accordingly, by this term is denoted the integrity with which Adam was endued when his intellect was clear, his affections subordinated to reason, all his senses duly regulated, and when he truly ascribed all his excellence to the admirable gifts of his Maker. And though the primary seat of the divine image was in the mind and the heart, or in the soul and its powers, there was no part even of the body in which some rays of glory did not shine.[12]

Even non-Christian thinkers recognize certain aspects of the image of God in man. For example, Plato knew that man is more than just a physical body; Aristotle recognized man's reason; and Kant sought to defend man's freedom.

We Know That God Exists

According to the Scriptures, we don't really need to convince anybody that God exists, because deep down we all know this already. Through his creation, God has revealed himself to

11. Robert Raymond, *A New Systematic Theology of the Christian Faith* (Nashville: Thomas Nelson Publishers, 1998), 425–29.

12. John Calvin, *Institutes of the Christian Religion*. 2 vols., ed. John T. McNeill, trans. Ford Lewis Battles (Philadelphia: Westminster Press, 1967), 1.15.3.

every human being. The problem is that we suppress this truth and try to hide it. Some people even seek a scientific explanation for it; now they are talking about the "God gene."[13]

> For the wrath of God is revealed from heaven against all ungodliness and unrighteousness of men who suppress the truth in unrighteousness, because that which is known about God is evident within them; for God made it evident to them. For since the creation of the world His invisible attributes, His eternal power and divine nature, have been clearly seen, being understood through what has been made, so that they are without excuse. For even though they knew God, they did not honor Him as God or give thanks, but they became futile in their speculations, and their foolish heart was darkened. Professing to be wise, they became fools, and exchanged the glory of the incorruptible God for an image in the form of corruptible man and of birds and four-footed animals and crawling creatures. (Rom. 1:18–23)

Notice that when Paul spoke to the Epicurean and Stoic philosophers in Athens (Acts 17), he took advantage of the fact that all human beings have a sense of God's existence. He noticed that among all their idols, they had dedicated one to the "unknown God." He realized that this betrayed a sense of the true God, and he turned this into a point of contact.

> So Paul stood in the midst of the Areopagus and said, "Men of Athens, I observe that you are very religious in all respects. For while I was passing through and examining the objects of your worship, I also found an altar with this inscription, 'TO AN UNKNOWN GOD.' Therefore what you worship in ignorance, this I proclaim to you." (Acts 17:22–23)

Once, when I was talking with a Buddhist girl from Vietnam, I experimented with this concept. First, I asked her to tell me the story of Buddha. When she finished, I asked her if God

13. Jeffrey Kluger, "Is God in Our Genes?," *Time*, Oct. 25, 2004, 62–72. The article refers to the book by Dean Hamer, *The God Gene: How Faith Is Hard-Wired Into Our Genes* (New York: Doubleday, 2004).

let Buddha into heaven after he died. I almost was surprised when she said yes. I repeated the question to make sure. I said, "You mean that God was pleased with Buddha and allowed him into heaven when he died?" Again she agreed. I said, "Then you believe there is a God!"

We Have the Law of God Written on Our Hearts

Man has a moral sense—a conscience—and therefore also a sense of guilt. Even though our values may be quite distorted, all people have a general sense of right and wrong. As we saw in our survey of the history of philosophy, the desire to distinguish between right and wrong is one of the last things man desperately holds on to, even when he is skeptical about knowing truth. Many movies portray the battle between good and evil. In fact, world religions show some common moral values. Famous literature also reveals the common problem of a guilty conscience. In spite of Freud's attempt to explain away man's true conscience by saying it has been imposed by society, it is an inherent aspect of human makeup. The notion of right and wrong is so undeniable that scientists seek desperately for an evolutionary explanation. Now they speak of the "giving gene," which supposedly developed over time as some animals tended to defend each other within their own herds and thus survived the others.[14] However, our basic innate sense of right and wrong does not come from a natural process of the survival of the fittest, nor does it come from society. It comes from God himself, who has made us in his image.

> For when Gentiles who do not have the Law do instinctively the things of the Law, these, not having the Law, are a law to themselves, in that they show the work of the Law written in their hearts, their conscience bearing witness and their thoughts alternately accusing or else defending them. (Rom. 2:14–15)

14. Olivia Judson, "The Selfless Gene," *The Atlantic*, Oct., 2007, 90–98.

Shakespeare's Lady Macbeth urged her husband to commit murder and eventually went insane because of her sense of guilt. She imagined her hands were permanently stained with blood, and she rubbed them desperately to remove it. She cried, "Out, damned spot!" However, it was useless, and she eventually committed suicide.

Tolstoy's main character in *Resurrection*, Nekhluyudov, sensed compunction for his shameful past. He had seduced a maid in his aunt's house, then sat on a jury that unjustly condemned the same woman for robbery. He had misled another young lady about his romantic intentions. He also realized he was living in contradiction with his beliefs about wealth. And so he searched his soul:

> "But am I really"—he stopped and stood still—"am I really such a scoundrel?—Well, am I not?" he answered himself.
>
> Never before had there been such discord between what his conscience called for and the life he was leading, and he was horrified when he saw the distance between the two.
>
> The distance was so great, the defilement so complete, that at first he despaired of the possibility of being cleansed. "Haven't you tried to improve and be better, and nothing came of it?" whispered the voice of the tempter within. "So what is the use of trying any more?"[15]

Even tribal groups far removed from civilization manifest a sense of guilt and a need somehow to make a sacrifice to cover their sins. One group may send out a dog on a raft to die for them. Others may cut off the head of a chicken. Some even sacrifice their own children. One of the most astounding things I have ever seen was a frozen indigenous child found in the Andes mountains of Chile. The experts believe he is hundreds of years old. He was dressed and seated in a way that shows he had been sacrificed to the gods.

15. Leo Tolstoy, *Resurrection*, trans. Rosemary Edmunds (London: Penguin Books, 1966), 140–41.

Man's mind is not a "tabula rasa"—a blank slate. Our hearts and minds know God exists and that he is holy and sovereign. Therefore, we have a fundamental understanding of good and bad, of right and wrong, no matter how much we have twisted this knowledge. No matter how hard we try to erase or hide it, these truths remain engraved on our hearts and minds.

We Do Not Want to Submit to God

We need to keep in mind that the image of God has been damaged by the fall and contaminated by sin. Even our reason and our conscience no longer function perfectly. Although we know God exists, until the Holy Spirit works miraculously in our hearts, we continue to deny God and refuse to honor him. Our fundamental problem is spiritual, rather than intellectual. We do not *want* to accept the truth.

> There is none who understands, there is none who seeks for God. (Rom. 3:11)

> They are without excuse. For even though they knew God, they did not honor Him as God or give thanks. (Rom. 1:20–21)

To avoid recognizing God as our creator and sovereign Lord, we invent our own personal paradigms of reality—worldviews—that exclude God.

> Their thinking became futile and their foolish hearts were darkened. Although they claimed to be wise, they became fools. (Rom. 1:21–22 NIV)

Once, I began talking with a young man from the neighborhood who had joined us for outdoor basketball. He insisted that he did not believe in God or miracles. I asked him what his understanding of miracles was and what would possibly convince him that miracles happen. He defined a miracle as something he could not explain scientifically. I asked what he would think if I could kill my friend and then raise him from the dead—raising my fist and acting like I might really do it! While he was hesitating to answer, I decided to help him out and suggested, "You would probably search the rest of your life to find a 'scientific' explanation, wouldn't you?" "Yes, probably," he admitted. "Then there really is nothing that would convince you that miracles can happen, is there?" "No, I guess not," he confessed. The honesty of this young man provides a profound insight into how non-Christians think. They set up their own rules to defend what they chose to believe.

THE VITAL CONFLICT OF THE NON-CHRISTIAN

A few years ago, a candidate for president in Chile withdrew from the campaign, saying he had begun to experience a "vital contradiction." Although he wanted to be president, it did not fit who he was. He had been an excellent minister of finances, but to be president was just not for him.

The non-Christian also experiences a "vital contradiction." He cannot really live with his own convictions. Although he denies God with his own invented truths, deep down he knows God is there. Although he refuses to live according to God's ethical guidelines, his conscience constantly reminds him they are valid. Although he pretends that he is not guilty, in reality his burden of guilt is too heavy to bear. He might decide in his mind that he is his own god, but the whole creation shouts at him that he is not. He might even try to deny his own dignity and the possibility of knowing the truth, but since he is the image of God, every cell in his body urges him against thinking he is nothing more than an "accident" or "animal."

The non-Christian is like John Nash, when he was suffering hallucinations. The movie *A Beautiful Mind* dramatically tells the story of this mathematical genius and Nobel Prize winner who heard voices of people that didn't exist. (In the movie, he actually *sees* people.) To give importance to his life, he began to imagine that he was helping the U. S. Government decipher spy codes to help avoid a nuclear holocaust. How could one convince John Nash the people he imagined were not real? He interpreted every attempt to do so as an attack on him and as siding with the spies. He always found a way to fit events into his own false scheme. Even his wife could not help him. However, she did continue to love and support him, in spite of how disheartening it was. Finally, there was a breakthrough. He suddenly realized that one of the people in his imaginary world was a young girl who was not growing up. After many years, she continued to be a young girl about ten years old. This detail made him begin to question the validity of his make-believe world, and finally he sought professional help.

This gives us a guideline for apologetics. We shouldn't let the non-Christian think he is all right when really he is "ill." We need to persist in loving him and at the same time help him see his inconsistency. We should look for something that makes him come to his senses. Our task is to show him the contradictions involved in living according to his false scheme. Then he can listen to our description of the Christian message and understand it is a worldview with which we can live consistently.

The non-Christian is like the prodigal son (Luke 15:11–32) who took his share of the inheritance and went far away. He tried to start a new life, pretending his father did not exist, but he could not go on like that forever. The first questions people normally ask you are related to your family and where you are from. No one can pretend he just came into existence! How long can you hide your history? Can you imagine a conversation with the prodigal while he was feeding the swine? Cornelius Van Til helps us envision this:

> When the prodigal son left his father's house he could not immediately efface from his memory the look and the voice of his father. How that look and that voice came back to him when he was at the swine trough! How hard he had tried to live as though the money with which he so freely entertained his "friends" had not come from his father! When asked where he came from he would answer that he came "from the other side." He did not want to be reminded of his past. Yet he could not forget the past.[16]

This is the non-Christian's dilemma. He knows where he came from, but he is trying to deny it. However, there comes a moment when he has to admit the truth. He has to "come to his senses," as the prodigal son did. And when he does, God the Father comes running to receive him with open arms and celebrates with a banquet!

Group Exercise

Look at a pencil or some other object in the room. Ask who thinks the object really exists. Ask why he or she thinks it exists, and keep asking why he believes what he believes, until he reaches his final answer. Try it with others in the group. What does this exercise reveal about each person's theory of knowledge (epistemology)? How does God fit into the picture?

Review Questions

1. If we were to use one word to describe the non-Christian for the purpose of apologetics, what would it be?
2. If we were to use one phrase to describe the root of man's problem regarding his search for truth, what would it be?
3. If the non-Christian thinks truth is outside himself, what problem does he face?

16. Cornelius Van Til, *The Defense of the Faith* (Phillipsburg, NJ: Presbyterian and Reformed Publishing Co., 1979), 231.

4. If the non-Christian thinks truth is in his own mind, what will he have to admit?
5. If the non-Christian denies the possibility of truth, what problem does he face?
6. What is wrong with saying, "What is true for you is true for you, and what it true for me is true for me"?
7. What is the inevitable dilemma of impersonal monism?
8. What doubt did Darwin express about the convictions of the human mind?
9. Mention the characteristics of man explained in this chapter, and give a Bible reference that supports each one.
10. In what way is the non-Christian like John Nash?
11. In what way is the non-Christian like the prodigal son?

Questions for Reflection

1. What was your tendency before becoming a Christian? Did you believe truth was outside your mind, that the truth was in your own mind, that it was impossible to know the truth, or that everything is true? What problems did this perspective cause you?
2. How has your understanding of non-Christians changed as a result of reading the first four chapters of this book? Explain.

Part 2

Certainty in Christian Apologetics

The fear of the Lord *is the beginning of knowledge.*

Proverbs 1:7

Now faith is being sure of what we hope for and certain of what we do not see.

Hebrews 11:1

5

Representative Apologists (Part 1)

Many advisers mean security. Prov. 11:14 (Good News)

What can we learn from some of the foremost apologists? This chapter begins a two-chapter survey of some of the most interesting arguments offered since the second century for the truthfulness of Christianity. This survey is selective. It is neither an encyclopedia of apologists nor a thorough review of the people and positions we will examine. Instead, it explains some arguments and concepts that have been helpful to me. The order of presentation is predominately chronological.

As early as the second century, apologists like Justin Martyr (ca. 100–165) defended Christianity against the accusation of "atheism," since Christians did not worship the multiple gods worshipped by the Romans. Justin pointed to fulfilled prophecies as proof of the validity of Christianity, and he carefully explained Christian customs, beliefs, and ethical principles.[1] Irenaeus (ca.

1. Edwin M. Yamauchi, "Justin Martyr; Defender of the Faith," *Great Leaders of the Christian Church*, ed. John Woodbridge (Chicago: Moody Press, 1988), 40–42.

130–202) wrote against the Gnostic heresy.[2] Tertullian (ca. 155–230) also defended Christianity against false accusations and the heresies of his day.[3] Although these early apologists were well educated—having studied Greek philosophy extensively—and were used by God in their day to open the hearts and minds of many non-Christians, we will begin our survey with the giants of medieval Christian philosophy and apologetics—Augustine, Anselm, and Aquinas—who have blessed the church with a legacy of apologetic arguments that continue to be useful today.

AUGUSTINE (354–430)

Augustine of Hippo disputed the dualistic philosophy of Manichaeism and in doing so developed answers to the problem of evil. Mani held that good and evil have existed from all eternity. This supposedly avoids the contradiction of an all-powerful and good God who creates evil. Augustine addressed Manichaeism by asserting that evil is not a created substance but a "defect" of good, an "accident" (in the sense of being a temporary negative situation), a "privation of good." For example, sickness is a privation of health. When a person becomes well, the sickness does not continue in some other form but ceases to exist.

> Nothing evil exists in itself, but only as an evil aspect of some actual entity.[4]

Furthermore, Augustine argued that God allows evil for an ultimately good purpose.

2. Everett Ferguson, "Irenaeus; Adversary of the Gnostics," *Great Leaders of the Christian Church*, 44–47.

3. Gerald L. Bray, "Tertullian and Western Theology," *Great Leaders of the Christian Church*, 50–54.

4. Augustine, *Enchiridion*, chapter 4, *Confessions and Enchridion* (Philadelphia: Westminster Press, 1955), 344.

> For the Omnipotent God, whom even the heathen acknowledge as the Supreme Power over all, would not allow any evil in his works, unless in his omnipotence and goodness, as the Supreme Good, he is able to bring forth good out of evil.[5]

These arguments still are helpful in our efforts to address the problem of evil. God is not the "author" of evil (James 1:13),[6] and ultimately he causes evil to fulfill a good purpose within his perfect plan. To explain that evil is not part of the *physical creation* may not be the best way to express this argument (although it is true), since it still doesn't answer the question why God allowed evil to occur in the first place, but at least it points to the biblical teaching that God made all things good (Gen. 1:31).

Anselm (1033–1109)

Anselm is known for his "ontological argument" for the existence of God. Basically, the argument is as follows:

1. "God" is defined as the greatest conceivable being.
2. Real existence (existence in reality) is greater than mere existence in the understanding.
3. Therefore, God must exist in reality, not just in the understanding.[7]

Some consider this argument to be valid, but others consider it to be a linguistic illusion. Those who refute it (and I agree with them) say that just because you can imagine something, or define it, doesn't mean it really exists.[8]

5. Augustine, *Enchiridion*, chapter 3, *Confessions and Enchiridion*, 342.

6. See WCF, 3.1.

7. Anselm, *Proslogium*, chapters 2 and 3, *Proslogium; Monologium: An Appendix in Behalf of the Fool by Gaunilon; and Cur Deus Homo*, trans. Sidney Norton Deane (Chicago: The Open Court Publishing Co., 1903), 7–9.

8. See Alvin Plantinga, *God and Other Minds: A Study of the Rational Justification of Belief in God* (Cornell University Press, 1990). He concludes that none of the more

Thomas Aquinas (1225–74)

Aquinas applied Aristotelian logic to theology. He assumed man could come to the conclusion that God exists by observing nature and using reason ("natural theology"). He is known for five key arguments:

1. *Motion.* Everything that moves has been moved by something or somebody. If we continue looking for the first mover, we discover that it must be God.
2. *Cause.* In a similar way, everything has a cause. If we continue the process of seeking the cause of everything, we will eventually find the first cause, who is God.
3. *The impossibility of nothing existing.* While it is possible for many things not to exist, it is not possible that nothing exists, for if at a time in the past nothing existed, then nothing could exist after that, since nothing comes from nothing. If anything exists now, then something always existed. If we back up far enough, we come to the point where we must assume that one first thing necessarily existed without an outside cause, and that must be God.
4. *Ideal standard.* All things are compared according to good, better, best. Something with which everything else is compared must be the best of all, and that must be God.
5. *Design.* All things seem to have a purpose. When unintelligent things act for a purpose, they point to a designer, who must be God.[9]

---

obvious ways of stating this argument succeed, but he does not rule out the possibility that there may be some version of the argument that is valid. See page 64.

9. Aquinas, *Summa Theologiae*, Question 2, Article 3.

The first three arguments have been called "cosmological" arguments. The fifth is called the "teleological"—not "theological"! The word comes from the Greek word *telos*, meaning "end" or "purpose." Some consider the fourth argument a version of the "ontological" argument, although it sounds quite different from Anselm's argument. I understand Aquinas to be saying that something is better than everything else, and we consider that to be God.

These arguments can be quite helpful. They show the logic of believing in a superior being who started everything. The teleological argument is especially helpful, since it points to intelligent design. According to Romans 1:18–20, God has revealed himself in his creation, and mankind senses something of his "invisible qualities"—his "eternal power and divine nature." Psalm 19:1 says, "The heavens declare the glory of God; the skies proclaim the work of his hands." When I doubted the existence of God, it was by looking at the stars that I sensed his presence. So, we certainly need to take advantage of the kind of reasoning that points to evidence for God's existence in his creation. In fact, the sense of a superior being is so divinely programmed into man that we really don't have to work very hard to convince most people of this. Some people may have suppressed the knowledge of God more than others, but most people soon concede they believe in some kind of superior being.

However, we have to be careful how we use these arguments. We have to admit they are not sufficient to show very much about that "superior being." If we use them by themselves, without referring to the scriptural concept of the one-and-only, personal, triune, saving God, then we have not accomplished a lot. In fact, we may have immunized our friend against the gospel by giving him just enough knowledge to invent his own concept of a superior being and to avoid facing the true God. We might make a Muslim out of such a person, a deist, a Jew, a Hindu, or just about any kind of religious believer. Remember that when Paul was speaking to the Athenians, he didn't simply point out the altar to the "unknown God" and say, "I'm so glad you believe in God!" Rather, he said, "Now what you worship as something unknown, I am going to proclaim to you" (Acts 17:23).

John Calvin (1509–64)

My wife, Angelica, studied French in college, and since Calvin was a key figure in French history, his teachings were included as part of her required reading. Although her professor was critical of Calvin, Angelica found Calvin convincing. In fact, this was the beginning of her conversion to Christ. I mention this because usually Calvin is not seen as an apologist but as a systematic theologian. However, his *Institutes* really should be seen as a *defense* of the faith. Calvin integrated his "apologetics" with a convincing presentation of the gospel.

Calvin did not rely primarily on reasoning or evidences to convince the non-Christian of the truth of the gospel. Compared with Aquinas, Calvin greatly reduced the role of human reason. However, he did not *reject* reason. In fact, he was very good at presenting well-reasoned arguments and evidences to *confirm* the gospel. It was precisely this aspect of Calvin's theology that caused my wife to start thinking. His combination of logic and passion was persuasive.

Calvin highlighted the fact that God has revealed himself to all men. "There is within the human mind, and indeed by natural instinct, an awareness of divinity."[10] Man himself, being the very image of God (a "clear mirror of God's works"), is the highest revelation of God in all of creation.

10. John Calvin, *Institutes of the Christian Religion*, 1.3.1.

> For each one undoubtedly feels within the heavenly grace that quickens him. Indeed, if there is no need to go outside ourselves to comprehend God, what pardon will the indolence of that man deserve who is loath to descend within himself to find God?[11]

Thus, general revelation is sufficient to leave man without excuse, according to Calvin. "We see that no long or toilsome proof is needed to elicit evidences that serve to illuminate and affirm the divine majesty."[12] However, the evidence of God in creation does not lead man to *salvation*. The Scriptures, as used by the Holy Spirit, are needed to communicate the gospel and to illuminate man's heart and mind, producing faith in Christ.

Calvin's defense of the Scripture reveals his view of apologetics. "They who strive to build up firm faith in Scripture through disputation are doing things backwards."[13] He asserted that only the testimony of the Holy Spirit will convince someone of the authority of the Bible.

> Since for unbelieving men religion seems to stand by opinion alone, they, in order not to believe anything foolishly or lightly, both wish and demand rational proof that Moses and the prophets spoke divinely. But I reply: the testimony of the Spirit is more excellent than all reason. For as God alone is a fit witness of himself in his Word, so also the Word will not find acceptance in men's hearts before it is sealed by the inward testimony of the Spirit.[14]

In fact, Calvin insisted that "it is not right to subject it [the Scripture] to proof and reasoning."[15]

> Therefore, illumined by his power, we believe neither by our own nor by anyone else's judgment that the Scripture is from God; but

11. Calvin, *Institutes*, 1.5.3.
12. Calvin, *Institutes*, 1.5.9.
13. Calvin, *Institutes*, 1.7.4.
14. Calvin, *Institutes*, 1.7.4.
15. Calvin, *Institutes*, 1.7.5.

> above human judgment we affirm with utter certainty (just as if we were gazing upon the majesty of God himself) that it has flowed to us from the very mouth of God by the ministry of men.[16]

In other words, anyone who comes into the very presence of God does not ask for proof of his existence or proof of his deity. His very glory is "proof" enough. The same thing happens with the Bible; as we read it, we recognize God's majestic authority.

After having said this, Calvin went on to present "firm proofs" of the credibility of Scripture. He believed that even if he were to argue with "the most crafty sort of despisers of God, who seek to appear shrewd and witty in disparaging Scripture," he would have plenty of arguments to "silence their clamorous voices."[17] His "proofs" include the following. (1) The wisdom of Scripture is "superior to all human wisdom." It is "crammed with thoughts that could not be humanly conceived." (2) The Scripture is very old, taking us back to the time of Moses, predating other religious writings. (3) Miracles attest to the authority of God's messengers. (4) Biblical prophecies were fulfilled, for example, the fall of Jerusalem and the name of Cyrus, mentioned in Isaiah. (5) Scripture has been preserved over many years. (6) The New Testament shows "simplicity and heavenly character." (7) The church has given "unvarying testimony" to the authority of the Scriptures. From this we see that, for Calvin, conviction of the authority of Scripture is "above" human reason, but not *against* it.[18]

G. K. CHESTERTON (1874–1936)

In the first half of *The Everlasting Man*,[19] Chesterton, a Catholic journalist and apologist, invites the reader to assume that

16. Calvin, *Institutes*, 1.7.5.
17. Calvin, *Institutes*, 1.7.4.
18. Calvin, *Institutes*, 1.8.1–12.
19. G. K. Chesterton, *The Everlasting Man* (New York: Doubleday and Company, 1955). See the online version of this book at http://www.worldinvisible.com/library/

man is a mere animal and then shows how that false assumption helps us see the astonishing differences between men and animals. In the second half, he reasoned similarly about Jesus. He shows that if we assume Jesus is a mere man, we will soon be overwhelmed at the differences between him and any other human being.

Chesterton argued that we cannot consider Jesus equal to other founders of religions, for example, Muhammad, Confucius, or Buddha, since none of them claimed to be God. In fact, normally the people we consider the greatest have been the least likely to make such a claim. The only people who consider themselves divine are lunatics. But Jesus obviously was not a lunatic.

> No modern critic in his five wits thinks that the preacher of the Sermon on the Mount was a horrible half witted imbecile that might be scrawling stars on the walls of a cell. No atheist or blasphemer believes that the author of the Parable of the Prodigal Son was a monster with one mad idea like a Cyclops with one eye. Upon any possible historical criticism, he must be put higher in the scale of human beings than that. Yet by all analogy we have really to put him there or else in the highest place of all.[20]

C. S. Lewis (1898–1963)

C. S. Lewis is one of the most widely read Christians of the last century. His children's books—The Narnia Chronicles—and science fiction—The Space Trilogy—are treasured by non-Christians and Christians alike, and they have been translated into many different languages. The recent movie *The Chronicles of Narnia: The Lion, the Witch, and the Wardrobe*, based on the first book of this series, has been very successful. Lewis's apologetic books are original, profound, and a pleasure to read. We will focus on four books that give us some heavy ammunition for apologetics.

---

chesterton/everlasting/content.htm.

20. Chesterton, *The Everlasting Man*, 202.

The Problem of Pain[21]

Lewis begins this book by explaining how an argument from nature for the existence of God would not work for him. Since there is so much suffering, it would only lead him to believe in a weak God or an evil God. "Either there is no spirit behind the universe, or else, a spirit indifferent to good and evil, or else an evil spirit."[22] But he turns this around and asks how people could still believe in an all-powerful loving God, considering the problem of pain. He suggests that this sense of God must come from God himself.

Then he argues that evil could be avoided only by altering the environment and depriving man of free will. Lewis insists that although in one sense God can do anything, in another sense he cannot do something that is intrinsically impossible. He cannot make a four-sided triangle, for example. There is no limit to his power, but he cannot make man with free will and at the same time withhold free will. Neither can he make man in an environment that does not follow certain predictable laws without taking away man's freedom. God could have programmed man in such a way that evil thoughts were impossible, so that his brain simply refused to function when he attempted to think something evil. Or maybe he could have prevented suffering by constantly manipulating the nature of things. But these options would take away true free will—our ability to choose what we desire in accordance with our abilities.

> We can, perhaps, conceive of a world in which God corrected the results of this abuse of free will by His creatures at every moment; so that a wooden beam became soft as grass when it was used as a weapon, and the air refused to carry the sound waves that carry lies

21. C. S. Lewis, *The Problem of Pain* (New York: The Macmillan Company, 1962). Originally published in 1940, it was his first apologetics book. A 2001 edition is available from HarperCollins.

22. Lewis, *Problem of Pain*, 15.

> or insults. But such a world would be one in which wrong actions were impossible, and in which therefore, freedom of the will would be void.[23]

Lewis concludes,

> Try to exclude the possibility of suffering which the order of nature and the existence of free wills involve, and you find that you have excluded life itself.
>
> Perhaps this is not the "best of all possible" universes, but the only possible one.[24]

Lewis considers pain "God's megaphone," a "terrible instrument" to remind us that something is wrong here. It "removes the veil" and "plants the flag of truth within the fortress of a rebel soul."[25] Pain keeps us from settling in this world and points us to eternity.

> Our Father refreshes us on the journey with some pleasant inns, but will not encourage us to mistake them for home.[26]

With regard to hell, Lewis insists that "the doors of hell are locked from the inside."[27] People can only blame themselves for deciding to reject God.

Miracles[28]

Lewis argues for miracles in this book by showing that naturalism contradicts itself. Naturalism affirms that nature is the only reality; it denies the spiritual and supernatural dimensions.

23. Lewis, *Problem of Pain*, 33.
24. Lewis, *Problem of Pain*, 34, 35.
25. Lewis, *Problem of Pain*, 95.
26. Lewis, *Problem of Pain*, 115.
27. Lewis, *Problem of Pain*, 127.
28. C. S. Lewis, *Miracles* (New York: Macmillan, 1968). Originally published in 1947. A 2001 edition is available from HarperCollins.

Lewis, however, says we must be consistent. If we believe only in the natural, we must include our own thoughts as a part of the natural process. But if my thoughts are caused by the impersonal movement of atoms (an irrational cause), why should I believe my thoughts are valid? This leads me to doubt the very premise I am defending. Lewis says,

> If all that exists is Nature, the great mindless interlocking event, if our own deepest convictions are merely the bye-products of an irrational process, then clearly there is not the slightest ground for supposing that our sense of fitness and our consequent faith in uniformity tell us anything about a reality external to ourselves. Our convictions are simply a fact about us—like the colour of our hair. If Naturalism is true we have no reason to trust our conviction that Nature is uniform.[29]

Lewis also argues:

> The Naturalist cannot condemn other people's thoughts because they have irrational causes and continue to believe his own which have (if Naturalism is true) equally irrational causes.[30]

In other words, as we mentioned previously, the theory of a closed universe is self-destructive because it is self-refuting. It is like saying, "Everything I say is a lie." It saws off the epistemological branch you are sitting on.

Lewis points out that naturalism has a similar problem with moral judgments. If naturalism is true, there is no reason to believe a moral system based on naturalism is better than any other moral system. In fact, Lewis says, "If Naturalism is true, 'I ought' is the same sort of statement as 'I itch' or 'I'm going to be sick.' "[31]

29. Lewis, *Miracles* 108.
30. Lewis, *Miracles*, 22.
31. Lewis, *Miracles*, 36.

This argument is powerful. Many people have naturalistic worldviews or believe in some kind of monism or in a "closed universe." Pointing out how these common positions are indefensible is a good starting point to force people who hold them to reconsider their belief systems.

Surprised by Joy[32]

This is the personal testimony of how Lewis came to believe in God. He was intrigued by an inexplicable sense of joy that often returned to him, especially as he remembered pleasant moments of his youth. Where does joy come from? It certainly can't be just a result of an impersonal process of the universe. He concluded that God must exist and that joy comes from him. Here we find the inverse of the problem of pain. Just as non-Christians ask how evil can exist, we can ask them how joy could exist, given their worldviews.

Mere Christianity[33]

In this popular book, Lewis argues that man's sense of right and wrong points to God. There is a common notion that "man ought to be unselfish," yet this "law" is not something we invented. Materialism cannot give an adequate explanation of this, but Christianity can.[34] Lewis goes on to explain what Christians believe, then deals with issues of Christian morality.

32. C. S. Lewis, *Surprised by Joy* (Orlando, FL: Harcourt Brace and Company, 1955).

33. C. S. Lewis, *Mere Christianity* (New York: HarperCollins, 2001, original copyright, 1952).

34. Lewis also develops this argument in *The Abolition of Man* (New York: HarperCollins, 2001), originally published in 1944. In this book, Lewis rejects the tendency to consider all moral judgments subjective and argues there really is such a thing as objective moral values. As an illustration, he argues that when one says that a waterfall is "sublime," he is not talking about his own feelings about the waterfall, but he is saying something about the waterfall itself. A similar argument can be made for moral issues. See pages 3–5.

Again, Lewis gives the free-will answer to the problem of evil. Why would God allow evil? He says that people in authority often allow something that is according to their will in one sense but against their will in another sense. For example, a mother may want her daughter to keep her room tidy, but at the same time she allows her the freedom to mess it up. "This is not what you willed, but your will has made it possible."[35]

Notice that Lewis's apologetic approach appeals to the image of God in man, especially to our belief that we are free to make decisions, to our sense of joy, and to our sense of right and wrong. Although non-Christians may attribute these characteristics to sources other than God, the Bible teaches they are reflections of God's image in us.[36]

Cornelius Van Til (1895–1987)

Van Til reminds us of the story of the emperor who had no clothes. The royal tailors deceived the emperor into believing he had a beautiful new suit of clothes and that only morons could not see the cloth. As the emperor sauntered through the streets, no one dared tell him he was completely naked, until a simple child bravely shouted the truth. Van Til has been compared to the little child who dared to expose the pretended autonomy of non-Christian thought.[37]

I can remember when Dr. Van Til would pace back and forth in front of the class and imitate Eve before the fall. "I wonder . . . , I wonder . . . , I wonder . . . who is right, God or the serpent?" But what right did they have to question their creator? How could they set themselves up as judges of truth, even over God? After the fall, the situation is even worse because every aspect, faculty,

35. Lewis, *Mere Christianity*, 47.

36. Gen. 1:26–28; 2:15–25; 3:6; Rom. 2:14–15.

37. Rousas J. Rushdoony, *By What Standard?* (Philadelphia: Presbyterian and Reformed, 1965), 19.

and ability of man has been damaged, including our reason and will. Man cannot discover ultimate truth on his own, independently of God, but this is exactly what he tries to do.

Van Til insists there are no "brute facts"—facts without interpretation—just waiting for man to find them. Truth is not neutral. To know the truth is to be faithful to God; to believe a lie is to be unfaithful to him. God has original, absolute knowledge; man only has knowledge that he receives from God. Therefore, we must learn to "think God's thoughts after him."

In a sense, there is no real epistemological "common ground" between Christians and non-Christians. That is, we should not go over to the non-Christian's belief system, accept his approach to knowledge, and then try to persuade him of the truth. It won't work. Once we have accepted his basic postulates, we cannot come back to the truth. For example, if we agree with the non-Christian that logic is the ultimate tool for judging truth, we will not be able to agree with him about some mysterious but basic doctrines, such as the Trinity. If we agree that logic is our test, then essentially we have allowed man to become the judge of what is logical and therefore of what is true. If man is the judge, then God no longer is our authority and source of truth. This does not mean there is no dialogue between Christians and non-Christians or that we should not try to listen to the non-Christian or understand his thinking. But we cannot agree with his basic foundation.

However, Van Til allows for assuming the position of the non-Christian, for the purpose of argument. He says, "They can, *for argument's sake*, place themselves with the unbeliever on his presupposition in order then to show him that he cannot even raise an intelligible objection against the Christian view."[38] Richard Pratt has cleverly developed this strategy in *Taking Every*

38. Cornelius Van Til, *The Defense of the Faith* (Phillipsburg, NJ: Presbyterian and Reformed Publishing Co., 1979), 180.

Thought Captive.[39] With the purpose of making Van Til's apologetics useful for lay people, he centers his strategy around Proverbs 26:4–5, "Do not answer a fool according to his folly, or you will be like him yourself. Answer a fool according to his folly, or he will be wise in his own eyes." Pratt explains that these apparently contradictory verses simply mean that on the one hand, we should avoid actually adopting the convictions of a non-Christian but that on the other hand, it is a good apologetic method to temporarily adopt his position, with the purpose of showing that it leads to contradictions. In other words, we can say, "Let's assume your position is true for a moment. Where would this lead us?"

Van Til's position does not mean there is no point of contact between Christians and non-Christians. Christians and non-Christians alike are surrounded by God's self-revelation in creation and in our consciences. Deep in his heart, the non-Christian senses God's existence; he is aware of the moral law; and he feels guilty for his sin (Rom. 1, 2). Furthermore, every person is created in God's image.

According to Van Til, ultimately all reasoning is circular. That is, no one can prove the starting point for their system without presupposing the truth of their system. We all presuppose the truth of our epistemological starting points. Christians always should refer back to God's word—his self-revelation in words in the Bible—as our final authority. Why do I believe something? Because *God* says so. How do I know God says so? Because God says he says so! The Christian concept of truth always takes us back to God's self-revelation in the Bible, not to ourselves, as our epistemological starting point.

On the other hand, by definition, the non-Christian's epistemological starting point is himself, and so in the final analysis

39. Richard Pratt, *Taking Every Thought Captive* (Phillipsburg, NJ: Presbyterian and Reformed Publishing Co., 1979).

he must return to himself. Why does the non-Christian believe something? Because *he* says so! The non-Christian's concept of truth always takes him back to his own reason and imagination, not to God, as his epistemological starting point.

> In the last analysis, we shall have to choose between two theories of knowledge. According to one theory, God is the final court of appeal. According to the other theory, man is the final court of appeal.[40]

Van Til is not presenting a blind, irrational leap of faith—a kind of simplistic fideism. God's word (the Bible) "fits" God's general revelation that we, as his image, perceive and interpret. In fact, *only* by presupposing the truth of Christian theism can we explain the world. Any other presupposition leads to self-contradiction and confusion. His apologetic method often is called "presuppositionalism."

To defend the Bible, says Van Til, we must be careful to avoid submitting God's word to some supposedly higher authority. If we judge the Scriptures by logic, we have put logic above God. If we judge his word by our scientific principles, by our notion of right and wrong, by our interpretation of history, by our emotions, or by anything else, we have elevated the other principle above God; we have made our minds God's judge, and we are back in the garden of Eden!

> We do not use candles, or electric lights in order to discover whether the light and energy of the sun exist. The reverse is the case. We have light in candles and electric light bulbs because of the light and energy of the sun. So we cannot subject the authoritative pronouncements of Scripture about reality to the scrutiny of reason, because it is reason itself that learns of its proper function from Scripture.[41]

40. Cornelius Van Til, *The Defense of the Faith* (Phillipsburg, NJ: Presbyterian and Reformed, 1979), 34.

41. Van Til, *Defense of the Faith*, 108.

For Van Til, there is a huge difference in the way a non-Christian uses reason and the way a Christian uses it. The non-Christian uses reason to suppress the truth and misinterpret general revelation. Van Til insists, "The Scriptures nowhere appeal to the unregenerate reason as to a qualified judge."[42] However, the Christian can use logic (Van Til appears to use *logic* interchangeably with *reason* here) to confirm the gospel. "The Christian finds, further, that logic agrees with the story [of the gospel]." In fact, "According to the Christian story, logic and reality meet first of all in the mind and being of God. God's being is exhaustively rational."[43] In other words, although God is a rational being and the gospel message is rational, fallen man will not see it that way until the Holy Spirit changes his heart and mind. Even after conversion, a Christian may not always use his reason in the proper way, due to the continuing battle with sin. Therefore, reason is a valid God-given instrument, but it must be used with caution and always in submission to God.

Van Til challenged me to submit my very thought process to the Lord, and when I did, it was like a second conversion. I believe many Christians have not experienced such an epistemological conversion. Luther said that if God told him to eat crab apples and manure, he would do it since it was a command.[44] As I mentioned previously, I also would say, "If God tells me the moon is made out of green cheese, then I'll change my mind about the moon and about green cheese!" Of course, God will never make a statement that so clearly contradicts our normal use of language, reason, and observation, but this idea expressed my new attitude of absolute submission to him. My point is that

42. *Defense of the Faith*, 212.

43. *Defense of the Faith*, 215.

44. Ernest Gordon Rupp, "Martin Luther" (July 29, 2005). http://www.hfac.uh.edu/gbrown/philosophers/leibniz/BritannicaPages/Luther/Luther.html.

whatever God says is right. Who am I to question him? He is the creator; I am a creature.

Van Til's analysis provides a truckload of confidence when dialoguing apologetically with non-Christians, because it enables us to see clearly the epistemological root of their problem and to keep our feet firmly planted in the Scriptures. Van Til's writings encourage us to keep apologetics evangelistic. In a way, he is saying that non-Christians need to hear the gospel proclaimed in a clear and challenging manner. We should not allow non-Christians to continue to reject the gospel because of their pretended autonomy. We must show them that their way of thinking—their epistemology—is rebellion against their creator. I believe Van Til is correct. Everything comes back to the gospel, to what God's word teaches about his lordship over knowledge and knowing—about God's epistemological sovereignty over his creatures and his creation.

This was not merely Van Til's theory; it was his practice. Although many might perceive him as a deeply philosophical writer who is difficult to understand, his students remember how he would frequently tell us that he met someone on the train and invited him for a cup of coffee to share the gospel with him. His students also remember how he would take walks with us around campus to chat with us and how his favorite hymn was "Jesus loves me, this I know, for the Bible tells me so." Apologetics must never be separated from practical evangelism.

The only danger in adopting Van Til's approach is that some of his disciples have wrongly concluded that all other apologetic approaches are wrong, including the use of evidences. Although there is disagreement regarding what Van Til believed about using evidences, John Frame, the best authority on Van Til, asserts that Van Til did *not* reject the use of evidences.[45] Personally, I agree

45. John Frame, *Apologetics to the Glory of God: An Introduction* (Phillipsburg, NJ: P&R Publishing, 1994), 12–13.

with Frame. I believe Van Til is not saying it is *wrong* to use evidences. I believe he is saying that we should not use evidences as supposedly *neutral* data or arguments and that we cannot expect non-Christians to *accept* them, because the unregenerate person is blind both to the truth of the gospel (special revelation) and to the truth of evidences (general revelation). According to Van Til, even though the non-Christian is spiritually blind, we should still "reason" with him, since the Holy Spirit can use this to open his eyes.

> Scripture teaches us to speak and preach to, as well as to reason with blind men, because God, in whose name we speak and reason, can cause the blind to see. Jesus told Lazarus while dead to arise and come forth from the grave. The prophet preached to the dead bones in the valley till they took on flesh. So our reasoning and our preaching is not in vain inasmuch as God in Christ reasons and preaches though us.[46]

If we trust God to open the eyes of non-Christians to the truth of the gospel, we also can trust the Holy Spirit to open their eyes to the truth of evidences. Why not use all aspects of the truth—God's special and general revelation? Of course, the gospel message is absolutely necessary for salvation, and it has a definite priority, but sometimes evidence from general revelation can help clear the dust from the air so that non-Christians can see the truth more easily.

FRANCIS SCHAEFFER (1912–84)

Much of Francis Schaeffer's ministry was at a location called *L'Abri* ("shelter," in French) in Switzerland, where he and his wife, Edith, received the intellectual seekers of the 1950s–1980s. Schaeffer was an evangelist to people from all over the world. As such, he wrestled with their existential doubts and felt the anguish of their despair and uncertainty. He analyzed philoso-

46. Van Til, *Defense of the Faith*, 212–13.

phy, music, art, literature, and culture in general as these related to the Christian message and worldview. He was prophetic in his understanding of where what we now call "postmodern thinking" was leading Western civilization. He identified key aspects of the image of God in man and touched people with the truth of the gospel. He was especially good at pointing out the vital contradictions in non-Christian belief systems.

Nancy Pearcey, a disciple of Schaeffer, considers his apologetic method a "hybrid" of evidentialist and presuppositionalist methods. She traces some of his views back to Thomas Reid and the Scottish "Common Sense" philosophy that asserted some things are innately known by man and do not need complicated philosophical proof, for example, one's own personal identity, the existence of a real natural world, and the validity of the use of reason.[47]

The God Who Is There[48]

I personally consider *The God Who Is There* Schaeffer's most important book. In the first half, he shows there has been a change in the concept of truth in the modern era. Modern man no longer believes in absolutes and the law of non-contradiction. Schaeffer identified a "line of despair" in philosophy, art, music, general culture, and theology, below which there is no longer a "unified field of knowledge." Man is in a dark room with no windows. With regard to philosophy, Kierkegaard is the first philosopher Schaeffer identifies as being "below the line," where faith is not rational. In art, the door to modernistic thinking was opened by impressionists such as Gauguin, who painted "Where Do We Come From? What Are We? Where Are We Going?" and tried

47. Nancy Pearcey, *Total Truth: Liberating Christianity from its Cultural Captivity* (Wheaton, IL: Crossway, 2005), 297, 313. See also Thomas Reid, *Essays on the Intellectual Powers of Man* (Boston: J. C. Derby, 1855).

48. Francis Schaeffer, *The God Who Is There* (Downers Grove, IL: InterVarsity Press, 1998).

to commit suicide. Some contemporary music communicates chaos; for example, the *Premier Panorama de Musique Concrète*, which begins with a voice speaking Greek, then slowly fades, begins to tremble, and ends in chaos. Bergman's movie *Silence* is a series of pornographic images with no meaning.

In this context, apologetics (the second half of *The God Who Is There*) can show that Christianity makes sense—that it provides answers to confused modern men. How do we know Christianity is true? Because it all fits together. Schaeffer gives an illustration of a torn book found in an attic.

> Imagine a book which has been mutilated, leaving just one inch of printed matter on each page. Although it would obviously be impossible to piece together and understand the book's story, yet few people would imagine that what had been left had come together by chance. However, if the torn parts of each page were found in the attic and were added in the right places, then the story could be read and would make sense.
>
> So it is with Christianity: the ripped pages remaining in the book correspond to the abnormal universe and the abnormal man we have now. The parts of the pages which are discovered correspond to the Scriptures which are God's propositional communication to mankind, which not only touch "religious" truth but also touch the cosmos and history, which are open to verification.[49]

Schaeffer suggests that we find the "point of tension" in the non-Christian—the point where he cannot live consistently with his own beliefs—and help him see the incongruence between his beliefs and his life. For example, the musician John Cage believed everything comes from chaos, and he composed music by chance. However, when he went to pick mushrooms, he did not do it by chance. He carefully distinguished between poisonous mushrooms and healthy ones! Each person has constructed

49. Schaeffer, *God Who Is There*, 137–38.

a "roof" to protect himself, and we should carefully and lovingly "take the roof off," Schaeffer said.[50]

There is nothing quite like this book. It is a profound analysis of contemporary man, along with diverse cultural expressions, from a Christian point of view. Schaeffer spoke clearly to a generation that was confused and facing a crisis of doubt and uncertainty. He helped many Christians, like myself, see that Christianity was a consistent package of truth, that intelligent people still believed it, and that the non-Christian was absolutely lost in self-contradictions.

My only concern with Schaeffer's approach is that he seems to give reason a higher priority than I think it should have. A logical analysis of the world we live in seems to be Schaeffer's starting point. For example, when discussing his example of the torn book found in the attic, Schaeffer says:

> The whole man would be relieved that the mystery of the book had been solved and the whole man would be involved in the reading of the complete story; but man's reason would be the first to tell him that the portions which were discovered were the proper solution to the problem of the ripped book.[51]

Later, he wrote:

> The truth that we let in first is not a dogmatic statement of the truth of the Scriptures, but the truth of the external world and the truth of what man himself is. This is what shows him his need. The Scriptures then show him the real nature of his lostness and the answer to it. This, I am convinced, is the true order for our apologetics in the second half of the twentieth century for people living under the line of despair.[52]

50. Schaeffer, *God Who Is There*, 147–54.
51. Schaeffer, *God Who Is There*, 137.
52. Schaeffer, *God Who Is There*, 159.

That is, we begin our dialogue with a non-Christian on the basis of his observation and reason, and then we give the scriptural explanation. But this does not mean that we give more *authority* to reason, or even to general revelation, than we do to Scripture. Schaeffer apparently wanted to avoid a simplistic presentation of the gospel. Sometimes, we rush too quickly to share the message with someone who isn't ready. We need to learn their language, see their needs, and address them in their situation. Furthermore, we need to keep in mind, as previously argued, that each person is different and may respond to a different approach.

He Is There and He Is Not Silent[53]

This is my second favorite of Schaeffer's books. It sketches the non-Christian's problems and the Christian answers in the three major divisions of philosophy—metaphysics, ethics, and epistemology—and shows how the Christian worldview is the only consistent one.

With regard to metaphysics, there are only three possible explanations of the origin of the universe: Everything came from nothing; everything had an impersonal beginning; or everything had a personal beginning. The first option is "unthinkable." The second option would mean that everything is really just one impersonal thing, and this would lead to a loss of personal identity and significance for the particulars, including people and our thoughts. The only acceptable explanation is that everything had a personal origin.

Schaeffer presents a similar argument with regard to ethics. If the universe had an impersonal beginning, then morality makes no sense. We would not have an explanation or solution

53. Francis Schaeffer, *He Is There and He Is Not Silent* (Wheaton, IL: Tyndale, 1972), also published as part of a trilogy by Crossway (1990) and alone as a revised and updated version by Tyndale (2001).

for the existence of evil. Only Christianity gives a valid basis for absolute morals based on the absolute character of God. Only Christianity offers a valid explanation of the existence of evil without also making God evil. Man was not created evil, but made himself evil.[54] Furthermore, in Christianity we find hope that man can be changed for the good, and we have a basis for fighting against evil.

Christianity also solves the epistemological problem. Knowledge is possible because of a personal-infinite God who made the universe, made man in his image to live in it, and has communicated with him, especially in the Bible. Since God knows everything, he can communicate effectively with man, and his message is in total harmony with the rest of the universe and with man's experience. Man does not have to know everything to be sure of something, because God himself, the source of all truth, has graciously and effectively revealed certain truths to him. For example, since God knows absolutely everything about the resurrection of Jesus, he can allow us to know *something* about it in a valid way. That is, man can know something *truly* without knowing it *exhaustively*.

Schaeffer illustrates the difference between a blind, irrational leap of faith and the biblical concept of faith. Suppose that we are mountain climbing in the Alps, and suddenly a fog settles in. The guide says we will freeze to death by morning. To keep us warm, he moves us into a dense fog, but now we have no idea where we are. One person decides to drop down just anywhere, hoping to land on a ledge, where he might have the possibility of surviving (a blind leap of faith). Suppose that now we hear the voice of a man telling us from a distance that he knows where we can find a ledge. We cannot see the man, but we ask who he is and realize he is from a family who lives in the area. We ask more

54. Chapter eight of this book deals with this issue more thoroughly.

and more questions, until we begin to trust him. Only then do I drop where he indicates, and I find a safe ledge (Christian faith, based on trust in God).[55]

Schaeffer was brilliant at pushing non-Christians to see the inconsistency of their positions and at making the Christian postulates resonate with non-Christians' innate sense of significance, truth, and morality. He showed how current philosophical issues relate to our daily lives. Once, when a young man insisted that they were not really communicating—pretending to show that no real communication was possible—Schaeffer astutely asked him for a cup of tea. When the man brought the tea, he simply said, "Now we are communicating!" He would do anything to break through to a person.

Francis Schaeffer is one of my heroes. His books helped me through my doubting years. He showed me that Christianity is a complete, harmonious package of truth, consistent with my experience, and his writings gave me the desire to believe Christian truth. Schaeffer showed me that I was being brainwashed into thinking that truth was relative, and he opened my understanding to contemporary culture. He awakened a desire in me to make my own life something different and creative.

GROUP EXERCISE

Let one person play the role of the skeptic, and let two other people play the roles of the apologists studied in this chapter. Practice a possible dialogue that could have taken place between three such people. Afterwards, discuss which apologetic approach seemed more effective.

55. Schaeffer, *He Is There and He Is Not Silent*, 99–100.

Review Questions

1. Explain the arguments of Augustine regarding the problem of evil.
2. Note the three steps of the ontological argument of Anselm.
3. Mention the five arguments of Thomas Aquinas for the existence of God.
4. What is the danger in using these arguments, according to the author?
5. According to Calvin, why is it not necessary to give "toilsome proof" of the existence of God?
6. According to Calvin, what form of revelation is necessary for someone to come to salvation?
7. According to Calvin, how does someone come to believe in the authority of the Scriptures?
8. What reasoned "proofs" does Calvin give to confirm the authority of Scripture?
9. Explain the argument of G. K. Chesterton for the divinity of Jesus.
10. According to C. S. Lewis, what would we lose if we had a world in which God made sure evil did not exist?
11. According to Lewis, what is the benefit of suffering?
12. Explain how naturalism contradicts itself, according to Lewis.
13. How did C. S. Lewis come to believe in God?
14. Explain the argument that Lewis uses in *Mere Christianity* for the existence of God.
15. What is the main problem in the thinking of the non-Christian, according to Van Til?
16. In what sense is there no "common ground" between the believer and the non-Christian, according to Van Til?
17. What is our "point of contact" with the non-Christian, according to Van Til?

18. In what sense is all reasoning "circular," according to Van Til?
19. Why should we not use criteria outside of the Bible to prove the Bible, according to Van Til?
20. What is the only danger in adopting the apologetic method of Van Til, according to the author?
21. What is the "line of despair," as explained by Francis Schaeffer?
22. Explain the illustration of Francis Schaeffer about the torn book.
23. What does Schaeffer mean when he says we should find the non-Christian's "point of tension"?
24. What is the author's concern about Schaeffer's apologetic approach?
25. Summarize the main argument of the book *He Is There and He Is Not Silent*.
26. Explain Schaeffer's illustration of the mountain climbers in danger in the Alps.

Questions for Reflection

1. Mention the argument that has helped you most from the apologists studied in this chapter. How did it help you?
2. Explain any concerns that you might have about any apologist presented in this chapter.

6

Representative Apologists (Part 2)

The second group of apologists consists of contemporary authors. Although many of their arguments have been presented by earlier writers, these men have updated them and contextualized them for a new generation.

Norman Geisler

Geisler has produced an arsenal of arguments that are quite helpful for defending our faith. He has written over sixty books and hundreds of articles.

In *When Skeptics Ask*, he presents evidence from science, archeology, and biblical passages. He places much weight on logic and the law of non-contradiction. He refers to the classical arguments for the existence of God and adds an argument from the moral law, giving credit to Immanuel Kant. The idea is that a sense of "ought" cannot come from the natural universe. It must come from a supreme lawgiver, who is God.[1] The fact that most people have many ethical principles in common reveals

1. As we have seen above, C. S. Lewis used the same argument. Aquinas put it another way: there is something better than everything else, and that "something" is God.

the divine source of morality. Geisler points to the second law of thermodynamics as an argument for creation. Heat dissipates, and the universe is slowing down. If it had always existed, then it already would have run down.

In dealing with the problem of evil, Geisler cites Augustine and develops the argument that evil is not a "substance" that God created. Geisler says,

> Evil is, in reality, a parasite that cannot exist except as a hole in something that should be solid. In some cases, though, evil is more easily explained as a case of bad relationships. If I pick up a good gun, put in a good bullet, point it at my good head, put my good finger on the good trigger and give it a good pull . . . a bad relationship results. The things involved are not evil in themselves, but the relationship between the good things is definitely lacking something. In this case, the lack comes about because the things are not being used as they ought to be. . . . Evil is a lack of something that should be there in the relationship between good things.[2]

In an argument similar to that of C. S. Lewis, Geisler suggests that a world without the possibility of evil would only be possible in a world without free will. He challenges us to consider the options: God could have chosen not to create anything, or God could have created creatures that are not free. Theoretically, God could have created "free" creatures who could not sin, but this is not "actually achievable."

> He [God] could have set up some mechanism so that just when they were about to choose something evil, a distraction would come along to change their decision. Or maybe He could have programmed creatures to do only good things. But are such creatures really free?[3]

2. Norman Geisler and Ron Brooks, *When Skeptics Ask* (Grand Rapids: Baker Books, 1990), 61.

3. Geisler, *When Skeptics Ask*, 73.

Geisler considers that "Forced love is rape; and God is not a divine rapist." He concludes,

> This may not be the best of all possible worlds, but it is the best way to the best world. If God is to both preserve freedom and defeat evil, then this is the best way to do it.[4]

With regard to the Bible, Geisler argues that we accept it on the basis of Jesus' testimony. He confirmed the Old Testament (Matt. 5:18; 2 Tim. 3:16; 2 Peter 1:21) and promised the New Testament (John 14:25–26). All apparent difficulties in the Bible have valid explanations. For example, the two different genealogies of Jesus in Matthew and Luke can be explained by showing that Matthew gives the descent from Joseph, while Luke gives the lineage of Mary.[5] Furthermore, genealogies in the Bible generally were not intended to be complete, for example, the genealogy in Genesis 5. Other supposed errors in data can be explained by the fact that numbers frequently were rounded or stated generally during the biblical period. Purposeful "imprecision" is not the same as an error.[6] Geisler deals with many other examples of supposed errors in the Bible.

Geisler provides us with many sound arguments and much up-to-date evidence. My only concern is the place he assigns reason and logic. In the introduction to *When Skeptics Ask*, he proposes there is a difference between evangelism and "pre-evangelism." Whereas evangelism is based on revelation, pre-evangelism (apologetics) is based on reason.[7] Later he says, "Logic is a necessary presupposition of all thought" and "How do we know that logic applies to reality? We know it because it is undeniable."[8] He

4. Geisler, *When Skeptics Ask*, 73.
5. Geisler, *When Skeptics Ask*, 168.
6. Geisler, *When Skeptics Ask*, 165.
7. Geisler, *When Skeptics Ask*, 10.
8. Geisler, *When Skeptics Ask*, 270.

asserts that you have to use logic to deny logic. After explaining the principles of Aristotelian logic, especially pointing to the fact that "all logic can be reduced to one single axiom—the law of non-contradiction,"[9] he says:

> These principles become the foundation for all knowledge. From this point, logic and evidence can confirm that God exists and that Christ is His Son. Truth has an absolute foundation in undeniable first principles and it can be tested through logical means because it ultimately corresponds to reality. Christianity claims to be true and it bids all to come in and dine at the table of truth.[10]

I agree that logic is a valid instrument for human reasoning, and I believe that it is part of God's image in man.[11] However, I believe the only reason we know we can trust logic is because *God says we can*. That is, the Bible suggests that the laws of logic, especially of non-contradiction, are valid. It doesn't say so explicitly, but the communication and the argumentation presented to us in Scripture assume the validity of logic. Paul uses logic, especially in Romans. For example, he says, "For if, when we were God's enemies, we were reconciled to him through the death of his Son, how much more, having been reconciled, shall we be saved through his life!" (Rom. 5:10). Here Paul appeals to our sense of logic: If God treated us with such love when we were enemies, obviously he will treat us even better, now that we are friends.

The problem is that after the fall we can misuse our reasoning abilities. Not only can we make logical mistakes, but we can use logic and reason to try and suppress our knowledge of God. Our reasoning abilities need to be submitted to God's word for correction and so that we can learn their limits and the divinely authorized realms in which they should be used. If we allow rea-

9. Geisler, *When Skeptics Ask*, 270–72.

10. Geisler, *When Skeptics Ask*, 272.

11. See the section in chapter 4 on the image of God in man.

son and logic to act as independent judges of truth, then what will happen to the doctrine of the Trinity or to the doctrine of the divine and human natures of Christ, or to many other theological *mysteries* that do not contradict reason but that seem to go beyond reason and that cannot be explained merely by *rational* means? Although these doctrines are not irrational or illogical, we would probably not become convinced of them if logic is our main guide.[12] To say that logic is the "foundation for all knowledge" stabs me in the heart. It flies in the face of the biblical teaching that God himself is the source of all truth. Proverbs 1:7, "The fear of the LORD is the beginning of knowledge." I certainly do not believe that Norman Geisler denies this, but his *theory* of apologetics is inconsistent with his theology. I can use most of the arguments and evidence in Geissler's book, as long as I am faithful to my commitment to the epistemological *authority* and the *priority* of God's word. But I am uncomfortable with Geisler's theory of apologetics. What is our final answer? When someone asks me why I believe what I believe, is my final answer going to be "because it is logical" or "because God says so"? If my final answer is *logic*, then my final answer is really, "because *I think so*," and we repeat the tragedy of the garden of Eden.

JOSH MCDOWELL

McDowell has been a popular apologist for Campus Crusade for Christ for more than thirty years and has spoken internationally to college students. He does not necessarily present new and original arguments, but he has written more than sixty-five books that are virtual encyclopedias of data and evidence to support the truth of Christianity. His own conversion came when he tried to disprove the resurrection and became convinced that the evidence pointed to its validity.

12. Geisler agrees with the doctrines of the Trinity and the two natures of Christ.

In *Evidence that Demands a Verdict*,[13] McDowell begins with evidence for the credibility of the Bible—it is unique, and it is confirmed by history and archeology. Later chapters of the book revisit this subject and present evidence of fulfilled prophecies. The middle section focuses on Chesterton's and Lewis's "trilemma" argument: Jesus was either a lunatic, a liar, or the Lord. Since Jesus' life and teachings do not fit the pattern of a lunatic or a liar, he must be who he said he was, God. Later, McDowell wrote a second volume with a similar title especially to answer the accusations of biblical higher criticism that portray and interpret the Bible as nothing more than human religious writings that are filled with errors and contradictions. Finally, McDowell combined these two into one volume and updated it. *New Evidence that Demands a Verdict*[14] addresses the more recent issues raised by the "Jesus Seminar" (a group of scholars who pretend to research what Jesus really said or did, in contrast with the biblical accounts), as well as deeper philosophical questions, such as the nature of truth, skepticism, and postmodernism.

McDowell presents many examples of how Jesus fulfilled the prophecies regarding the Messiah. Some of the most compelling examples are the following:

He would be born of a virgin.

> Therefore the Lord himself will give you a sign: The virgin will be with child and will give birth to a son, and will call him Immanuel. (Isa. 7:14)

He would be born in Bethlehem.

13. Josh McDowell, *Evidence that Demands a Verdict* (San Bernadino, CA: Here's Life Publishers, 1972).

14. McDowell, *New Evidence that Demands a Verdict* (Nashville: Thomas Nelson, 1999).

But you, Bethlehem Ephrathah,
    though you are small among the clans of Judah,
out of you will come for me
    one who will be ruler over Israel,
whose origins are from of old,
    from ancient times. (Mic. 5:2)

He would enter Jerusalem riding on a donkey.

Rejoice greatly, O Daughter of Zion!
    Shout, Daughter of Jerusalem!
See, your king comes to you,
    righteous and having salvation,
    gentle and riding on a donkey,
    on a colt, the foal of a donkey. (Zech. 9:9)

He would be wounded for our sins yet would not defend himself.

Surely he took up our infirmities
    and carried our sorrows,
yet we considered him stricken by God,
    smitten by him, and afflicted.
But he was pierced for our transgressions,
    he was crushed for our iniquities;
the punishment that brought us peace was upon him,
    and by his wounds we are healed.
We all, like sheep, have gone astray,
    each of us has turned to his own way;
and the Lord has laid on him
    the iniquity of us all.
He was oppressed and afflicted,
    yet he did not open his mouth;
he was led like a lamb to the slaughter,
    and as a sheep before her shearers is silent,
    so he did not open his mouth. (Isa. 53:4–7)

McDowell gives other evidence for biblical prophecies whose fulfillments are confirmed in secular historical books, for example, the destruction of the city of Tyre. Ezekiel 26 indicates that Tyre would be destroyed by Nebuchadnezzar, converted into a bare rock—a place to spread fishnets, and that finally it would be totally destroyed and lost. McDowell cites secular accounts of Nebuchadnezzar's attack and later fulfillments of this prophecy by Alexander the Great and others.[15]

Henry Morris, John Whitcomb, and Phillip Johnson

Over the last half a century, many believing scientists have combated the theory of evolution, in part by documenting scientific facts that condemn it. In *The Genesis Flood*, the late Henry Morris, former director of the *Institute for Creation Research*, and John Whitcomb, a theologian, defend the position that the earth was created with "apparent age" by pointing to fallacies in the arguments presented by evolutionists regarding fossil records. Morris and Whitcomb argue that the Noahic flood explains things such as the otherwise baffling presence of thousands of frozen mammoths in Siberia. They believe that during the catastrophe the climate changed so quickly and drastically that it caused the onset of the ice age. The animals did not have time to migrate and consequently were frozen.[16] According to the evolutionary scheme, they would have had time to seek a warmer climate.

Morris and Whitcomb also point out the problem of harmonizing the theory of evolution with the laws of thermodynamics, which are accepted universally by physicists. According to the second law of thermodynamics, things tend to run down and become more disorderly (this principle is called "entropy"). But

15. McDowell, *Evidence that Demands a Verdict*, 267–319.

16. Henry Morris and John Whitcomb, *The Genesis Flood* (Phillipsburg, NJ: P&R Publishing, 1989), 288–95.

this is the opposite of what the theory of evolution proposes—that things become more and more organized and complex.[17]

In *Science and the Bible*, Morris also points out one of the most serious problems facing evolutionists—the lack of transitional fossil forms. There is a lack of evidence of gradual change from one species to another—the very essence of the evolutionary scheme. There are only fossils from animals that are quite distinct among themselves. Instead of gradual changes, the evidence points to sudden jumps. The development of the horse has been given as a classic example of evolution, but research cannot provide the in-between forms.

Furthermore, the fossil layers often are not ordered according to increasing complexity, as would be the case if evolution were true. Instead, scientists frequently find different species that supposedly evolved over great periods of time in the same historical age and in places far away from one another.[18]

Although not a scientist, Phillip E. Johnson, a retired University of California Berkeley law professor and author, has been a key spokesman for the intelligent design movement, which seeks to promote public awareness of an alternative to evolution and campaigns to offer this as a second option in public school curricula. In *Darwin's Nemesis*,[19] Johnson recently has been celebrated for his leadership in this cause, having begun his efforts in 1991 with his book *Darwin on Trial*.[20] In this book, Johnson does not deal with biblical arguments for creationism but uses his training as a lawyer to expose the lack of objectivity on the part of evolutionists. Instead of examining the evidence impartially, evolutionists have distorted it to fit their fundamental assumption that there is a naturalistic explanation for everything.

17. Henry Morris, *The Genesis Flood*, xxi, 222–27.

18. Henry M. Morris, *Science and the Bible* (Chicago: Moody Press, 1986), 51–55.

19. William A. Dembski, ed., *Darwin's Nemesis: Phillip Johnson and the Intelligent Design Movement* (Downers Grove, IL: InterVarsity Press, 2006).

20. Phillip Johnson, *Darwin on Trial* (Downers Grove, IL: InterVarsity Press, 1991).

Antonio Cruz and Michael Behe

Antonio Cruz, a Spanish biologist/theologian, has published fascinating, scholarly, up-to-date books and articles in the areas of a Christian view of science, evolution, philosophy, and postmodernism. Although his writing at times is technical, we can simplify and use some of his most important arguments. I had the privilege of working in the office next door to him for a year when he was giving conferences throughout Latin America, and I consider him one of the best speakers and writers of our day.

Dr. Cruz shows that evolutionists are running out of arguments and losing supporters, even in the secular scientific world. He shows that all creation exhibits intelligent design and that you have to be blind or stubborn not to see it. He says,

> There is an elephant in the scientific laboratories and the research centers called "intelligent design." But many do not want to see it because they have been told that any hypothesis that leads to God cannot be scientific. Nevertheless, the DNA molecule did not appear by accident, but was planned by someone.[21]

Cruz explains that the structure of the atom itself is perfectly designed with no room for alterations.

> If the mass of the neutron were reduced by merely 0.1% of what it is, the protons would be converted into neutrons and this would cause all the stars of the universe to collapse, forming giant black holes or neutronic stars. For life on earth to be possible, the neutrons of the atoms must have the precise mass that they have. The initial conditions of the universe must have been very special so that now there can be life on the earth.[22]

21. Antonio Cruz, *¿La ciencia encuentra a Dios?* [*Does Science Find God?*] (Barcelona: CLIE, 2004), 219 (translated by the author).

22. Cruz, *¿La ciencia encuentra a Dios?*, 181–82.

Cruz argues that complex organisms have existed from the beginning and that there is no evidence of a gradual process from simple to complex organisms, as evolutionists hold.

> If the cat and the dog derived from a common ancestor, as Darwinism tells us, where is the collection of gradual fossils that must have existed between the ancestor and the cat, on one hand, and between the ancestor and the dog, on the other? The issue of lost links, something that concerned Darwin himself so much, having attributed it to the imperfection of the fossil records, has finally been admitted by the evolutionist paleontologists, and some have responded that intermediate fossils have not been found because they never existed.[23]

On the contrary, the evidence points to sudden jumps. Some evolutionists, such as Stephen Jay Gould, have proposed a new version of evolution called "punctuated equilibrium." According to this version of the evolutionary theory, species maintained equilibrium during long periods of time and then experienced sudden changes.[24] The following drawings show the difference between gradualism and punctuated equilibrium.

According to Gould, how did these changes occur? Why have we not found fossils that support his hypothesis? Cruz explains Gould's solution, then provides his own response.

> What was needed was a change so drastic that it would be capable of converting one species into another. And this is what happened [according to the theory of Gould]: a small genetic mutation in the

23. Cruz, *¿La cienca encuentra a Dios?*, 282.

24. Stephen Jay Gould, *The Structure of Evolutionary Theory* (Cambridge, MA: Harvard University Press, 2002), 745ff.

> embryo could completely change the adult. In other words, one day a female lizard laid an egg, and when it cracked open, a rat appeared.
>
> [Cruz answers.] Needless to say, nobody has ever demonstrated even one case of the appearance of a new species in this way (or in any other).[25]

Cruz believes God created more species than now exist and that many of them have disappeared over time, especially because of the Noahic flood. While some species have experienced minor changes ("microevolution"), there is no evidence of jumping from one species to another ("macroevolution").[26]

Dr. Cruz argues against the theory proposed by some Christians that God created new species intermittently over a period of millions of years. He believes this theory conflicts with the biblical account of the fall. The Bible teaches that death was a punishment for sin, but if the animals lived and died during so many years before the appearance of man, they would have experienced punishment for sin before the fall.[27]

Cruz prefers the "gap theory" and the theory of an old earth but clarifies that the Bible does not tell us how old the universe is. Cruz argues that God made the initial materials of the universe, and then after possibly several billion years, he miraculously created the plant and animal species. This gap of time could have occurred between verse one of the first chapter of Genesis and verse two. He suggests that Exodus 20:11 could be translated, "Because God worked on the heavens and the earth during six days," instead of "Because in six days, God created the heavens and the earth," since the original Hebrew does not have the preposition "in."[28]

25. Cruz, *¿La ciencia encuentra a Dios?*, 283.
26. Cruz, *¿La ciencia encuentra a Dios?*, 180.
27. Cruz, *¿La ciencia encuentra a Dios?*, 176.
28. Cruz, "Seis días trabajó Jehová los cielos y la tierra." *¿La Ciencia Encuentra a Dios?*, 179.

One of Cruz's most helpful arguments against Darwinism is based on the concept of "irreducible complexity."[29] Cruz credits biochemist Michael Behe for promoting this concept.[30]

The central concept of irreducible complexity is that many living organisms function as a complete system, with different elements that all depend on each other, so that it is impossible for the organism to function properly unless all of these elements are in their right place and functioning properly. Often the mousetrap is given as an example of an apparatus that is irreducibly complex. It will not function as a mousetrap unless all the pieces exist and are properly fit together. If you remove the spring or the latch, for example, it will no longer trap mice. The eyeball is a good example of a living organism that displays irreducible complexity. The eye could not work without the optic nerve, or the retina, or the pupil, for example. Cruz argues:

> Such a system could not have been produced by evolution from the simple to the complex, because any precursor that was missing a part would be totally inefficient. It would have had to originate from the very beginning as an integrated unity to be able to function properly.[31]

Darwin himself admitted the importance of the concept of irreducible complexity, even going so far as to say that if this could be proved, it would falsify his entire theory of evolution.

29. Antonio Cruz, *Sociología: una desmitificación* (Barcelona: CLIE/Logoi, 2001), 210–14.

30. See Michael J. Behe, William A. Dembski, and Stephen C. Meyer, *Science and Evidence for Design in the Universe* (San Francisco: Ignatius Press, 2000), Michael J. Behe, *Darwin's Black Box: The Biochemical Challenge to Evolution* (New York: Simon and Schuster, 2006), and Michael J. Behe, *The Edge of Evolution: The Search for the Limits of Darwinism* (New York: Free Press, 2007).

31. Cruz, *¿La ciencia encuentra a Dios?*, 23.

> If it could be demonstrated that any complex organ existed, which could not possibly have been formed by numerous successive, slight modifications, my theory would absolutely break down.[32]

Michael Behe, a Roman Catholic biochemist, explains that previously he saw no conflict between Darwinism and his faith. He believed God created life and set into motion the physical laws that include the evolutionary process. However, he began to question Darwinism when he read *Evolution: A Theory in Crisis*, by Michael Denton.[33] He became more interested in the subject when Phillip Johnson invited him to meet other scientists who were questioning evolution. Soon, he was involved in the intelligent design movement and realized that his contribution was the concept of irreducible complexity.[34] He is now a scientific spokesman for the movement, but he tries to separate his scientific arguments from religion. Behe continues to believe in an old earth (4.6 billion years) and in a common descent of all species.[35] However, his problem is with the idea that "random mutation and natural selection powered the changes in life."[36] He believes this is especially apparent on the level of cell structure, something scientists did not yet understand in Darwin's day. As Behe

32. Charles Darwin, *The Origin of Species by Means of Natural Selection* (Boston: Adamant Media Corporation, 2000), 146 (facsimile of 1875 edition published in London by John Murray), quoted by Cruz, *¿La cienca encuentra a Dios?*, 24.

33. Michael Denton, *Evolution: A Theory in Crisis (*Bethesda: Adler and Adler, 1986). Denton is not a creationist.

34. Michael Behe, "From Muttering to Mayhem: How Phillip Johnson Got Me Moving," in *Darwin's Nemesis*, 37–47.

35. Michael Behe, "Darwin Under the Microscope," *The New York Times*, October 29, 1996, 25. See also http://www.arn.org/docs/behe/mb_dm11496.htm, Nov. 29, 2007, "Kansas Evolution Hearings," http://www.talkorigins.org/faqs/kansas/kangaroo10.html, Nov. 29, 2007, and "Michael Behe" in Wikipedia: http://en.wikipedia.org/wiki/Michael_Behe, Nov. 29, 2007).

36. Behe, "Darwin Under the Microscope."

argues, "there is no unintelligent process which could produce the complexity that we see in the cell."[37]

Russell Humphreys

"Answers in Genesis"[38] is an unusually helpful and up-to-date resource for studying evolutionary matters and for learning to defend creationism. Although the site promotes the "young earth" theory (the world was created with the appearance of maturity), they do not make this a dominant issue. They answer questions in language that lay people can understand but with the backing of serious scientific investigation. Common questions such as, "What happened to dinosaurs?" "Does carbon 14 dating contradict the young earth theory?" or "Who did Cain marry?," are addressed with a combination of conservative biblical theology and respectable scientific evidence. Current articles deal with aggressive anti-Christian writers, such as Richard Dawkins.

According to "Answers in Genesis," one of the most interesting current debates among defenders of the young earth position is how to explain the distance of the stars within the young earth scheme. If some stars are millions of light years away and we can see their light, does this prove the universe actually is millions of years old? Dr. Russell Humphreys, a physicist, proposes the theory of a "stretched universe" to address this question. His solution is based on Einstein's general theory of relativity, which teaches that time is not a constant and that gravity and accelerated motion distort time. This theory has been rigorously tested, and multiple observations support Einstein's description of the universe. In his book, *Starlight and Time*,[39] Humphreys suggests that at the beginning of creation, everything was tightly compacted in a point cen-

37. Behe, "Kansas Evolution Hearings."

38. www.answersingenesis.org.

39. D. Russell Humphreys, *Starlight and Time* (Green Forest, AR: Master Books, 1994).

tered near the earth. This would create a very strong force of gravity, and it would slow down time. (A "black hole" is such a tight concentration of matter, with such strong gravity, that not even light can escape, and in a sense, this causes time actually to stand still.) Referring to passages such as Isaiah 42:5,[40] Jeremiah 10:12,[41] and Zechariah 12:1,[42] Humphreys argues that God then *stretched out* the universe. This in turn would weaken gravity and speed up time. In other words, as the universe was stretched out, the acceleration of matter and the reduction in gravity would dilate time from the earth's frame of reference. Thus, while the stretching of the matter in the universe would occur instantaneously from the point of view of a clock contained in the stretched matter, from the point of view of a clock on the earth, this stretching would take billions of years. Although the writers of "Answers in Genesis" are cautious about adopting the "stretched universe" theory wholeheartedly, it is interesting to see plausible options. This theory actually coincides with secular physicists' current theories about the relativity of time and about "white holes" (the reverse of black holes, where instead of collapsing, things expand).[43]

R. C. SPROUL

Sproul is known for his clear and practical theological teaching. His apologetic approach is similar to that of Norman Geisler. He coauthored a book called *Classical Apologetics*,[44] in which he

40. "This is what God the LORD says—he who created the heavens and stretched them out."

41. "But God made the earth by his power; he founded the world by his wisdom and stretched out the heavens by his understanding."

42. ". . . The LORD, who stretches out the heavens . . ."

43. Don Batten (editor), Ken Ham, Jonathan Sarfati, and Carl Wieland, "How can we see distant stars in a young universe?" http://www.answersingenesis.org/docs/405.asp#f12 (Oct. 22, 2007).

44. R. C. Sproul, John Gerstner, and Arthur Lindsley, *Classical Apologetics: A Rational Defense of the Christian Faith and a Critique of Presuppositional Apologetics* (Grand Rapids: Zondervan, 1984).

defends and "reconstructs" the traditional reasoned approach, or the "natural theology" approach, of theologians such as Thomas Aquinas.

Sproul believes both in the "primacy of the mind" and in the "primacy of the heart." "The mind has a primacy of *order*, while the heart has a primacy of *importance*."[45] According to Sproul, man needs reason, just like he needs oxygen, and therefore apologetics must approach him with reasons.[46]

According to Sproul, genuine saving faith has three aspects, and theologians have assigned each aspect a Latin name. *Notitia* refers to the cognitive, intellectual *understanding* of the data or to the content of the gospel message. *Assensus* refers to giving personal intellectual *assent* to the truth of this content. *Fiducia* refers to personal *trust* in Christ for salvation. Apologetics, which Sproul calls "pre-evangelism," is vital for the first two aspects. Apologetics cannot produce the third kind of faith, which is necessary for salvation.[47] Sproul reminds us that God has revealed himself through the creation (Rom. 1:18–20), and he asserts that non-Christians can understand this natural revelation, even without the light of Scripture. Thus all of creation becomes "common ground" between the Christian and the non-Christian.[48]

In his later book, *Defending Your Faith,*[49] Sproul shows more specifically how to use this classical apologetic approach. He first establishes four principles of knowledge that he believes are assumed in Scripture: "1) the law of non-contradiction; 2) the law of causality; 3) the basic (but not perfect) reliability of sense perception; and 4) the analogous use of language."[50] The fourth

45. Sproul, *Classical Apologetics*, ix.
46. Sproul, *Classical Apologetics*, 16.
47. Sproul, *Classical Apologetics*, 21.
48. Sproul, *Classical Apologetics*, 70–72.
49. R. C. Sproul, *Defending Your Faith: An Introduction to Apologetics* (Wheaton, IL: Crossway, 2003).
50. Sproul, *Defending Your Faith*, 30.

point refers to the fact that we can legitimately speak about God without having perfect knowledge of him. Some theologians argue that God is so different from man that we cannot know anything about him or say anything meaningful about him. But Sproul argues there is enough similarity between God and man to make some "connection" (some "point of analogy")—to enable meaningful discourse about him.[51]

Next, based on Romans 1, Sproul defends "natural theology" as the study of God's revelation in creation. He argues that Aquinas has been misunderstood and that he became the "Protestant punching bag of the twentieth century."[52] Sproul insists that Aquinas did not make a "separation" between faith and reason, only a "distinction." He blames Kant, not Aquinas, for such a separation.

Sproul then practices the classical approach, first by presenting arguments for the existence of God. He analyzes four options to explain reality: (1) it could be an illusion; (2) it could be self-created; (3) it could be self-existent (that is, it has always existed); and (4) it could be created by something that is self-existent. Reason will not allow us, as Descartes showed, to believe that *everything* is just an *illusion*. At least I exist, because otherwise I could not be thinking. The option that reality created itself is absurd because it violates the law of causality and the law of non-contradiction. "For something to create itself, or to be its own effect as well as its own cause, it would have to exist before it existed."[53] To say that the universe was created by "chance" is just another way of saying it was created by nothing. To say that reality is self-existent is to concede that something has always existed and that everything else was brought into existence because of it. Sproul argues that this first cause could not be formless, eternal

51. Sproul, *Defending Your Faith*, 33.
52. Sproul, *Defending Your Faith*, 79.
53. Sproul, *Defending Your Faith*, 110.

matter, because matter has no *personality*. The "observable purpose" in the world we experience points to the fact that the first cause is an intelligent designer, a personal God. Furthermore, the moral law within man's heart (Rom. 1–2) points to a lawgiver and a morally perfect judge.

Up to this point, Sproul has argued for a personal, eternal, creator God. Now he focuses on the Bible as our authority in order to create the foundation for a complete Christian system of thought. Sproul prefers to avoid a "circular argument" that quotes the Bible to defend the Bible. However, he appeals to the "internal" evidence and to the "external" evidence of its authenticity. Internal evidence includes the "amazing coherence and symmetry," the "heavenliness of the matter," and the inner "ring of truth" of its contents. External authentication includes historical and archeological findings. But the key to accepting the authority of the Scriptures is in trusting the testimony of Jesus.

> To state the argument in a nutshell: first, we must show that the biblical record is historically reliable, then we must move to the biblical writers' description of Jesus' flawless character. Once that is established, we can judge his claims of prophecy to be reliable because his character is reliable, as attested by the historically reliable biblical accounts. If, then, the accuracy of his teaching is established, we can easily accept his teaching on Scripture—that it is the very Word of God.
>
> In this progression the authority of the Bible, in its highest sense, rests on the testimony of Jesus.[54]

Sproul is a master at making complex things easy to understand, and this is what he has done with classical apologetics. My concern with him is the same as my concern with Norman Geisler. Although Sproul has much to offer in the way of helpful arguments, I am uncomfortable with his emphasis on reason. I

54. Sproul, *Defending Your Faith*, 181.

am imagining a heated debate between a Christian and a non-Christian, both of whom are trying to show how brilliant they are and how logical their systems are. I like Sproul's emphasis on Jesus' testimony as that which validates Scripture, but I would be uncomfortable beginning a discussion about the Bible by allowing the non-Christian to acknowledge merely that the Bible is "historically reliable." I find it hard to believe that such a discussion would lead to an acceptance of the inspiration of Scripture, because it grants the non-Christian the right to be the judge of Scripture from the very beginning. Liberal theologians begin with this approach to Scripture, then they proceed to question miracles and the authority of Jesus' own words. Maybe we cannot expect the non-Christian to look at the Bible as anything more than just "reliable" at the beginning, but I would avoid *granting* him this right, as if it were perfectly acceptable. Sproul himself clarifies that he does not intend to subject God or the Bible to human tests. "It is one thing to use God's gift of reasonable thinking in apologetics; it is quite another to presume that our reasonable thinking is the ultimate standard of truth."[55]

John Frame

John Frame has taken the best from Van Til but has modified his approach to make it more practical, friendly, and open to the proper use of evidences and reasoned arguments. I personally consider Frame the wisest theologian I know. In *Apologetics to the Glory of God*,[56] he suggests that apologetics has three aspects: *proof*—giving a rational basis for our faith, *defense*—answering objections, and *offense*—attacking the foolishness of unbelieving thought. Frame believes that apologetics should be based on

55. Sproul, *Defending Your Faith*, 168.

56. John Frame, *Apologetics to the Glory of God* (Phillipsburg, NJ: P&R Publishing, 1994). Frame also deals thoroughly with epistemology in his *The Doctrine of the Knowledge of God* (Phillipsburg, NJ: P&R Publishing, 1989).

Scripture, not on supposedly "neutral" arguments. Frequently, apologetics tries to start with "unbiased" evidence. However, in that case:

> Logic, facts, experience, and such become the sources of the truth. Divine revelation, especially Scripture, is systematically excluded.[57]

As Van Til has shown, there is no real "neutrality." Nevertheless, we can use evidence as long as we do not surrender our Christian presuppositions.

Frame recounts several arguments for the existence of God, beginning with the moral argument. Ethical values are hierarchically structured. As we climb the ladder to a maxim which is higher than any others, we ask where the authority of the absolute moral principle comes from. There are only two possible answers: (1) the source is personal or (2) the source is impersonal. If the source is impersonal, "What of ethical significance can we learn from the random collision of subatomic particles?"[58] We conclude that the source must be personal, and only the Christian God is both personal and absolute.

Next, Frame presents the "epistemological argument." The human mind correlates with the world and can make sense of it. How could this come from chance? The hypothesis of absolute personality explains the data far better than ultimate impersonality. These two arguments remind us of Francis Schaeffer.

Frame also makes a unique contribution in the defense of Scripture, focusing on the Bible as a *covenant* document. As we survey the history of God's people and the plan of redemption, *it is to be expected* that God would leave a written covenant. He has always related to his people through covenants. In the Bible, the first written covenant began at Mount Sinai after the Israelites'

57. John Frame, *Apologetics,* 4.
58. Frame, *Apologetics*, 98.

liberation from Egypt. The Lord gave the Israelites the tablets on which were written the Ten Commandments, and these were placed in the most sacred place, the ark of the covenant. God continued to add to this document until we had the complete Old Testament. Jesus himself commands that Scripture should never be broken (John 10:33–36). Finally, Jesus tells us that he is making a new covenant (Luke 22:20; 1 Cor. 11:25). Obviously, we would expect this to be written down as well.

> What of the New Testament? In the nature of the case, it could not talk about itself as a completed collection of writings. Yet it leaves no doubt that it is God's purpose to give such a collection to the church.[59]

Frame gives extended attention to the problem of evil.[60] First, he surveys different attempts to solve the problem, such as "process theology," which proposes that God is not totally sovereign but interacts with the creation over time. According to Frame, to excuse God by saying he cannot prevent evil is not an acceptable solution. Others deny evil (Eastern religions), which obviously doesn't fit reality. Some suggest this is the "best of all possible worlds" (Leibniz), but why does a perfect world require evil? After all, God is perfect without evil. Evil is not logically necessary, and we do not know if this really is the "best possible world." How about the free-will defense? Frame insists that the Bible never uses the free-will argument when the issue of evil comes up.

Frame wants to give us a biblical answer, not a philosophical or speculative one. What does the Bible really say about the "problem of evil"? He begins by reminding us that God does not owe us an explanation and that man has no right to complain. Job and Romans 9 put us in our place. Frame suggests we need

59. Frame, *Apologetics*, 125.
60. Frame, *Apologetics*, 149–90.

to look at history and time—past, present, and future—through God's eyes.

> I have always felt that a great many mysteries in theology boil down to the mystery of time.[61]

Time makes suffering hard to bear.

> Certainly a great part of the problem of suffering lies in the fact that our suffering is drawn out in time. We cry out to God, and he does not seem to hear. Or, rather, he in effect tells us to wait and wait and wait.[62]

But time provides the platform for the plan of redemption. As for the past, we see that in the Old Testament God lets suffering draw out but that he is solving the problem in Christ. In a sense, the "problem of evil" is more like a problem of "justice versus mercy" in the history of Israel. God will put an end to evil by showing justice. But he also will show mercy. How? The answer is not clear until the New Testament—by having his own Son suffer the justice and thereby showing mercy to his people. Frame says, "Christ is the theodicy of Romans 3:26." The verse says, "He did it to demonstrate his justice at the present time, so as to be just and the one who justifies those who have faith in Jesus."[63] But why did God wait so long?

> As for the wait, well, in retrospect it almost seems necessary. The tension must be built up to the nth degree so that we can feel to the utmost the liberating power of salvation.
>
> But here is the lesson for us: If God could vindicate his justice and mercy in a situation where such vindication seemed impossible, if he could vindicate them in a way that went far beyond our expec-

61. Frame, *Apologetics*, 180.
62. Frame, *Apologetics*, 180.
63. Frame, *Apologetics*, 182–83.

> tations and understanding, can we not trust him to vindicate himself again?[64]

How about the present? God is even now using evil for his own good purposes.

> We cannot always understand why God has chosen evil events to accomplish these good purposes. We do know that God never foreordains an evil event without a good purpose (Rom. 8:28).[65]

As for the future, we have the promise that eventually God will end all evil!

> It may be that when we see God face to face, we shall see a face of such supreme trustworthiness that all our complaints will simply disappear. . . . At any rate, we may be assured that in the last day there will be no problem of evil.[66]

There are many other apologists who have made great contributions to the defense of the faith. We mention some of them in the book, without dedicating a special section to them. Nancy Pearcey[67] defends the Christian concept of a unified truth, as opposed to a "two-story" dichotomy. Doug Groothuis[68] contrasts the Christian worldview, especially the Christian view of truth, with postmodernism. Paul Little has written several books and has spoken to many young people on behalf of InterVarsity, teaching practical pointers about defending the faith.[69] We

64. Frame, *Apologetics*, 184.

65. Frame, *Apologetics*, 187.

66. Frame, *Apologetics*, 189.

67. Nancy Pearcey, *Total Truth: Liberating Christianity from its Cultural Captivity* (Wheaton, IL: Crossway, 2005).

68. Doug Groothuis, *Truth Decay: Defending Christianity Against the Challenges of Postmodernism* (Downers Grove, IL: InterVarsity Press, 2000).

69. Paul E. Little, *How to Give Away Your Faith* (Downers Grove, IL: InterVarsity Press, 2006, originally published 1966), *Know Why You Believe* (Downers Grove, IL: InterVarsity Press, 2000, originally published 1967).

have referred to James Sire's helpful study of alternate worldviews, *The Universe Next Door*.[70] Sire is profound, practical, and a pleasure to read. His books reveal a clear understanding of the postmodern generation through his constant interaction with college students. See *Why Good Arguments Often Fail: Making a More Persuasive Case for Christ*,[71] *A Little Primer on Humble Apologetics*,[72] and *Why Should Anyone Believe Anything at All?*[73] Walter Martin[74] was an authority on cults, and Peter Jones[75] has written excellent books on New Age beliefs and other current issues. Besides the apologists mentioned above (Geisler, McDowell, and Frame), there are other contemporary theologians who defend biblical inerrancy, for example, J. I. Packer[76] and John MacArthur.[77] Charles Colson's book, *How Now Shall We Live?*,[78] is a powerful presentation of the Christian worldview and a thought-provoking analysis of many contemporary issues, including evolution, science, philosophy, and ethics. Ravi Zacha-

70. James W. Sire, *The Universe Next Door: A Basic Worldview Catalog* (Downers Grove, IL: InterVarsity Press, 1997).

71. James W. Sire, *Why Good Arguments Often Fail: Making a More Persuasive Case for Christ* (Downers Grove, IL: InterVarsity Press, 2006).

72. James W. Sire, *A Little Primer on Humble Apologetics* (Downers Grove, IL: InterVarsity Press, 2006).

73. James W. Sire, *Why Should Anyone Believe Anything at All?* (Downers Grove, IL: InterVarsity Press, 1994).

74. Walter Martin and Ravi Zacharias, *The Kingdom of the Cults: The Definitive Work on the Subject* (Bloomington, MN: Bethany House, 2003, original version 1965).

75. Peter Jones, *The Gnostic Empire Strikes Back: An Old Heresy for a New Age* (Phillipsburg, NJ: P&R Publishing, 1992), *Stolen Identity: The Conspiracy to Reinvent Jesus* (Colorado Springs, CO: David C. Cook, 2006).

76. J. I. Packer, *God Has Spoken: Revelation and the Bible*, 3rd ed. (Grand Rapids: Baker, 1993), *Fundamentalism and the Word of God* (Leicester: InterVarsity Fellowship, 1958).

77. John MacArthur, *The Truth War: Fighting for Certainty in an Age of Deception* (Nashville: Thomas Nelson, 2007).

78. Charles Colson and Nancy Pearcey, *How Now Shall We Live?* (Wheaton, IL: Tyndale, 1999).

rias[79] is one of the most popular apologists today. His engaging writing is loaded with up-to-date illustrations. Basically, he follows Norman Geisler's arguments, especially in pointing out the logical inconsistency of the non-Christian position. Alvin Plantinga, professor at Notre Dame and a leading Protestant philosopher, has written books to defend the existence of God[80] and to answer the problem of evil.[81] There are many more! If I have left out your favorite apologist, please forgive me!

In the next chapter, we will begin to examine practical applications. How should we do apologetics? How can we use the things we have learned so far?

Group Exercise

Role play a dialogue between a skeptic and two of the apologists from this chapter. Then discuss the methods used.

Review Questions

1. What argument does Geisler use to answer the problem of evil?
2. Geisler says that this may not be the best of all possible worlds, but it is the best ________ to the best of all possible worlds.
3. How does Geisler explain the imprecision in the Bible regarding genealogies and numbers in general?
4. What is the author's concern about Geisler's apologetic method?
5. Explain the "trilemma" of Josh McDowell.

79. Ravi Zacharias, *Can Man Live Without God?* (Nashville: W. Publishing Group/Thomas Nelson Publishers, 1994).

80. Alvin Plantinga, *God and Other Minds: A Study of the Rational Justification of Belief in God* (Ithaca, NY: Cornell University Press, 1990).

81. Alvin C. Plantinga, *God, Freedom, and Evil* (Grand Rapids: Eerdmans, 1977).

6. Mention three examples of fulfilled prophecies regarding the Messiah.
7. What is the position of Henry Morris regarding the age of the earth?
8. What evidence is there in Siberia of the Noahic flood?
9. According to Morris, what is the problem evolutionists face with regard to the fossil evidence?
10. What has Phillip Johnson contributed to the evolution debate?
11. What is the "elephant" in the science laboratories, according to Antonio Cruz?
12. Explain the argument of irreducible complexity, as Antonio Cruz uses it to refute the theory of evolution.
13. What does Cruz say about the design of atoms?
14. Explain Russell Humphrey's theory about how we can see stars that are so far away if the universe is so young.
15. Explain the apologetic approach of R. C. Sproul.
16. Explain the argument of John Frame to support the authority of the Scriptures.
17. According to Frame, what is the lesson of the Old Testament regarding the problem of evil?
18. According to Frame, what is our future hope with regard to suffering?

Questions for Reflection

1. Which of the apologists studied in this chapter has helped you most? Why?
2. What do you think of the author's opinion about Geisler's apologetic approach?
3. Do you have any concerns about any of the apologists studied in this chapter? What are they?

7

A Suggested Approach

Many kinds of diets are recommended in our day, including the "Atkins" diet, the "apple diet," the "Bible" diet, and the "hallelujah diet." In my experience, extreme measures do not give long-lasting results; it is better to consume a balanced variety of many kinds of food in appropriate amounts. That is, I prefer an "integrated" diet. For apologetics, I also suggest an "integrated" approach. As long as our highest authority is the word of God, we can offer a diversity of evidences and arguments.

Our goal in apologetics is to point the non-Christian to Christ. To do this, we can use special revelation and general revelation. Although apologetics is inseparable from evangelism, it is not exactly the same. Many times we simply explain the message of the gospel; this is *evangelism*. But our task becomes *apologetics* when the person questions the message and challenges us to defend it.

Special Revelation

Special revelation is what God has revealed in Scripture, in Christ, and by any other method of direct verbal revelation. Although general revelation points to the existence of God—his power, and his moral law, special revelation primarily focuses on the gospel of salvation in Christ. We now have special revelation in the form of the Bible.

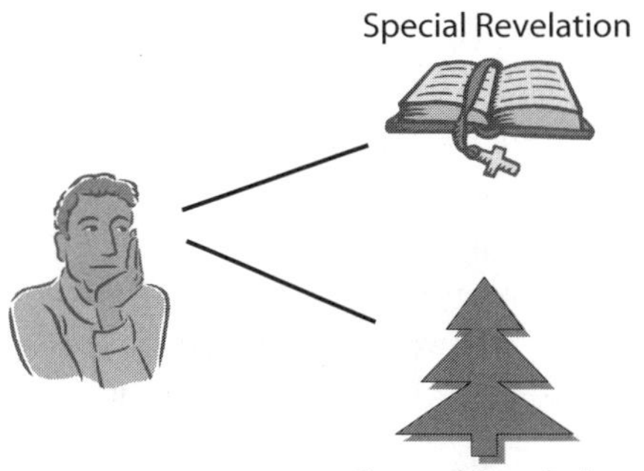

Although fallen man is apt to misinterpret anything, special revelation contained in Scripture is verbal and therefore less susceptible to misunderstanding. On the one hand, two people who look at the same sunset may perceive two completely different messages. One may think of *peace*, and another may think of *death*. On the other hand, when two people read, "Abraham was the father of Isaac" (Matt. 1:2), their interpretations normally are not going to vary quite so much. Of course, they may disagree about exactly how this happened, but the main idea is clear. This is why apologetics should always come back to the Scriptures and to the gospel message. Furthermore, we have no promise that God will convert people as they look at a beautiful sunset, but we do have the promise that the Holy Spirit will accompany the gospel message.

> For I am not ashamed of the gospel, for it is the power of God for salvation to everyone who believes, to the Jew first and also to the Greek. (Rom. 1:16)

> From childhood you have known the sacred writings which are able to give you the wisdom that leads to salvation through faith which is in Christ Jesus. (2 Tim. 3:15)

Paul is clear about the priority of preaching the gospel. Only the message of the cross can break through the barriers of sin.

> For the word of the cross is foolishness to those who are perishing, but to us who are being saved it is the power of God. . . . For since in the wisdom of God the world through its wisdom did not come to know God, God was well-pleased through the foolishness of the message preached to save those who believe. (1 Cor. 1:18, 21)

> For I determined to know nothing among you except Jesus Christ and him crucified. (1 Cor. 2:2)

Our message must be clear: Man is a sinner who deserves eternal condemnation. God sent his Son to live a perfect life in our place and on the cross to be punished for sin in our place. Jesus rose again, victorious over sin, Satan, and death, and he will return to establish the eternal form of his kingdom. By trusting him as our personal Lord and Savior, we are saved and given eternal life. This salvation is by grace alone, through faith alone, in Jesus alone.

General Revelation

Nevertheless, in our apologetic task we also should take advantage of every aspect of general revelation to help clear the air of obstacles to the gospel. General revelation is God's self-revelation in creation. This includes nature, history, and man—whatever we can investigate with our five senses. When understood properly, scientific studies point to the creator. When done properly, historical investigation validates the biblical accounts. Man himself is part of general revelation. In fact, he is its culmination. Therefore, non-Christians can learn much from themselves since they are part of this revelation. That is, the very hearts and minds of those who are searching for truth contain vital information about themselves that also points to God. Non-Christians can see the image of God in themselves, for example, in their capacity to reason, feel, enjoy, love, struggle, and communicate. Although the effects of the fall have damaged the creation and our capacity to interpret it, all of these aspects point to God.

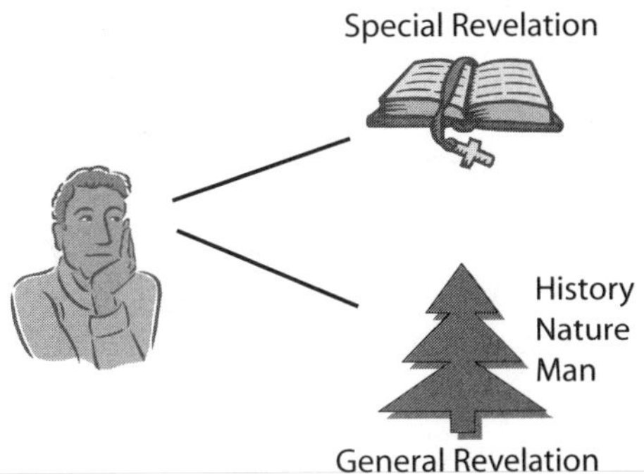

The Different Aspects of Man to Which We Can Appeal

Just as there are different aspects to revelation, there also are different aspects of man to which we can appeal as we defend the gospel. These are like different channels of television, each one capable of receiving different signals. First, God has endowed us with our five senses to observe the creation. Direct contact with nature often reveals God's majesty to us (Psalm 19:1–3), as it did to me when I was in college, gazing at the stars.

Second, we have the ability to reason. We have an innate sense of logic, an intuitive notion that makes us want to avoid contradictions. We innately believe that if A is true, we cannot also assert that A is not true. This is part of the image of God in man. Our reasoning ability is like a computer, and logic is like the programming language that guides it—the rules by which it functions. Paul "reasoned" with the Jews in the synagogues (Acts 17:2; 18:19) and with the Greeks at the marketplace in Athens (Acts 17:17).

Third, we also have the capacity to feel emotions such as love, hate, joy, and fear. Sometimes, we can appeal to these emotions to help explain the gospel or to help a person come to saving faith. For example, people may feel lonely, empty, or disoriented, and we can point them to genuine fulfillment in Christ. My mother-in-law was brought to saving faith because she saw the happiness in our family that she did not have. Paul writes that the kingdom of God is a matter of "righteousness and peace and joy in the Holy Spirit" (Rom. 14:17). Furthermore, although it may not be popular today, many people have committed their lives to Christ because of a *fear* of eternal condemnation. Jesus certainly did not apologize for warning people about hell (Matt. 10:28; Luke 12:5).

Fourth, man has a will that we must address at some point. After all, the non-Christian does not submit to God because he does not *want* to (Rom. 3:11–12). We can help him see this by asking searching questions. We also can give him *positive* motivations for wanting to become a Christian. Jesus offered the Samaritan woman at the well "living water" that would eternally quench her thirst (John 4:10–14). This is not an exhaustive theological analysis of the different aspects of man. It is a reminder of four key aspects we need to consider in our apologetic task.

Notice especially that reason is not the only thing to which we can appeal. Man is not merely a reasoning animal. For example, our emotions often escape logical explanation. This becomes clear when we are in love. Being in love is not something we can explain very well, so we write poems and sing songs about it. Also, sometimes our will goes *against* our reason. Once I was so frustrated by a lady sitting in the back seat, constantly telling me how to drive, that my will to disobey her overrode my reasoning, and I made a wrong turn out of blind refusal to submit to her! After I exited the main road, I was astonished at what I had done. It took fifteen minutes to get back on the right road. Reason is a crucial aspect of apologetics but not the only one.

After explaining these aspects of man to which we can appeal, we have to consider the effects of the fall on them. After the fall, our spirits are "dead"; the "natural man" cannot apprehend God's supernatural message.

> But a natural man does not receive the things of the Spirit of God, for they are foolishness to him; nor can he know them, because they are spiritually appraised. (1 Cor. 2:14)

Every aspect of man has been affected by sin, which is like a heavy cloud that impedes television reception. Furthermore, fallen man often uses the tools that God has given him to deny his very creator. For example, just as a computer can be used for good or evil, man's reason also can be turned against God, insisting that it is not "logical" to believe in him.

Why, then, should we evangelize? Why do apologetics? The answer is that God is working in the world to repair the damage of the fall. We do not know exactly how, when, or in whom he is operating (the Holy Spirit is like the wind, John 3:8), but we must evangelize faithfully and trust God for the results. As God acts in the heart and mind of a person, the clouds of confusion are removed so he or she can understand the gospel. This is why prayer has a vital place in apologetics. Also, as we said at the beginning of the book, man is like a closed house; to enter with our message, we must pray and look for the opening the Spirit has made.

Furthermore, remember that God has implanted two important points of contact in the heart of every person—a knowledge of his existence (Rom. 1:18–25) and a sense of right and wrong (Rom. 2:14–15). We always should try to help the unbeliever recognize these two fundamental truths. He may deny them, but we know they are permanently engraved on his heart.

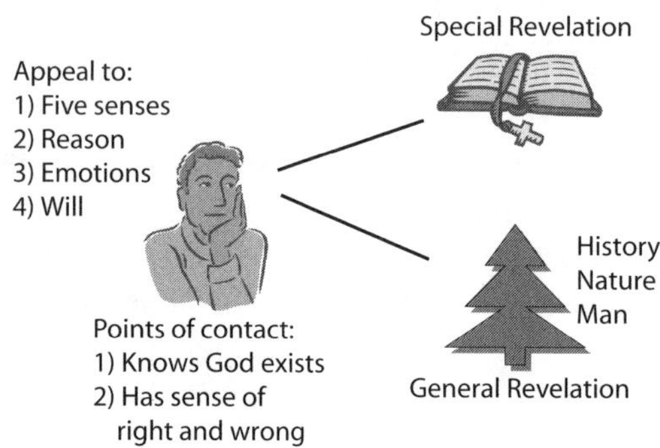

THE CHRISTIAN ANSWER TO UNCERTAINTY

As we defend our faith, we must cling tightly to the Christian view of truth and never let go. Only the Christian view of being and truth allows for true freedom and true knowledge. Christianity is the only worldview that does not self-destruct because of inherent self-contradictions. Christian ontology is not impersonal monism; it affirms there are two kinds of reality—God and his creation. Therefore, man is not simply a cog in a vast machine or a drop of water in a huge spiritual river. We are God's creatures, made in his image—free to think, reason, choose, and feel. The biblical concept of the truth centers on God, not man. Man does not discover truth on his own. God, who knows all truth because he is the creator, sustainer, and governor of all things, chooses to reveal some truths to us.

God has revealed the truth about himself in the Bible, and he promises to open the eyes of those who truly seek him to this truth. In spite of problems interpreting the Bible, human weakness, and a multitude of factors present in any context, God assures us that we can know the truth. He takes the initiative to reveal it to us, and the Holy Spirit enables us to understand it and believe it.

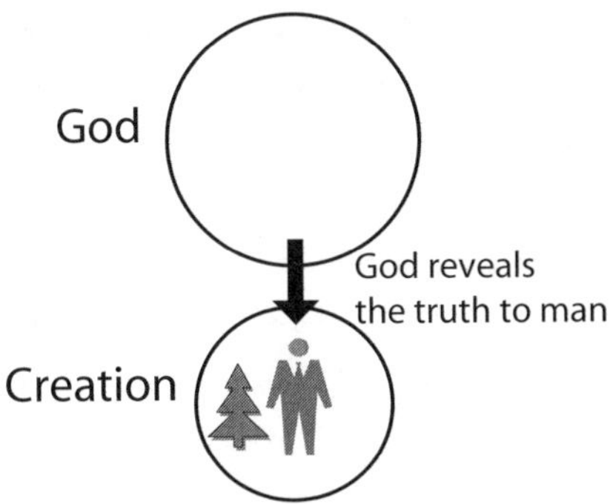

Knowing the truth is not merely an intellectual process—accepting the verbal propositions in God's word. It also includes a moral component—submitting our hearts to God and his authority as expressed in his word. A friend once told me that truth is like a virtuous woman who undresses only in the context of a relationship of marriage and fidelity. Truth is revealed in a context of a personal relationship of faithfulness to God. If we are not faithful disciples, we will not learn the truth.

> If you continue in My word, then you are truly disciples of Mine; and you will know the truth, and the truth will make you free. (John 8:31–32 NASB)

> Your word is truth. (John 17:17)

> The fear of the LORD is the beginning of knowledge. (Prov. 1:7)

> But when he, the Spirit of truth, comes, he will guide you into all truth. (John 16:13)

Knowing the truth also means living it. When we say we believe God loves us and is in control of all things and then become anxious about our finances or about a son or daughter driving home at night, then in one sense we are not "knowing" these truths at that moment in the fullest biblical sense of *know*.

Finally, we must remember that Jesus is the truth in person. ("I am the way, and the truth, and the life." John 14:6) All truth relates to him somehow. Paul speaks of Christ, "in whom are hidden all the treasures of wisdom and knowledge" (Col. 2:3). Jesus reveals to us what God is like. He is the "radiance of His glory and the exact representation of His nature" (Heb. 1:3). Furthermore, throughout the history of mankind, God's goal has been to establish his kingdom through the person and work of Christ. This means every event in history should be interpreted in the light of Christ and God's plan of redemption.

But after having made these observations, in this age of postmodern influence, which is affecting even Christian thought, it is more important than ever to insist that there *is* an intellectual dimension to knowing the truth. Many postmodernists would deny absolutes, deny the propositional aspect of truth (that is, deny that it can be stated verbally in a way we can understand it rationally), and make truth completely subjective. But this view centers truth around me again, and it removes all certainty. It leaves non-Christians with a concept of truth similar to Nietzsche's analogy of "coins which have lost their pictures and now matter only as metal, no longer as coins."[1] A bare piece of metal does not communicate a clear message.

However, the Bible does give us a clear message, and it assumes that knowing the truth includes giving assent with our reason to objective content. Look at some evidence for this. Jude urges his readers to "contend for *the faith* that was once for all

1. Friedrich Nietzsche, "Truth and the Extra-Moral Sense," in *The Portable Nietzsche*, ed. Walter Kaufmann (New York: Viking, 1968), 46–47. Quoted by Douglas Groothuis, *Truth Decay: Defending Christianity Against the Challenges of Postmodernism* (Downers Grove, IL: InterVarsity Press, 2000), 29.

entrusted to the saints" (Jude 3), implying there is a body of beliefs that constitute the gospel, which we can express and defend. Remember also how the author of the letter to the Hebrews speaks of faith: "Now faith is being sure of what we hope for and certain of what we do not see" (Heb. 11:1 NIV). He then proceeds to name something that faith makes us sure of: "By faith we understand that the universe was formed at God's command, so that what is visible was not made out of what was visible" (Heb. 11:3 NIV). This is a propositional truth. Then the author goes on to list heroes of the faith, like Noah, Abraham, and Moses, who believed God's *promises* and acted on them. Notice what John writes about Jesus: "the one whom God has sent speaks the *words* of God" (John 3.34). This implies that divine revelation includes the very words used to reveal the truth.

In other words, knowing the truth is a step of faith—trusting God as the source of truth. This means we not only believe *in* God, but we *believe God*. That is, knowing the truth also includes an intellectual acceptance of the propositions that God reveals to us. It includes *more* than that, but it certainly does not *exclude* that. And this brings us back to the Scriptures as our vital, supernatural connection with the mind of God himself.

When Paul talks about saving faith, it includes giving assent to some important historical facts and their proper interpretation. These are the *notitia* (content) and *assensus* (intellectual assent) aspects of faith that Sproul explains. To be saved, one must "hold firmly" to the doctrine of Jesus' death and resurrection for the forgiveness of our sins.

> Now, brothers, I want to remind you of the gospel I preached to you, which you received and on which you have taken your stand. By this gospel you are saved, if you hold firmly to the word I preached to you. Otherwise, you have believed in vain. For what I received I passed on to you as of first importance: that Christ died for our sins according to the Scriptures, that he was buried, that he was raised

on the third day according to the Scriptures, and that he appeared to Peter, and then to the Twelve. (1 Cor. 15:1–5 NIV)

Douglas Groothuis explains that the Hebrew word for truth, *'emet*, contains the two inseparable notions of "faithfulness" and "conformity to fact." He also insists that the Greek word *aletheia*, frequently used in the New Testament for "truth," has similar implications.[2] He quotes Roger Nicole: "The biblical concept of truth (*'emet-aletheia*) is like a rope with several intertwined strands. . . . involving factuality, faithfulness, and completeness."[3] And again: "It is because truth is conformity to fact that confidence may be placed in it or in the one who asserts it, and it is because a person is faithful that he or she would be careful to make statements that are true."[4]

Some people might think it seems arrogant to claim that we know the truth, but in reality it takes humility to admit that we depend completely on God to know anything. Furthermore, it would be a lack of faith, and it would offend God, to doubt what he has spoken. That is how the fall began in the mind of Adam and Eve. To me, it is like having assurance of salvation. Although some consider it arrogant to claim such assurance, in reality it is not. In the first place, salvation is not something we earn but something Jesus has accomplished for us. It is not arrogant to claim we have received a free gift. In the second place, it is *good* to believe God's promises, not arrogant. In a similar way, to claim assurance of knowing the truth (not all truth, just what God has chosen to reveal) basically means we take God at his word. This should not be considered arrogant, and we must make sure that

2. Groothuis, *Truth Decay*, 61–64.

3. Roger Nicole, "The Biblical Concept of Truth," 296, quoted by Groothuis, *Truth Decay*, 64.

4. Roger Nicole, "The Biblical Concept of Truth," in *Scripture and Truth*, ed. D. A. Carson and John W. Woodbridge (Grand Rapids: Zondervan, 1983), 290. Quoted by Douglas Groothuis, *Truth Decay*, 61.

as Christians we do not become proud of it and that we do not communicate an attitude of superiority because of it.

Challenging the Inconsistency

Apologetics should be both offensive and defensive. We give answers to non-Christians, and we challenge them with questions to help them see the inconsistency of their position. Remember that Proverbs 26:4–5 teaches that we should sometimes avoid answering a fool "according to his folly," so that we do not become like him (that is, we should defend the gospel on its own terms and not give in to non-Christian presuppositions), and at other times we should "answer a fool according to his folly, or he will be wise in his own eyes" (that is, we should take an offensive approach to apologetics, showing the non-Christian the error of his own thinking by carrying it out to its contradictory consequences). The non-Christian is confused, like John Nash (see the discussion of *A Beautiful Mind* in chapter four), and he denies things he knows are true, just as the prodigal son was probably doing.

As we defend the Christian faith, we can ask non-Christians why they believe what they believe. When they explain why, saying, for example, that it is logical, we can ask why they trust logic. We can keep pushing them to their final answer. This is not a game. We need to do this with much love and respect. Otherwise, we will lose the opportunity to explain the gospel. But if we continue asking until there are no more questions, where does the non-Christian end up? What is his "final answer"? He will have to back up to something beyond which he has nothing more to say.

One way or another, that final answer for the non-Christian will be reduced to the fact that he believes it simply because he thinks it's true. He may say something like, "I believe it because it just seems true to me," or "I believe it, period," or "I believe it because I want to." In any case, the non-Christian essentially makes himself the judge of what is true and false and right and wrong.

This eliminates all *certainty* for the non-Christian, because to be sure of *anything*, he needs to know *everything*. It also eliminates *consistency*, because he knows deep down that he is not God and that he cannot simply decide for himself what the truth is.

The Christian alternative is to accept God as the judge and source of truth. When you keep backing up a Christian to his "final answer," it should be that "God says so." It is true because *God says so*. How do I know God says so? Because *he says he says so*! As a Christian, I cannot back up any further than God himself; I cannot elevate something above him. If I appeal to an authority superior to God, I have just contradicted my own worldview and destroyed the foundation underneath me.

If non-Christians accuse Christians of appealing to our *own personal understanding* of what God says, and therefore of appealing finally to *ourselves*, we should ask them to get in touch directly with the word of God and read it for themselves. We have to admit that our understanding may be fallible, but this does not make our source fallible.

We now have a basis for understanding the weakness of the non-Christian position and the strength of the Christian position. We also have become more aware of the variety of channels through which we can communicate the message of the gospel. Finally, we have seen that the power to open a non-Christian's heart and mind comes from the Holy Spirit working through the gospel message.

THE "DEFEND" APPROACH

Because each person and situation are unique, I do not wish to encourage a "canned" presentation. However, I would like to suggest several general aspects of any dialogue with a non-Christian that we should keep in mind. We may sometimes need to change the order in which we use these different steps, or we may need to leave out some aspect. It depends on how the conversation goes. Furthermore, these points may be covered over a period of time, in a series of conversations.

1. Demonstrate interest. Ask questions to get acquainted. Find out about the non-Christian's family, interests, and religious background. Most people enjoy talking about themselves and their family, but be careful not to meddle into private areas that are sensitive or to make the person uncomfortable. Be genuinely interested in the person, not just in a hurry to "convert" him. People can always tell when we are not sincere. People are fascinating! Remember they are made in God's image and worthy of our love and respect.

2. Explain your faith. Share your testimony. Try to find a natural transition to share about your own life, family, and religious experience. As the conversation continues, most people will begin asking you questions. However, they might not ask about spiritual things, and you may need to insert this aspect. Explain how you understand the gospel. Do not treat non-Christians as "unclean gentiles" or assume they are not believers. Talk with them as if you expect them to understand and share your spiritual interests. This is a tip I learned from my wife, Angelica. She realized that as Protestant missionaries, we tended to erect unnecessary barriers by unconsciously assuming people were not Christians. Many people in Latin America consider themselves Christians, even though they may not understand the gospel. So if you treat them like non-Christians, it offends them. However, if they are not Christians but you talk to them as if they were, they get an inside view of what it really means to be a Christian.

For example, if you talk to them in a natural manner about your personal relationship with the Lord, they suddenly realize they do not have such a personal relationship. Or if you talk to them about prayer and Bible reading, they may realize they are missing this spiritual depth. Without putting them down, they see what a vital Christian life is like and realize they do not have it.

Our testimony should be more than words. Part of our apologetic task is to break down barriers by showing love and joy. But we have to be careful. Our love must be sincere, because the non-Christian is watching closely for hypocrisy. We should not have to work so hard at it; it should come naturally. We certainly should not make special efforts to show how "holy" we are. The non-Christian also is watching closely for a "holier than thou" attitude, and, frankly, often we project this without realizing it. I believe legalism and arrogance are two of the greatest "turn-offs" for non-Christians, but authentic love and joy are disarming. Philip Yancey says, "Evangelicals are responsible citizens whom most people would appreciate as neighbors but don't want to spend much time with."[5] I would like to think he is wrong, but I am afraid he is right about many of us. Before we started our last church-planting project in Chile, we talked to some friends who have been very successful church planters in California. We have never forgotten their suggestion: "The people have to *know* you, they have to *like* you, and they have to want to *be* like you."

3. Furnish answers to his questions. Most likely, at this point the person will become curious and ask questions. He or she may express doubts or even criticism of the Christian faith. It is important to accept these comments gracefully and not take them personally. Do your best to provide reasonable answers. This is where apologetics will help us.

5. Philip Yancey, *Soul Survivor: How My Faith Survived the Church* (New York: Doubleday, 2001), 57.

4. Expose his basic presuppositions. Now it's your turn to ask questions. I recommend asking the person *why* he believes what he believes. Then ask again why he believes the second principle. Continue down this pathway until he comes to the end, until he cannot give any other reason. For example, he might believe in evolution. When you ask why, most likely he will give scientific evidence. Then you can ask why he trusts scientific evidence. Eventually, he will somehow reveal his basic starting point. This will have to be one of two things—an outside authority or his own mind. Most people will fall into the second category, unless they are followers of some other religion. If it is his own mind, he either thinks truth starts within his own mind (subjective), or he thinks it starts outside himself (objective). In either of these two cases, he is the ultimate judge of the truth. If possible, try to bring the person to recognize this. This process will likely make the person uncomfortable. You are stripping away his cover, forcing him to expose his deepest convictions. Furthermore, these convictions probably have remained practically unconscious until now, and it may be extremely unnerving to face them. You must be gentle but without backing down.

5. Navigate through the inconsistencies of the non-Christian view. Again, you must be absolutely sure you do not show pride or disdain. It is all too easy to communicate a sense of superiority that will totally close the door. No one likes to feel ridiculed or attacked. If we do not show love and humility, it does not really matter whether our arguments are solid or not; the person with whom we are talking will stop listening to us. With gentleness, we need to show the non-Christian where his position is inconsistent. In this process, you will be like a medical doctor who has to discover the patient's sickness. You will not help the patient by denying his sickness, but keep in mind that no one likes to hear bad news. You are like John Nash's wife, pointing out that the imaginary child in his pretend world had not grown up. Something is seriously wrong with the non-Christian's scheme. In the final analysis, the non-Christian has been hanging on to beliefs that are self-contradictory, and he has developed a worldview he cannot live with consistently. For example, if he believes in evolution because he believes in science, and he believes in science because he trusts his senses and logic, you can point out that if evolution were true, his own thoughts would be part of that impersonal process and therefore lose their meaning. If evolution is true, then his thoughts are no more significant than a grape growing on a vine.

6. *Direct the person to Christ.* It would be terribly cruel to expose the contradictions of the non-Christian and leave him with no solution and no hope. He needs to know that Jesus has died for us and risen again. His unbelief is not neutral; it is a rejection of his creator. Remind him of the story of Adam and Eve, and gently show him that he also is questioning his creator in an illegitimate way. But the good news is that in Christ there is forgiveness and restoration. He can be reconciled with God by trusting in Jesus and in what he has done on the cross. He can begin a new life with the important things in proper perspective. His train can be put back on the tracks. His planet can be returned to its proper place in the solar system. He must be born again and submit his heart and mind to God. Charles Spurgeon said that before he understood the gospel, his mind was "one great confused chaos" but that after becoming a Christian, "I got a shelf in my head to put everything upon it just where it should be." He added, "When I had discovered Christ and Him crucified, I had found the centre of the system, so that I could see every other science revolving in due order."[6]

6. C. H. Spurgeon, *Autobiography, Vol. I, The Early Years* (Edinburgh: Banner of Truth Trust, 1973), 108.

These points can be easily remembered by the acrostic *DEFEND*:

> **D**emonstrate interest.
> **E**xplain your faith.
> **F**urnish answers.
> **E**xpose his presuppositions.
> **N**avigate through his inconsistencies.
> **D**irect him to Christ.

Group Exercise

Using the question about the existence of God, have two students practice an apologetic dialogue using the steps of the "DEFEND" approach. One of them can play the role of an atheist or an agnostic. The other plays the role of a Christian sharing his faith. Afterwards, talk about how the Christian could improve his defense of the faith.

Review Questions

1. What is the "integrated approach" to apologetics?
2. What is the difference between "special" revelation and "general" revelation?
3. Why should special revelation have a priority in our defense of the faith?
4. Mention three aspects of general revelation that are sources of evidence for apologetics.
5. Mention four aspects of man to which we can appeal as we do apologetics.
6. Mention the two "points of contact" God has implanted in the heart of every person.
7. What is the Christian answer to the problem of

epistemological uncertainty?

8. In what sense is "knowing the truth" more than just an intellectual process?
9. What does it mean that is Jesus the "truth"?
10. Why is it important to insist there is an intellectual dimension to knowing the truth?
11. How can we summarize the biblical teaching of what "knowing the truth" means?
12. In what sense should apologetics be "offensive"?
13. Name and describe with a phrase each step of the DEFEND strategy of apologetics.

QUESTIONS FOR REFLECTION

1. Did this chapter help you understand what it means to "know the truth" in the biblical sense? In what ways has your thinking changed about this?
2. How do your non-Christian friends understand what it means to "know the truth"?
3. What do you think of the suggested apologetic approach in this chapter? Is there some aspect you are not sure of, or is there some aspect you would add? Is this something you think you could put into practice?

8

THE QUESTIONS OF GOD AND THE BIBLE

PRACTICE WITH TYPICAL QUESTIONS

Now let's see how we might handle the questions posed in the first chapter, following the guidelines to "defend" our faith. In this chapter we will look at the first two, the existence of God and the authority of Scripture.

Question #1 How can you prove that God exists?

Although this is a fundamental question, the dialogue needs to go beyond philosophical debate.

Demonstrate interest in the person. In the initial stages of your conversation, you should try to find out about the spiritual background of your friend, especially whether he or she believes in God. Be especially sensitive to any tragedy that may have caused him to reject God. Keep in mind also that a serious problem in a person's relationship with his parents may produce obstacles to a relationship with a loving God.

Remember that until the Holy Spirit changes his heart, a non-Christian does not want to submit to Christ. A college girl told me of a friend who, although she was a pastor's daughter, began to say she no longer believed in God about half way through her first year of college (every Christian parent's nightmare). She began to use drugs and have sexual relationships with young men. I asked the girl which came first, her new life style or her lack of faith in God, and she said her changed life style. I suspect she felt her faith in God limited her freedom, so it was convenient to deny him. This is why we need to show our joy to non-Christians—our true freedom and happiness is in our relationship with Christ and in living according to his guidelines. I am sure the girl is not really happier now, and I hope she comes back to Christ soon, before making a real mess of her life. This is also why prayer is a key aspect of apologetics.

Explain your faith. Explain how you came to believe in God. This is your personal testimony, and it is probably the most important thing you can share with your friend.

Furnish answers. First, ask the person to look inside himself to see if he does not already know that God exists. The Bible teaches that God has revealed himself to everyone (Rom. 1:18–25). "Deep down," everyone knows that God exists. Everyone has an "altar to the unknown God" in his heart (Acts 17:23). The problem is that non-Christians repress this truth (Rom. 1:18–23).

While spending a week in Mexico recently to teach a course on apologetics, one of the students asked me to accompany him to visit a friend with whom he had been sharing the gospel. I decided I should practice what I was preaching, so one evening we drove over to his friend's house. As we talked about the gospel, the man repeated several times, "I would like to believe, but

I just can't." When I asked him why he couldn't, he said, "I don't know. I just can't." After more than an hour of friendly conversation about things of the faith, we returned to the seminary. On the way, I told the student that I didn't accept his friend's argument that he "wanted" to believe, but just "couldn't." I said, "I don't know this man very well, but I suspect there's some sin in his life that he doesn't want to give up." After years of pastoral experience, I now begin to look for moral problems when someone talks to me that way.

The cosmological and teleological arguments may then be used as additional evidence that the God of the Bible exists. How did everything get here? How could things so complex just happen to exist by chance? Look at the human body, the eye, the balance of nature. Why is water the only substance that expands when it freezes? If it didn't, ice would sink, lakes would freeze down to the bottom, and all life in them would perish. Look at the precise balance of gravity and centrifugal force that keeps the earth from flying out of its orbit. Remember the similar balance within the atom itself. Think also of the marvel of man, his emotions, his reason, his creativity, and his appreciation for beauty. All of these amazing characteristics point to an intelligent designer. Here we are pointing to general revelation that has God's fingerprints all over it.

Finally, we might explain that any "proof" we offer tends to put the proof above God. God reveals himself clearly in creation and in Scripture, and he does not need for us to convince anyone that he exists. If we use logic to prove God, then logic becomes our god. If we appeal to science, then science becomes our god. To try and "prove" God's existence is like Nietzsche's crazy man who went looking for God with a lantern.[1] Rather than continue with more "arguments," recommend that your friend ask God to

1. Friedrich Nietzsche, *The Gay Science* (Cambridge: Cambridge University Press, 2001), 119–20.

open his eyes to God and his truth by doing the following. Ask him to gaze at the stars at night, watch the clouds, and observe the waves on the shore. And, above all, ask him to read the Bible.

One summer I was a counselor at a youth camp in the mountains of Pennsylvania. After the campfire service the last night, a young man came up to talk. His father was a pastor, and he was the president of his youth group, but he confessed that he no longer believed in God. I was at a loss for words, knowing that he already had heard anything I could say to him and much more. Remembering my own experience under the stars, I suggested he go for a walk to see if he did not sense God's presence. The next morning he thanked me and said that he had experienced a personal encounter with God.

Expose the presuppositions of the non-Christian. Ask what he believes and *why, why, why* . . . until you come to his final answer. If he is honest, he will admit that basically he decides for himself what is true. Ask: *What would convince you that God exists*? This question will help uncover his presuppositions. Most people will have a hard time answering this because it leaves them vulnerable to being convinced. However, some will answer they would believe if God would answer their prayers or if God would perform a miracle in front of them. If so, ask how they would know if their prayers were answered or how they would define a miracle. Help them see they have probably constructed their standards of evaluation in such a way they will reject evidence for God before objectively reviewing it.

Navigate through the inconsistencies. Show the serious problems of denying a personal God and creator. As we have mentioned several times previously, doing so leads to an impersonal, closed universe, which leads to a denial of the significance of a person's own thoughts. In such a universe, our thoughts would be nothing more than "accidents"—impersonal movements of atoms, nothing more than part of the ticking of a giant, cosmic clock. To deny God is to close yourself up in a box and lose the proper use of reason, like the head in Francis Bacon's painting. It also leads to a denial of morals and human dignity. In an impersonal, deterministic universe, how could you explain love, joy, and a sense of right and wrong? Why would you even bother to talk?

Show the non-Christian that he is pretending to be the judge or source of truth but that deep down he knows he is not. If he thinks he is the judge of truth that comes from outside his own mind, ask him if there is a star one million light years directly north of the North Pole. He will probably admit that he does not know. Then you can point out there are many things he does not know, and you can ask how he can be sure that God does not exist. In fact, how can he be sure of anything? How can he be sure he will not learn something tomorrow that totally changes today's outlook? If he claims to be the source of the truth, ask him if he would be willing to go stand on the railroad tracks and wait for a train. Ask him if he could simply determine that a train is not really coming. If he admits that he could not, then he has admitted that he is not really the source of truth but that the truth is outside his own mind.

Furthermore, to deny God is to reject the inner sense of a deity and his moral law that has been engraved on man's heart. The non-Christian is trying to suppress the knowledge of his creator, similar to the way in which the prodigal son had run away from his father. The non-Christian's need for love, significance, and security can only be satisfied by God.

Direct him to Christ. Explain that his life is like the erroneous, geocentric view of the universe, before man realized the sun is its center (heliocentric). He is living as if the universe orbited around him, when actually he and the universe orbit God, so to speak. He needs to experience a Copernican revolution and recognize that God is his center of gravity. All humans are guilty of denying God, just as Adam did. Our fundamental problem is spiritual and moral, not intellectual. Jesus died and rose to bring forgiveness to those who have denied, rejected, and rebelled against their creator. The non-Christian must repent and trust in Jesus for forgiveness and a new life.

Question #2: How can you be sure that the Bible is true? What about the apparent contradictions and errors?

This question strikes at the foundation of our faith. If the Bible is not true, we lose our source of truth. In answering this question, do not forget the initial steps to apologetics:

Demonstrate interest in the person. Find out if the person has read the Bible at all. Be careful not to make him feel ignorant if he has not read much of it.

Explain your faith. Share how you became interested in the Bible and how much it means to you personally.

Furnish answers. The person may challenge you or give a simplistic dismissal of the Bible—it is outdated; it is full of errors; it is too mysterious or irrational.

First, show the non-Christian that the Bible claims to be the word of God. Refer to key passages such as 2 Timothy 3:16–17 and 2 Peter 1:21 to show that the New Testament considers the Old Testament ("the Scriptures") to be inspired—breathed out by God himself—his very words. Jesus considered the Old Testament to be the word of God (Matt. 5:18; John 10:35), and indirectly he promised to reveal what we call the New Testament to his apostles (John 14:25–26).

As John Frame suggests, *it is to be expected* that God would leave us a written covenant.[2] God has always related to his people through covenants. The composition of the Bible began at Mount Sinai with the tablets of the Ten Commandments and continued until we had the complete Old Testament. Deuteronomy clearly reflects the form of a written covenant, and Paul refers to the writings of Moses as the "old covenant" (2 Cor. 3:14–15). Since Jesus tells us that he is making a new covenant (Luke 22:20; 1 Cor. 11:25), we also would expect this to be written down. In fact, the names Old *Testament* and New *Testament* (in Greek, *diathēke*) were used by the early Christians because they considered them the Old *Covenant* and the New *Covenant*.

We cannot expect an endorsement by Jesus of the documents of the New Testament, because they were not written until after his death. However, we do see comments within the New Testament itself that indicate certain New Testament documents were considered to be the word of God. Peter refers to the writings of Paul as part of the "Scriptures."

> Regard the patience of our Lord as salvation; just as also our beloved brother Paul, according to the wisdom given him, wrote to you, as also in all his letters, speaking in them of these things, in which are some things hard to understand, which the untaught and unstable distort, as they do also the rest of the Scriptures, to their own destruction. (2 Peter 3:15–16)

Paul quotes two passages as "Scripture" in 1 Timothy 5:18.

> For the Scripture says, "You shall not muzzle the ox while he is threshing," and "The laborer is worthy of his wages."

2. John Frame, *Apologetics to the Glory of God: An Introduction* (Phillipsburg, NJ: P&R Publishing, 1994), 98.

The second phrase, "The laborer is worthy of his wages," is an exact quote from Luke 10:7. Although other biblical passages include similar thoughts, the only passage that contains the exact same words is Luke 10:7.

As for the canon (the official list of books included in the Bible), this is a complex issue that requires thorough study. For the moment, it is sufficient to say that although the list of the Old Testament books was not officially accepted by a council until after Christ, centuries before Christ the Jews considered the Old Testament to be complete. As for the New Testament, although it took several centuries for church leaders to come to an official agreement about its exact contents, early in the post-apostolic era there was a general consensus regarding which key books were canonical. We trust that the Holy Spirit guided the process to identify the inspired writings and that he continues to guide his people to recognize his voice in his word.

To substantiate the authority of the Bible, you also can show fulfilled prophecies, such as the ones that Josh McDowell mentions about Jesus.

- He would be born of a virgin. (Isa. 7:14)
- He would be born in Bethlehem. (Mic. 5:2)
- He would enter Jerusalem riding on a donkey. (Zech. 9:9)
- He would be wounded for our sins but would not defend himself. (Isa. 53:4–7)

The example of the destruction of Tyre also might be helpful, since secular history confirms it (Ezek. 26).

You also might refer to supporting archeological evidence as well. Whereas over the last centuries secular archeologists have tended to question a lot of biblical data, such as the existence of David and the city of Jericho, the more evidence they find, the more it confirms biblical history. For example, archeologists have found inscriptions in stone that refer to David[3] and to the ruins of Jericho.[4] A recent special edition of *U. S. News & World Report* mentions archeologists have located the village of Nazareth and have discovered more and more historical evidence of Jesus, Pontius Pilate, and the high priest Caiphas.

> Not only does much more information exist today about the places Jesus frequented, there are many specific discoveries that seem to bear out the sparse details we have about Jesus's childhood, ministry, and horrifying death.[5]

There are many web sites that provide more than sufficient archeological data to support the Bible.[6]

The Bible gives us a complete package of truth that fits the world we live in. It explains the origin of the universe, the origin of evil, and the solution for evil. It describes man in his wonderful complexity and gives wise advice for living in harmony with our fellow man. You may wish to refer to the illustration of Francis Schaeffer about the torn book and the loose pages that was presented in chapter five.

G. K. Chesterton offers an illuminating illustration that shows how the Bible helps us understand our world (I have modified this slightly). Imagine that you awakened with amnesia on the beach of an abandoned island where you found remnants from another place—jewelry, books, photographs, coins, and fine clothes. You would try to reconstruct the past and discover what had happened. If one of the books were the journal of the

3. Jeffery L. Sheler, "Is the Bible True?" (August 31, 2005). http://www.uhcg.org/news/is-bible-true.html.

4. Bryant Woods, "The Walls of Jericho" (July 26, 2006). http://biblicalstudies.qldwide.net.au/cs-walls_of_jericho.html and "Jericho." http://www.crystalinks.com/jericho.html.

5. Amy D. Bernstein, "Decoding Christianity," *U. S. News & World Report*, Collectors Edition, *Mysteries of Faith: Secrets of Christianity* (2007), 9.

6. See, for example, the web site *Archaeology and the Bible* (August 31, 2005). http://www.christiananswers.net/archaeology/home.html.

captain of the ship, you would probably read it in one sitting before you did anything else. You would conclude that you came from a fairly advanced world and were shipwrecked. This is man's situation. We live in a wrecked world, and the Bible explains the whole story. When we read it, we can understand the remnants in this world that point to another, better world. Furthermore, the Bible even tells us how to get back to where we belong.[7]

The seeker may ask about specific passages that seem to be errors or contradictions. Do not feel obligated to explain everything right away. You may need to study the passage more carefully before giving an answer. Or you might need to admit that you are not sure of the best explanation but that you can offer some options. Some of the most common accusations are related to supposed contradictions in the gospels. Most of these problems can be solved by realizing that the gospel writers did not always report exactly the same details. Other common accusations are related to genealogies and dates. As Geisler points out, frequently the biblical authors did not pretend to give exhaustive genealogies, and many dates and periods of time were rounded off in ancient times.[8]

If the non-Christian insists that you cannot use the Bible to prove the Bible, you need to explain that you really would not be consistent if you allowed some other authority to become the rule by which you judge God's word. As soon as you put logic or science or secular history above the Scriptures, you have violated the position you are trying to defend—the Bible is our absolute, inspired authority. This does not mean other evidence does not help confirm the truth of the Bible. It means that nothing can be put *above* the Bible. In other words, we have to let God speak for himself.

7. G. K. Chesterton, quoted by Philip Yancey in *Soul Survivor* (New York: Doubleday, 2001), 51, 52.

8. Norman Geisler and Ronald M. Brooks, *When Skeptics Ask: A Handbook on Christian Evidences* (Grand Rapids: Baker Books, 1990), 165.

This means we should encourage our friend to read the Bible for himself, and we should pray that the Holy Spirit speaks to him as he comes into direct contact with God's word.

Expose the presuppositions of the non-Christian. Now is the time to talk about epistemology. Since this has been the central focus of this book, you should be prepared to carry out a serious dialogue about it. How do you know if something is true? Ask your friend what method he uses to determine truth. Ask how he can have certainty regarding what he believes. Without being obnoxious, ask him *why*, *why*, *why*, . . . until he backs up to his final answer. Push him to see his starting point—his initial presupposition. Inevitably, this will be either that he thinks it is so (subjective truth) or that the evidence he processes seems that way to him (objective truth). In either case, he needs to see that he is making himself out to be the final judge of what is true.

Navigate through the inconsistencies. Show the non-Christian that he cannot be sure of anything and that he cannot live consistently with his worldview, as long as he sets himself up as the ultimate point of reference. Furthermore, he knows in his heart that he is neither the source of truth nor its final judge. Ask him about the star a million light years north of the North Pole or about the train coming down the tracks. Ask him how he knows he will not discover something tomorrow that will change what he believes today. If he admits total uncertainty, then ask him how he can be certain that Christianity is not true. Show him that any belief system that leaves him in the center eventually will collapse on top of him.

Now you should show how the Christian view of truth contrasts with the non-Christian's view. God is the creator, the source of all truth. He reveals sufficient truth to us so that we can know him and follow him, though he does not reveal everything about himself and about the world to us. We can live in harmony with the Christian epistemology and the truth God has revealed in the Scriptures. All other systems are self-destructive.

Direct him to Christ. Plead with him to take a fair look at the Bible. Let the Lord himself speak to him as he reads it. According to John 10:3–5, the Lord's sheep will hear his voice, recognize it, and follow him. Our job is to point the non-Christian to the Good Shepherd.

The non-Christian needs to see that his way of thinking is sinful, because he is pretending to discover the truth on his own, apart from his creator. Remind him of the story of Adam and Eve in the garden of Eden, and help him see that he is placing himself above God, just as they did. The non-Christian's problem is more spiritual and moral than intellectual. This is why Jesus died on the cross and was raised from the dead in order to forgive our sin of rebelling against God and turning from him. Only through faith in Christ can the non-Christian find forgiveness and begin a new life centered in Christ.

Recent Attacks on Scripture

My doctor always sees me reading books while I wait for him, and recently he asked my opinion about Dan Brown's popular novel *The Da Vinci Code*, as well as other books, such as *Misquoting Jesus* and *The Jesus Mysteries*. Much of the recent controversy revolves around the Gnostic literature, found in a cave in Egypt in 1945, called the *Nag Hammadi* library, so the issue itself is not exactly new. But the novel has popularized a new wave of doubt regarding the Bible and its historic integrity. The most recent debate centers on a translation of the *Gospel of Judas*. I felt that I should research some of these books in order to give my doctor a serious answer. I must say that the number of volumes related to this topic on the shelves of Barnes and Noble impressed me. Let me share the answer I prepared for my doctor.[9]

Doctor C________,

1. As you know, *The Da Vinci Code*[10] is *fiction*. Although Dan Brown does say at the beginning, "All descriptions of artwork, architecture, documents, and secret rituals in this novel are accurate," he does not pretend to make a serious defense of the idea that Jesus had a child with Mary Magdalene, that his descendants have continued until today, that the original New Testament documents did not teach the divinity of Christ, that the original copies were destroyed and replaced by others that were modified to teach this doctrine, and that the church has been covering up these things for two thousand years, as the story goes.

Although I found the thriller engaging to read, my problem is the way Dan Brown carelessly mingles fact and fiction, leaving the reader confused. I can more easily distinguish the fantasies related to the Bible and church history, but I found myself uncertain about other things, such as art history and the life of Leonardo Da Vinci. As they read *The Da Vinci Code,* I imagine the same thing happens to many people with regard to the New Testament manuscripts and other Christian data, especially in light of the seemingly innocent note before the prologue. My daughter is reading the novel now, and when she asked me about some of the details, I said, "If you aren't absolutely certain about some detail in his novel, just assume it isn't true." I think that is

9. I have since talked with my doctor. He was very appreciative of the letter and seemed convinced that these books did not make a valid case against Christianity and the Scriptures.

10. Dan Brown, *The Da Vinci Code* (New York: Doubleday, 2003).

the safest guideline. Even though it is only a novel, it betrays Dan Brown's feminism and anti-Catholicism throughout.

2. The main point of *Misquoting Jesus*[11] is that we do not have the original manuscripts of the New Testament and thus we really cannot be sure about the life and teachings of Jesus. There is nothing new in this concern about the New Testament manuscripts. We know that the originals are nowhere to be found. But there are more than 5,000 copies that contain all or portions of the New Testament. Although the scribes who made the copies were quite careful, over the centuries some errors were introduced into the text.

Some people are shocked to learn there are different versions of the biblical writings. They feel this undermines their faith in the Bible. It made me nervous for several years. Nevertheless, after studying the topic more thoroughly, I realized there is no need to be nervous. In the first place, the differences among the versions are almost all insignificant, and none of them would *change* any important doctrine. Most of the variations are similar to the difference between writing "Jesus" instead of "Christ" or something similar. No other books from antiquity are supported by so many copies and by the level of confidence these copies provide us in establishing the content of the originals. Second, I believe God did not allow us to have the original documents because people would have worshiped them as religious objects. Finally, although we do not have the original manuscripts, we can trust that God has left us with reliable versions of his word. The Bible is like a cassette tape with a message from your father. It is not exactly the same as hearing him in person, and if you make copies of the copies, something of the quality may be lost. In fact, there may be words that you are not quite sure you understand. Nevertheless, there will only be few words that are doubtful, and

11. Bart D. Ehrman, *Misquoting Jesus: The Story Behind Who Changed the Bible and Why* (New York: Harper Collins, 2005).

those details do not change anything important in the message. Furthermore, as his son, you recognize your heavenly Father's voice, his way of thinking, and you accept the communication as authoritative, as if you were hearing him in person.

The Greek New Testament has notes at the bottom of the page that explain all the different variations in the Greek manuscripts. These notes are called the "textual apparatus."[12] The study of the textual apparatus is called "textual criticism," and this has developed into a serious and reliable science. The accusation that Jesus has been significantly "misquoted" is a distortion of the facts.

3. *The Jesus Mysteries*[13] is a twisted and poorly documented attempt to destroy our confidence in the historical Jesus. The authors overtly declare their New Age inclinations: "According to Pagan astrology, Christianity was created at the beginning of the Great Month of Pisces. This Age is presently coming to an end and the New Age of Aquarius is dawning. . . . Established religion is discredited and in decline."[14]

The authors claim Jesus was not a historical person and that Christianity is a compilation of myths taken from ancient mystery religions. According to the authors, the biblical accounts of Jesus are based especially on the stories of Osiris-Dionysus, dating from many years before Jesus. Most of the references given by

12. For example, in Romans 1:7, we find the following note in the Greek New Testament (fourth version edited by Kurt Aland, Matthew Black, Carlo Martini, Bruce Metzger, and Allen Wikgren, distributed by United Bible Societies) that shows two versions, one in which the text reads "in Rome" and the other where "in Rome" is omitted. The letter "A" in brackets indicates that the scholars are very sure that the original text included "in Rome." Here is the note: {A} ἐν Ῥώμῃ p$^{\text{10, 26vid}}$ ℵ A B C D$^{\text{abs1}}$ Ψ 6 33 81 104 256 263 424 436 450 1175 1241 1319 1506 1573 1739 1852 1881 1912^{vid} 1962 2127 2200 2464 [K L P] Byz Lect it$^{\text{ar, b, d, (mon) o}}$ vg syr$^{\text{p, h, pal}}$ cop$^{\text{sa, bo}}$ arm eth geo slav Origen$^{\text{gr, lat}}$ Chrysostom Theodoret; Ambrosiaster Pelagius Augustine // omit (see 1.15) G it^{g} Origen $^{\text{acc. to 1739}}$

13. Timothy Freke and Peter Gandy, *The Jesus Mysteries: Was the "Original Jesus" a Pagan God*? (New York: Three Rivers Press, 1999).

14. Freke and Gandy, *The Jesus Mysteries*, 253.

the authors are from just several centuries before Christ, but it is hard to identify the authors' chronological scheme. The authors find parallels to these non-biblical writings in the following events: god becomes man, his mother is a virgin, he was born in a cave before three shepherds on December 25, he turned water into wine, he rode triumphantly into town on a donkey, he died as a sacrifice for the sins of the world, he descended into hell, he rose from the dead on the third day, he celebrated a ritual of bread and wine, and he will return as judge during the last days.[15]

I have to admit when I first read this, I was shocked by these parallels—not shaken in my faith but curious about their explanation. As I began to examine the arguments in detail, I realized this book should not be taken seriously. First, you cannot get beyond the secondary sources the authors cite to the actual mystery religion documents to which their citations refer. Although there are more than sixty pages of footnotes, every time I attempted to get back to the original source, I was disappointed by a reference to another secondary source. Second, the authors often speak of similarities as if they were exact parallels. For example, they say that like Christ, Dionysus also rode triumphantly on a donkey into town, with people shouting praise. But when you read what they are really saying, it is not Dionysus, after all, but a "basket containing the sacred paraphernalia, which would be used to create the idol of Dionysus." The authors conclude, "In this way, like Jesus entering Jerusalem, Dionysus rode in triumph to his death."[16]

Let's look at one example of an error-filled paragraph where the authors attempt to show that the story of Jesus' birth has its origins in the stories of Dionysus. Strangely enough, the authors do not tell us about Dionysus's *birth* at all but about his *marriage* in an ox stall. Then they say, "the word usually translated as

15. Freke and Gandy, *The Jesus Mysteries*, 5.
16. Freke and Gandy, *The Jesus Mysteries*, 44.

'stable' in the gospels is *katalemna*, which literally means a temporary shelter or cave."[17] They proceed to show how the cave was an ancient image for "the womb of mother earth." I cannot find *katalemna* in my Greek dictionaries. The closest thing I can find is *kataluma*, which is possibly the word they meant to use, since it is found in the birth story (Luke 2:7). But it does not mean "cave" at all; it means "inn" or "guest room." Furthermore, it is not where Jesus was born; it is a reference to the building or place where there was no room for Joseph and Mary! Finally, if you look at the original source to see if the authors failed to explain themselves accurately or if they used the wrong word, you will be disappointed. As usual, they only provide a footnote to a secondary source and no quotes from the original mystery religion documents. In other words, the authors' research seems restricted to secondary sources, which are consistently misinterpreted.

The Jesus Mysteries is riddled with this kind of sloppy and confusing documentation, so much so that one quickly tires of looking for solid, original-source documentation. Remember the common description of gossip. Gossip is like throwing a ton of feathers on the street; it takes forever to clean up the mess. Scholars have not taken *The Jesus Mysteries* seriously.[18]

But I want to go further than this. Let's assume for a moment that at least some of the parallels the authors draw are valid. How could we explain this? First, we should remember that some of these parallels could have been taken from Old Testament prophecies and incorporated into mystery religions. This could be true especially for writings that originated in the time of the Greek philosophers such as Plato (427–347 BC). The virgin birth, for example, was prophesied long before Christ. Isa-

17. Freke and Gandy, *The Jesus Mysteries*, 32.

18. See, for example, the following sites: http://www.bede.org.uk/books,jmyth.htm and http://arbitrarymarks.blogspot.com/2004/08/jesus-mysteries-part-two.html and http://www.skepticwiki.org/wiki/index.php/The_Jesus_Mysteries.

iah wrote: "Behold a virgin will be with child and will give birth to a son, and will call his name Immanuel" (Isa. 7:14). In the sixth-century BC, Zechariah prophesied that Jesus would come into Jerusalem riding on a donkey: "Rejoice greatly, O daughter of Zion! Shout in triumph, O daughter of Jerusalem! Behold, your king is coming to you; He is just and endowed with salvation, humble, and mounted on a donkey, even on a colt, the foal of a donkey" (Zech. 9:9). The ceremony of baptism frequently was used throughout the Old Testament, as was the sprinkling of blood, to symbolize cleansing (e.g., Ex. 24 and 29, as well as many references in Leviticus). The concept of a "scapegoat" is clearly taught in the Old Testament (e.g., Lev. 16).

Second, other concepts cited as parallels are so general that it is no surprise they might be found in many other religions, for example, God becoming man, miracles, dying to save others, and the resurrection from the dead. Additionally, love, humility, and purity are common moral principles.

Finally, we should remember that God revealed the gospel message to the first human beings, Adam and Eve, in the garden of Eden. When Adam and Eve fell into sin, God told the serpent, "And I will put enmity between you and the woman, and between your offspring and hers; he will crush your head, and you will strike his heel" (Gen. 3:15). This refers to the struggle between Jesus, who is the seed of the woman, and Satan along with his demons. Where was Jesus injured? On the cross. But who gained the victory in this struggle? The seed of the woman, because Jesus was only injured in the heel, but he crushed the head of his enemy. This was a prophecy of Jesus' victory. God also symbolized Jesus' sacrifice to cover our sins when he used animal skins to cover the nakedness of Adam and Eve (Gen. 3:21). This means all mankind could have received some communication of the gospel message since the time of the fall. The Bible also tells us that God has put a sense of his presence and a sense of right and wrong in people's hearts (Rom. 1:18–20; 2:14–15). This is why people feel guilty and sense a need for forgiveness. And this is why some tribes make sacrifices to expiate their guilt and why Christian themes appear throughout history in other religions.

4. The latest debate is about the *Gospel of Judas*.[19] This Gnostic document dates from around the end of the second century AD—a century later than the biblical gospels. The *Gospel of Judas* is quite fragmented, missing many words and entire lines. In the parts that are quoted, Jesus frequently laughs, almost giving the impression that he is ridiculing people. Strange references are made to the stars and to names such as *Saklas* and *Barbelo*. But the part of the book that has made the most striking impression is Jesus supposedly asking Judas to betray him. Even if we accepted the *Gospel of Judas* as historically true, it is not clear that the document really says that Jesus asks Judas to betray him. After many missing lines, Jesus says something about *evil* and then says, "But you will excel them all, for you will sacrifice the man that clothes me." Next he quotes, "Your horn has been raised, your wrath has been kindled, your star has shown brightly. . . ." Does Judas excel in good or in evil? Of course the interpretation that he excels positively would fit the Gnostic teachings, because according to Gnosticism, material things, including our bodies, are evil, and spiritual things are good. Therefore, to kill Jesus means liberating him from the prison of his body. But this interpretation seems at best uncertain.

I am not worried about the Bible. It has withstood attacks for two thousand years. Some people may be confused for a time, but eventually truth will prevail.

> The grass withers, the flower fades,
> But the word of our God stands forever. (Isa. 40:8)

19. See http://www9.nationalgeographic.com/lostgospel/document.html to download the English translation.

Bankers are trained to recognize false bills by carefully studying legitimate bills. Because of this, when they see a counterfeit they can spot it right away. Bankers can never look at all the counterfeits in circulation, but knowing what true bills look like enables them to spot the false ones. The same applies to religious teachings and literature. In order to learn to identify false teachings, we need to study true teaching—the Bible—more carefully.

> I tell you the truth, the man who does not enter the sheep pen by the gate, but climbs in by some other way, is a thief and a robber. The man who enters by the gate is the shepherd of his sheep. The watchman opens the gate for him, and the sheep listen to his voice. He calls his own sheep by name and leads them out. *When he has brought out all his own, he goes on ahead of them, and his sheep follow him* because they know his voice. But they will never follow a stranger; in fact, they will run away from him because they do not recognize a stranger's voice. (John 10:1–5 NIV)

True followers of Christ will recognize the voice of the Good Shepherd.

GROUP EXERCISE

Using the question about the authority of the Bible, have two students practice an apologetic dialogue using the steps of the "DEFEND" approach. One of them can play the role of a skeptic. The other plays the role of a Christian sharing his faith. Afterwards, talk about how the Christian might improve his defense of the faith.

REVIEW QUESTIONS

1. Mention briefly some possible answers to the question about the existence of God.

2. How can we expose the presuppositions of the non-Christian regarding his lack of faith in God?
3. Explain briefly the inconsistency of denying the existence of God. What are some of the consequences?
4. Mention some examples of how the Bible attests to its own authority.
5. Mention four Old Testament prophecies about Christ that were fulfilled in the New Testament.
6. Mention one example of archeological evidence that confirms the Bible.
7. Explain G. K. Chesterton's illustration about the shipwreck and explain what it shows about the Bible.
8. How can we answer the accusation that it is unfair to use the Bible to defend the Bible?
9. What is the author's concern about the novel, *The Da Vinci Code*?
10. How can we respond to the concern about different versions of the Bible?
11. What is the author's criticism of the book *The Jesus Mysteries*?
12. What is the author's response to the assertion that the *Gospel of Judas* teaches that Jesus asked Judas to betray him?

Questions for Reflection

1. How did you come to believe in God? What influenced you most?
2. Do you have friends who deny God's existence? What is their reason? How can you help them come to faith in God?
3. What is your own attitude toward the Scriptures? Do you consider it inspired and inerrant? If so, how did you come to believe this?
4. Do you have friends who question the authority of the

Bible? Are they familiar with the Bible? What problems do they have in accepting its authority?

5. How does it make you feel to realize there are slight differences among the biblical manuscripts? Does it make you distrust the Bible? Why or why not?

9

The Question of Other Religions

Question #3: What about other religions? How can you be sure that they are not legitimate?

This question has become increasingly common today because of the growing interest in Eastern religions and the New Age movement. Some people have said to me, "If I had been born in India or China, my family would belong to another religion. Just because I was born in the United States does not mean Christianity is right and other religions are wrong." Frequently, the illustration of the blind men and the elephant is used to support this type of religious relativism. The following poem is based on a fable told in India many years ago.

"The Blind Men and the Elephant"
by John Godfrey Saxe

It was six men of Indostan
To learning much inclined,
Who went to see the Elephant
(Though all of them were blind),
That each by observation

Might satisfy his mind.

The First approached the Elephant,
And happening to fall
Against his broad and sturdy side,
At once began to bawl:
"God bless me! but the Elephant
Is very like a wall!"

The Second, feeling of the tusk,
Cried, "Ho! what have we here
So very round and smooth and sharp?
To me 'tis mighty clear
This wonder of an Elephant
Is very like a spear!"

The Third approached the animal,
And happening to take
The squirming trunk within his hands,
Thus boldly up and spake:
"I see," quoth he, "the Elephant
Is very like a snake!"

The Fourth reached out an eager hand,
And felt about the knee.
"What most this wondrous beast is like
Is mighty plain," quoth he;
" 'Tis clear enough the Elephant
Is very like a tree!"

The Fifth, who chanced to touch the ear,
Said: "E'en the blindest man
Can tell what this resembles most;
Deny the fact who can
This marvel of an Elephant
Is very like a fan!"

The Sixth no sooner had begun
About the beast to grope,
Than, seizing on the swinging tail

That fell within his scope,
"I see," quoth he, "the Elephant
Is very like a rope!"

And so these men of Indostan
Disputed loud and long,
Each in his own opinion
Exceeding stiff and strong,
Though each was partly in the right,
And all were in the wrong![1]

This captivating story makes two valid points—no human being has *all* the truth, and everyone can learn from others. However, the illustration has been used to defend the idea that all religions are just different views of the same truth and that all roads lead to the same God.

Before we answer the question, remember we are assuming you already have done steps one and two.

Demonstrate interest in the person. Find out if your friend identifies himself with any religion. Let him explain what he believes and tell how he came to that religion.

Explain your faith. Share how you became a Christian. Share why Jesus is special to you. After this, let's assume the person raises the question of other religions. Now you can take the next step.

Furnish answers. Let's assume first that our friend is not really a dedicated follower of another religion but is wondering why he cannot embrace more than one religion.

1. John Godfrey Saxe, "The Blind Men and the Elephant," quoted in William Iler Crane and William Henry Wheeler, *A Sixth Reader: Wheeler's Graded Literary Readers, With Interpretations* (Chicago: W. H. Wheeler & Company, 1919), 85–87.

We should answer that as Christians, we realize other religions contain traces of truth—reflections of God's revelation, but we also believe there is only one way to God and it is through Jesus Christ. This is not our idea; it is Jesus' teaching: "Jesus answered, 'I am the way and the truth and the life. No one comes to the Father except through me' " (John 14:6 NIV).

Throughout the Bible, we find references to other gods, but in no case does God say, "That's fine. These other gods are just different ways of worshiping me." God always considers these religious manifestations as offensive spiritual adultery.

> I am the Lord your God, who brought you out of Egypt, out of the land of slavery.
>
> You shall have no other gods before me.
>
> You shall not make for yourself an idol in the form of anything in heaven above or on the earth beneath or in the waters below. You shall not bow down to them or worship them. (Ex. 20:2–4 NIV)

> "Now then," said Joshua, "throw away the foreign gods that are among you and yield your hearts to the Lord, the God of Israel." (Josh. 24:23 NIV)

Regarding the illustration of the elephant, it is important to remember there really is an *elephant* there. The men are *blind*, and when one says the elephant *as a whole* is "like a wall" and another thinks he is "like a spear," they have distorted things. Even the poem says, "Though each was partly in the right, and *all were in the wrong*!" They have *reduced* the elephant to something very different from what he really is. This is what other religions have done; they have distorted the truth so much that their teachings are radically incompatible with Christianity. The truth is that we are all blind to God until he opens our eyes.

The God of the Bible is offended when people pretend to worship him as if he were someone else, or when people worship him by other names, or when they describe him inaccurately. What father would like it if his son put a picture of a cow on the wall and labeled it "Dad"? The true God does not like to be represented by a cow, by the moon, or by a statue of anything he has created.

Show your friend that other religions contradict Christianity in fundamental ways. You cannot accept Christianity and at the same time accept other religions. At the end of this chapter, we will give a brief review of the basic teachings of popular religions. However, the main thing to emphasize is the way of salvation. Only Christianity teaches salvation by grace. All other religions and cults teach some kind of works-based salvation. The God of the Bible is a Trinity—three persons in one God, and only Christianity teaches that God the Father gave his Son to die for us!

Although Christianity may be accused of being exclusive, all religions are exclusive. Buddhism rejects the *Vedas* and the caste system of Hinduism. Islam excludes other religions and elevates the *Quran* above other sacred writings. When other religions reject Jesus as the only Lord and Savior, they are excluding true Christianity. It is like the young man mentioned earlier who did not deny the divinity of Jesus. In fact, he didn't deny the divinity of anyone! You cannot claim to accept the teachings of different religions that contradict each other. In doing so, you inevitably exclude some teachings.

Show your friend that the Bible teaches the true God has revealed himself to all people (Rom. 1:18–21). Tell him the story of Paul at Athens, where they had an altar to the "unknown God" (Acts 17:23). Explain that people who belong to other religions have a sense of the true God, but they have covered up this innate knowledge.

Explain how the Bible teaches the true God revealed himself to the first human beings on earth and that the first religion was Christianity, even though initially it was revealed in seed form, becoming more clearly developed over thousands of years. Any deviation from the biblical teaching is really a distortion of divine revelation. Even Adam and Eve were told about the Messiah to come (Gen. 3:15). God showed Abraham that he would provide a sacrifice in our place (Gen. 22:8). The tabernacle, the temple, and the sacrificial system of the Old Testament point to the Lamb of God who was to come.

This explains why we find clues to Christianity among different cultures and remote tribes all around the world. People make sacrifices and celebrate rituals that manifest their sense of guilt and their need for forgiveness and reconciliation with God.

Now let's assume that our friend is a dedicated follower of another religion. This calls for another approach.

This person probably is not seeking answers about Christianity; he may be trying to persuade us of his own religion. In this case, ask lots of questions about his beliefs. It is better not to attack his beliefs but to let him explain them. As he does this, he may realize, after all, that he is not so sure what he believes. Furthermore, like Christians, many non-Christians are not that familiar with the doctrines of their religion.

I recently spent a week in Kazakhstan teaching a course on apologetics. One of the biggest concerns of my students there was how to evangelize Muslims. As I talked with the students and listened to their testimonies, I came to understand what I had read in a helpful little book called the *Pocket Guide to Islam*. I believe the principle I learned in that book can be applied to other religions as well.

> Most Muslims who come to Christ are not won over by intellectual arguments which disprove the validity of Islam. Rather they have a personal encounter with Christ. Often this happens by reading the

> New Testament. Others have testified to the power of the love of Christ working through their Christian friends.[2]

It is important to let non-Christians see our personal relationship with a loving God. My wife, Angelica, (from a Catholic background) was drawn to Christ when she heard a group of students praying to God in a personal way. No other religion has a loving God like Christianity, so we should not hesitate to let non-Christians see that.

Nevertheless, we may be able to clear up misunderstandings about Christianity. For example, the Trinity is a common obstacle for Muslims, and we should learn to explain it as well as we can. (See "A Biblical Defense of the Trinity" later in this chapter.) Some Muslims may think we believe in three Gods or that we think Jesus the Son was born out of a divine sexual relationship.

Another obstacle for members of other religions is the identification of Christianity with Western culture. Unfortunately, much of Western "Christian" society is very immoral and materialistic. Furthermore, for someone from another background, Christianity may seem foreign and unattractive. They may find it hard to give up their customs and ethnic identity to become Christians. We should try to make this as painless as possible. Certainly, we should not expect them to change cultural customs such as dress, food, language, and tastes in art or music. Although anyone who becomes a Christian must die to himself and take on a new identity, it also is true that we should follow Paul's example of "becoming all things to all men."

> To the Jews I became as a Jew, so that I might win Jews; to those who are under the Law, as under the Law though not being myself under the Law, so that I might win those who are under the Law; to those who are without law, as without law, though not being without the

2. Patrick Sookhedeo, *A Christian's Pocket Guide to Islam* (Fearn, Ross-shire, Scotland: Christian Focus Publications, 2001), 73.

> law of God but under the law of Christ, so that I might win those who are without law. To the weak I became weak, that I might win the weak; I have become all things to all men, so that I may by all means save some. (1 Cor. 9:20–22)

Expose his presuppositions. Your friend may be assuming that the contradictions between world religions are insignificant, or he may be assuming that it does not matter if there are contradictions. He may think of Jesus as nothing more than a good man. Possibly, he has unwittingly swallowed the evolutionary scheme of world religions, and he thinks they evolved over time. If so, he may think that Eastern religions are older than Christianity and therefore more valid. Try to get behind the non-Christian's spoken convictions to his deeper assumptions. Find out what makes him believe what he believes. Keep asking until he reveals his most basic assumption. Help him see that he is probably pretending to decide the truth by himself, and in doing so he is denying God's sovereign rule over the truth.

Navigate through the inconsistencies. Ask your friend to think about his innate sense of right and wrong and his sense of guilt. Is there any other religion that can erase his guilt and soothe his conscience? Help him see that if he holds to a monistic view of reality, as do many religions, it leads to denying the validity of his own thoughts, as well as destroying the distinction between right and wrong.

We should avoid building a straw man to destroy and avoid pushing too far. Many representatives of other religions will not identify with these logical conclusions, just as we would not identify with some of the logical conclusions they might draw concerning Christianity. However, we can ask non-Christians questions to help them see how difficult it would be to live consistently with their postulates.

If logical contradictions don't really matter to the non-Christian, help him see that he cannot live that way either. Would he go pick mushrooms randomly, or would he carefully select the healthy ones? Can he accept two contradictory statements, for example, God created the world and God did not create the world? If not, then how can he accept two religions that contradict each other? If he believes Jesus was just a good man, show him that a "good man" would not claim to be God. If he did, he would be either a liar or a lunatic. Help him see that he cannot make himself the judge of truth without leading to total uncertainty or to a vital contradiction between life and ideology.

Direct him to Christ. Point to the unique and wonderful characteristics of Jesus Christ, who is full of grace and truth. Tell him again the story of Jesus' life, death, and resurrection. No other religion can be compared to the gospel! Encourage him to read the gospels or to watch a biblical movie about Jesus and to consider the validity of Jesus' claims.

We can use the same elephant story and turn it around to describe our condition *before* our spiritual eyes were opened. Before the Holy Spirit worked in our hearts, we were as confused as the blind men. But when the Holy Spirit gave us new life in Christ, we saw the truth.

A Review of World Religions

In order to complete our answer to this question, we should look at some popular current religions. Again, this will be only a brief summary.

Animism

The term comes from *anima* ("soul"), because animists believe that everything, including animals, plants, rocks, and all objects, have spiritual life. Some people estimate that forty percent of today's population is animist. Frequently, this religion includes witchcraft, magic, superstition, and rituals. Normally, animists believe in one creator god who is over many small gods. Nevertheless, man cannot relate to the creator but only to the smaller gods of health, weather, and all that affects our daily lives. In reality, animism is another form of pantheism, because everything that exists contains the universal soul of god.[3]

In Latin America, from the time of the colonization the Catholic Church has cultivated a syncretism of Christianity and the animism that existed among the indigenous peoples. Missionaries in Mexico took the image of Oztocteotl (god of the witch doctors) out of a cave, replaced it with an image of Christ, and told people that it had appeared miraculously. The problem (besides the fact that it was a lie!) is that this was only a change in form, not in content. This "Christ" has the same characteristics of the previous god. Now not only the Catholics visit this statue every year, so do the witch doctors! The famous Virgin of Guadalupe of Mexico is located in the same place where there was formerly a temple dedicated to Cihuacoatl (goddess mother earth, mother serpent), long before the conquistadors. In the image of this Virgin, she is standing on a symbol of the moon, an important indigenous deity, showing that she is superior but that she does not destroy it. This image expresses graphically how the Catholic Church simply added Christianity on top of animism, without eliminating the ancient beliefs.[4]

3. J. N. D. Anderson, *The World's Religions* (Grand Rapids: Eerdmans, 1968), 9–24. See also http://religion-cults.com/Ancient/Animism/Animism.htm.

4. Rodolfo Blank, *Teología y misión en América Latina* (Saint Louis, MO: Concordia, 1996), 80, 101–5.

Hinduism

Hinduism has no main founder or leader. The sacred Hindu texts are the *Vedas*, which are collections of hymns, incantations, and rituals that were written by different people between 1500 and 900 BC. Other later writings, such as the *Brahmanas*, the *Aranyakas,* and the *Upanishads,* are commentaries on the *Vedas*. Hindu gods are nature gods, and the sacrificial system was elaborated to gain favors from them. Eventually, three gods became the most important: Brahman is the creator; Vishnu is the preserver, who came to earth at least ten times; and Siva is the destroyer. The more philosophical writings teach that behind the visible phenomena of this world, there is one ultimate reality, *brahma*. Man needs to realize that he also is *brahma*—that his soul is really one with the soul of the universe.

> As rivers flow and disappear at last
> In ocean's waters, name and form renouncing,
> So too the sage, released from name and form,
> Is merged in the divine and ultimate existence.[5]

Hindus believe that man's actions in this life accumulate either good or bad *karma*, which determines one's status when one is reincarnated in his next life.[6] As J. N. D. Anderson says,

> Once again he is caught up in the round of desire, action, and consequences, as the water in the water-wheel is passed from one plate to the next, and finds no release.[7]

Buddhism

Buddhism has its roots in Hinduism but breaks away from some of its fundamental teachings. Gautama (563–483 BC), the

5. *Mundaka Upanishad,* quoted in Anderson, *The World's Religions,* 110.

6. Anderson, *The World's Religions,* 99–117. See also http://www.san.beck.org/EC7-Vedas.html#10 (Sept. 2, 2005).

7. Anderson, *The World's Religions,* 109.

Buddha (enlightened one), came from a wealthy family but was impressed with the suffering of others and decided to seek a way to end pain and escape the unending wheel of rebirth. First, he attempted asceticism, supposedly living on one grain of rice a day until his body became a skeleton. Eventually, he realized the only way to end suffering was to eliminate desire. This is why the statues of Buddha show no emotion. To achieve a complete release, one must meditate, concentrating on a single object until you transcend sensations of pleasure or pain and enter a state *beyond consciousness*. This is a state of full *enlightenment*, or *nirvana*, that provides deliverance from the cycle of rebirth. Gautama describes it as:

> a condition where there is neither earth nor water, neither air nor light, neither limitless space, nor limitless time, neither any kind of being, neither ideation nor non-ideation, neither this world nor that world. There is neither arising nor passing-away, nor dying, neither cause nor effect, neither change nor standing still.[8]

Personally, this is not a condition I would desire! I also wonder what happens when Buddhists emerge from this state and finish their time of meditation. Do they not reenter the world of suffering and endless reincarnation? What have they gained but greater frustration?

Buddhism can be considered more a way of life than a religion. It is centered on one's own personal spiritual experience of release from suffering and does not encourage any kind of worship of a divine being. One author describes it as a "non-theistic ethical discipline."[9]

8. *Sacred Books of the Buddhists*, 2.54ff. Quoted in Anderson, *The World's Religions*, 126.

9. Anderson, *The World's Religions*, 126. He quotes "Prof. Kraemar," but gives no source.

Islam

Muhammad (570–632 AD) supposedly received revelations that were to become the *Quran*, making him the prophet of the movement. Besides the *Quran*, Muslims also accept the *Pentateuch*, the *Psalms*, and the *Gospels* as divine revelation. They openly admit that the *Quran* contains contradictions. They attempt to explain this by saying that later revelation always replaces previous revelation.[10]

Muslims consider Jesus to be no more than another prophet, and they teach that his followers deified him against his will. Supposedly, the earliest documents of the Gospels were later modified by believers to teach the deity of Jesus.[11] Muslims deny the crucifixion of Christ; in fact, they deny his death altogether. To avoid the inevitable conclusion that this would make Jesus superior to Mohammed, who *did* die, they add the prophecy that Jesus will return, embrace Islam, and then die.[12]

The Islamic creed is simply, "There is no God but God (Allah), and Muhammad is the Prophet of God." Allah is so distant from his creatures, and man is so limited in comparison, that man cannot say much about Allah. *He created both good and evil*, and he governs the whole creation moment by moment, miraculously. In the fatalistic Muslim view of predestination, man has no real freedom of choice; choice is merely an illusion. Muslims tend to accept everything that happens as Allah's will and do not try to make the world better. When the earthquake erupted in the Indian Ocean on December 26, 2004, causing deadly tsunami waves to take thousands of lives and bringing devastation to hundreds of thousands more, some Muslim countries denied aid to the victims, believing Allah was punishing those people.

10. Sookhedeo, *A Christian's Pocket Guide to Islam*, 16, 28.
11. Sookhedeo, *A Christian's Pocket Guide to Islam*, 16.
12. Sookhedeo, *A Christian's Pocket Guide to Islam*, 39–40.

When people die, they must face judgment by Allah, who will balance their good deeds with their bad ones. If they are willing to give their lives in a *jihad* (holy war) against the infidels, they are guaranteed a place in Paradise.[13]

We have seen the atrocious practices of the extremist factions of Islam in the terrorist events of the last decade. The dangerous marriage of Islamic politics and religion has transformed the twenty-first century into a society of suspicion and fear. In the West, we were not prepared to confront people with convictions so strong they were willing to commit suicide to further their cause. In fact, Islamic fanatics have been persecuting Christians for centuries around the world. In countries like Sudan, Christians and Muslims have been fiercely fighting since 1983, and more than two million people have lost their lives. Muslims nail Christian children to trees or behead them. They pierce holes in the lips of believers, attach a padlock, and lock it. In 2001, former U. S. Secretary of State Colin Powell said of these conflicts, "There is perhaps no greater tragedy on the face of the earth today."[14] While certainly most Muslims do not agree with this kind of persecution, I believe we have underestimated the threat of the extremist militant factions.

Judaism

Judaism is somewhat familiar ground for Christians. We know that Jews accept only the Old Testament and do not recognize Jesus as the Messiah. Additionally, Jews do not believe in the Trinity, and they believe salvation is earned by performing good works and by sincerely repenting for their sin. Upon death, the wicked usually will spend twelve months in *Gehenna* (similar to

13. Anderson, *The World's Religions*, 52–98.

14. Jeff M. Sellers, "Bearing the Cross: Sudan: No Greater Tragedy," *Christianity Today*, June 11, 2001. See http://www.christianitytoday.com/ct/2001/008/43.95.html. (Nov. 6, 2007).

the Catholic idea of purgatory), and then join the righteous in *Gan Eden* (the garden of Eden) in the presence of God.[15]

Although Christians share many common beliefs with Jews—including the rich heritage of the Old Testament, belief in a personal creator God who made man in his image, and the moral law, we must be careful not to think we worship the same "God." It is not simply the case that Jews need to *add* Jesus and the New Testament to their belief system. Jews have distorted the concept of God and the Old Testament in fundamental ways. We have to insist that the Old Testament portrays a *triune* God, that it teaches salvation is by *grace*, and that Jesus is the *Messiah* in whose life and work all the Old Testament promises of a savior and kingdom find their fulfillment.

New Age

What is the New Age movement? It is neither an organized religion nor a systematized philosophy but a group of ideas and a network of communication. It is a mixture of Eastern religions and Western science and reason. Although it rejects oriental mysticism because of its failure to try to change the world, it does not follow the Western approach that tends to exclude the religious and mystical elements of human existence. The New Age movement rejects materialism, traditional culture, and nihilism. It is a Western version of oriental religions but with an emphasis on the individual. It has roots in ancient Gnosticism, which held that matter is bad, spirit is good, and that knowledge is the way of salvation. The New Age movement does not reject other beliefs but sees them as part of the process of human awakening. New Age followers have been expecting a change of ages. In the age of Aquarius, women will dominate.

New Age followers believe that many spiritual beings exist. Witches and magicians supposedly know how to control these

15. Anderson, *The World's Religions*, 25–51.

spirits. New Age believers practice "channeling"—the use of mediums to contact the spirits. Ultimate reality is "being"—consciousness—not material, not energy. This "being" manifests itself in two ways—the visible universe, accessible by means of the normal conscience, and the invisible universe, accessible through altered states of consciousness, for example, by means of drugs. Reality is like a hologram in which the whole picture is included in each tiny part. Any point of the universe contains the information of the whole universe. Therefore, the whole universe also is in my mind![16] Man is separated from "God" by ignorance. Man must realize that he is God.

> Know that you are God; know that you are the universe. (Shirley MacLaine)[17]

> I feel the power of the galaxy flowing within me . . . I myself am the process of creation, incredibly strong, incredibly powerful. (John Lilly)[18]

Some known representatives include:

- Alvin Toffler (futurist)
- Shirley MacLaine (actress)
- Elizabeth Kubler-Ross (death expert)
- Carl Jung (psychology)
- John Denver (singer)
- Steven Spielberg (movie producer)[19]

16. Douglas Groothuis, *Unmasking the New Age* (Downers Grove, IL: InterVarsity Press, 1986), 99.

17. Quoted by James Sire, *The Universe Next Door* (Downers Grove, IL: InterVarsity Press, 1997), 155.

18. Sire, *The Universe Next Door,* 162

19. Groothuis, *Unmasking the New Age*, and Sire, *Universe Next Door*. These names are referenced throughout both of these books. See the indices.

I am not suggesting that as Christians we should not listen to John Denver's songs or watch Steven Spielberg's movies. These are two of my favorites! However, we should learn to "test the spirits" (1 John 4:1). We can rejoice to find the reflections of God's truth within these artistic expressions yet reject their New Age messages.

New Age beliefs are distortions of Christianity, the first religion taught to the first human beings. Only orthodox Christianity preaches an absolute, personal, loving, trinitarian God and a gospel of salvation by grace alone through faith alone. Only Christianity has the true answer for the needs of the world—the need for forgiveness, salvation, and radical change. All other religions leave people guilty and hopeless. If Christianity were not true, then as Paul says, "Let us eat and drink, for tomorrow we die!" (1 Cor. 15:32).

A Biblical Defense of the Trinity

It may be helpful to establish a biblical defense of the Trinity, as we compare Christianity with other religions. Why is this doctrine important? Because each person of the Godhead deserves to be honored as God. This may not be the best place to begin our dialogue with representatives from other religions, but eventually we need to help them understand it, and we need to have it clear in our own minds. As I learned in Kazakhstan, for many Muslims the Trinity presents one of the biggest obstacles to becoming a Christian.

How should we explain this doctrine? Basically, there is one God in three persons who are equal in power and glory. The Westminster Shorter Catechism says:

> Question 5. Are there more gods than one?
> Answer: There is but one only, the living and true God.

> Question 6. How many persons are there in the Godhead?
> Answer: There are three persons in the Godhead: the Father, Son, and Holy Spirit; and these three are one God, the same in substance, equal in power and glory.

What is the biblical evidence for the Trinity? We harmonize passages that teach the following:

- God is one: Deuteronomy 6:4; 1 Corinthians 8:4.
- Jesus is God: John 1:1–14; John 5:22, 23; John 14:6–9; John 17:5, 20–22; Titus 2:13: Hebrews 1:8.
- The Holy Spirit is God: Acts 5:3–4; 2 Corinthians 3:16–17.
- The Holy Spirit is the Spirit of Christ: Romans 8:9–10.

One misunderstanding of the Trinity is that God takes different forms at different times. However, the Bible teaches that all three persons are present in the same place at the same time, as clearly shown at Jesus' baptism (Matt. 3:13–17).

Others passages that suggest the Trinity include Matthew 28:19 and 2 Corinthians 13:14.

Any attempted illustration of the Trinity falls short of explaining it. For example, some compare the Trinity to water, because it takes the form of liquid, solid, or gas. The problem with this illustration is that God always is Father, Son, and Holy Spirit at the same time; he does not change from one form to another. Another illustration is the egg, which has a shell, the white, and the yolk. The problem with this illustration is that the egg has three totally distinct and separable parts, each with quite distinct qualities, whereas the three persons of the Trinity are the same in substance. Others compare the Trinity to man, who supposedly has a body, spirit, and soul. In addition to this questionable threefold doctrine of man,[20] this illustration is weak because these dif-

20. Many people, including myself, prefer to make only one distinction—between the physical body and the inner spiritual person. To make a clear distinction between

ferent aspects of man do not share the same qualities in the same way the three persons of the Godhead do. For example, without the presence of the spiritual aspect, the physical body has no life of its own.

Although we cannot comprehend the doctrine of the Trinity, we know the Bible teaches it. In some ways, it should not seem so strange to us. For God to exist eternally as a loving God, there had to be more than one person. That is, from eternity there had to be someone to love. Also, for redemption to be effective, God had to give himself for us on the cross. The substitutionary atonement was possible because God the Father punished sin in the God-man Jesus Christ (Rom. 3:25; Heb. 2.9–18; 9:24–28).

Group Exercise

Using the question about other religions, have two students practice an apologetic dialogue using the steps of the "DEFEND" approach. One of them can play the role of someone who believes he can accept more than one religion or the role of a member of another religion. The other plays the role of a Christian sharing his faith. Afterwards, talk about how the Christian could improve his defense of the faith.

Review Questions

1. Explain the illustration of the elephant and the blind men. How is this used frequently to speak of world religions?
2. What did Jesus teach about the exclusivity of Christianity?
3. What is God's attitude throughout the Bible toward other religions?
4. What is the fallacy in using the illustration of the elephant

the "spirit" and the "soul" is not biblically sustainable. See Wayne Grudem, *Systematic Theology* (Leicester, England: InterVarsity Press, 2000), 472–86, and Louis Berkhof, *Systematic Theology* (Grand Rapids: Eerdmans, 1996), 193–95.

to show that all religions are legitimate?

5. Describe briefly the fundamental beliefs of each of the following religions:
   a. Animism
   b. Hinduism
   c. Buddhism
   d. Islam
   e. Judaism
   f. New Age
6. What are the key differences between Christianity and other religions?
7. Explain the biblical teaching about the Trinity.

Questions for Reflection

1. What are the most popular alternative religions in the context in which you live? Do you have friends who believe strongly in another religion? What led them to embrace this other religion?
2. Do you have friends that believe they can hold to more than one religion? What do you think has influenced them to think this way?
3. Can you think of other suggestions about defending Christianity against other religions?

10

The Questions of Evolution and Hell

I consider the last three questions the most challenging for apologetics. The question of evolution is probably the most common *scientific* objection to Christianity. On the other hand, the most serious theological and philosophical objections to Christianity are found in the questions of hell and the problem of evil. We will leave the problem of evil for the last chapter.

Question #4: What about the theory of evolution? Doesn't it prove that the Bible is wrong?

During the last two centuries, the theory of evolution has been promoted as a proven fact. Almost without question, the evolutionary scheme has imposed itself on every discipline. Areas such as linguistics, psychology, sociology, history, philosophy, religion, and practically every other discipline are studied through the lens of evolution. It also has become a political issue in the United States, since many evangelicals are asking their school boards to modify the standard curriculum to include "intelligent design" as an option to be taught in the science classes. Not surprisingly, this has caused a furious reaction. The news media are currently reporting frequently on this debate.[1]

The theory of evolution has made many people doubt the existence of God, including myself at one time. Joseph Stalin was a seminary student when he read Darwin and decided that "all this talk about God is sheer nonsense." Michael Shermer, director of the Skeptics Society and publisher of *Skeptic Magazine*, considered himself a "born-again Christian" at one time, but when he studied evolutionary biology in graduate school, he became a dedicated defender of Darwinism.[2]

Demonstrate interest. This issue may be volatile, and you need to establish a relationship of trust and mutual respect. Remember to spend time showing interest in the person.

Explain your faith. You need to explain that the two most important issues in this debate are whether God created the world and whether the Bible contains errors. These are fundamental tenets of our faith. However, even among evangelical Christians who believe the Bible, there are differences of opinion about the best way to harmonize scientific evidence with the biblical account of creation. It is essential to express our belief that there are no real contradictions between the Bible and scientific evidence. We may be interpreting the Bible incorrectly, and we may be interpreting the scientific evidence incorrectly, but as Francis Schaeffer says, there is no "final conflict".[3] That is, if we understand the Bible and scientific evidence properly, they will

1. There was a program about this debate on PBS television, *Nova* series, Nov. 13, 2007, called "Judgment Day, Intelligent Design on Trial." See also Claudia Wallis, "The Evolution Wars," *Time*, August 15, 2005, 27–35.

2. Nancy Pearcey, *Total Truth: Liberating Christianity from its Cultural Captivity* (Wheaton, IL: Crossway, 2005), 223.

3. Francis Schaeffer, *No Final Conflict*, originally published in 1975, reprinted in *The Complete Works of Francis Schaeffer* (Wheaton, IL: Crossway, 1984).

be in agreement. We are not afraid of scientific investigation, nor are we afraid to do a careful exegesis of Genesis.

Furnish answers. However we interpret the first chapters of Genesis, the Bible is clear throughout that God is the creator of the universe. The Bible also teaches that man was made in a special way, in the image of God, and with the "breath of life." Furthermore, the scientific evidence for the traditional theory of evolution is inconsistent.

1. As Henry Morris and Antonio Cruz have pointed out, the fossil evidence does not support the essential evolutionary tenet of the *gradual* transition from one species to another. On the contrary, instead of the picture of one large tree that grows steadily, one branch leading to another, as Darwinists propose,[4] the fossil evidence is more like a picture of an "orchard" (see below), in which each species starts independently.[5] To make partial adjustments to this evidence, some non-Christian scientists have embraced the theory of "punctuated equilibrium,"[6] which proposes that changes in species come in sudden jumps. Although this theory still assumes that all species evolved from a common ancestor, it is contrary to Darwin's classical statement of evolutionary theory.[7]

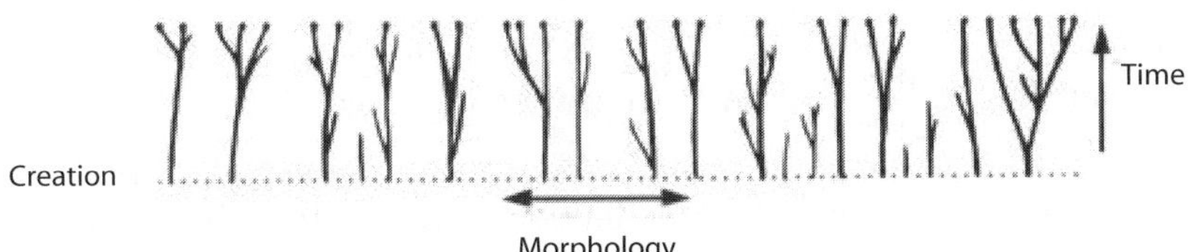

4. Such an illustration was shown to portray the evolutionary scheme in "Judgment Day, Intelligent Design on Trial," PBS television program, *Nova* series, Nov. 13, 2007.

5. Roger Patterson, "Classifying Life," http://www.answersingenesis.org/articles/ee/classifying-life (Nov. 15, 2007).

6. Stephen Jay Gould, *The Structure of Evolutionary Theory* (Cambridge, MA: Harvard University Press, 2002), 745 ff.

7. The following graphic comes from http://www.answersingenesis.org/articles/ee/classifying-life.

We need to understand precisely what evolutionists mean by "transitional forms." Essentially, evolutionists consider any fossil form between a fish and a man a "transitional form." Accordingly, evolutionists believe there are many transitional forms! For example, a recent issue of *Time* magazine has an article about a *tiktaalik* (or "fishapod") fossil that recently was found in northern Canada. According to the article, this is a fish with "primitive fingers" that "represents a crucial step in the progression from sea creatures to land animals to, eventually, humans."[8] But in reality, this fossil looks like an example of a fish with long fin bones. The fossil does not prove these animals were evolving into tetrapods that could walk, as the article argues. Furthermore, where are the expected countless forms with longer and longer "fingers"? However, if we say there are no transitional forms, evolutionists will cite this or other fossils as examples of transitional forms and doubt our objectivity. Our argument will be more convincing if we avoid confusing terminology and simply say if evolution is true, we would expect the evolutionary evidence to be more complete and to provide a smooth, progressive fossil line, rather than the sudden, large jumps from one fossil form to another.

2. Furthermore, in the fossil deposits, layers often do not correspond to the evolutionary scheme of progress from more simple to more complex forms. If evolution were a fact, we would expect the evidence to be more universal and more compelling.

3. I find that "irreducible complexity" makes gradual evolution according to natural selection difficult to believe. Natural selection cannot explain why a partially formed optic nerve, without the rest of the eye, or a partially formed eyeball would evolve in the first place or why this would make a certain species more likely to survive than its counterpart with no eye parts at all. Why would a fish that is developing short legs in place of fins

8. J. Madaline Nash, "Our Cousin the Fishapod" (*Time,* April 17, 2006), 58.

be more likely to survive (as it originally exists in the water) than fish that have fins but no legs? It is more likely that such useless parts would make the animals less likely to survive. I can see why the new, fully developed form might survive but not the intermediate forms. For example, scientists have produced fruit flies with an extra set of wings and have considered this to be evidence that supports the theory of evolution. However, the problem is that these wings do not function for flying. They are just appendages that weigh the insect down, and make it more difficult to fly.[9]

The bacteria flagellum mechanism is complex, surprisingly similar to a man-made motor, and frequently used by Christians as evidence of irreducible complexity. When you look at a picture of this amazing little organism, you cannot help but see the work of a master engineer. How could a merely natural process cause the development of such an organism?

The "bombardier beetle" is another example that is hard to explain by appealing to a natural process. This insect has two tubes that shoot chemicals to repel enemies. When combined, the chemicals are explosive. But the beetle has an inhibitor substance that impedes the explosive reaction until the chemicals are spurted into a "combustion chamber" and combined with an enzyme. It is difficult to imagine a gradual evolutionary process that could produce this species. If the beetle did not have the inhibitor or the chamber in which to mix the chemicals, wouldn't this cause uncontrollable, spontaneous explosions? What would cause these components to develop in the appropriate order and the chemicals to be formed and the tubes to fire the chemicals? This insect is bizarre, and it is more reasonable to explain its existence in terms of divine creation.[10]

9. Nancy Pearcey, *Total Truth*, 160–61.

10. Wayne Grudem, *Systematic Theology* (Leicester: InterVarsity Press and Grand Rapids: Zondervan, 1994), 281–82.

However, after watching the PBS television program, "Judgment Day, Intelligent Design on Trial,"[11] I believe we need to be careful how we use "irreducible complexity" as an argument for "intelligent design." First, when we say a particular organism is "irreducibly complex," we should not imply there can be no organism that lacks all the parts and that does function properly. In that sense, "irreducible" is not the best word to use, because it implies that it is impossible to have a similar but "reduced" form. For example, we might use the mousetrap, the bacteria flagellum,[12] or the "bombardier beetle" as examples to show that these would not function properly without all their parts. However, evolutionists can show that a mousetrap without all the same parts still can be used as a tie clasp, for example, even without the metal hook that holds the "hammer" back until the trap is sprung. They also may be able to point to bacterial forms that are similar to one we label irreducibly complex, but that lack all the same parts, and to show that these forms function perfectly well.[13] With this, they challenge the argument that some organisms are irreducibly complex.

To be more precise, this should not be our argument. Our point should be to question what would cause the gradual addition and survival of new parts to make a more complex organism. Natural selection is not a very convincing explanation. In other words, to use the same mechanical illustration, what would explain the hook being added to the mousetrap if it already seems to function properly as a tie clasp? A human might add parts

11. "Judgment Day, Intelligent Design on Trial," PBS television program, *Nova* series, Nov. 13, 2007.

12. This is the example Michael Behe used in the trial in Dover, PA, 2005, according to "Judgment Day, Intelligent Design on Trial." See also Nancy Pearcey, *Total Truth*, 185–87, for an explanation of the scientific evidence, and Jonathan Sarfati and Michael Matthews, "Argument: 'Irreducible Complexity'," http://www.answersingenesis.org/home/area/re2/chapter10.asp (Nov. 14, 2007).

13. This is what happened to Michael Behe in the trial in Dover, PA, 2005, according to "Judgment Day, Intelligent Design on Trial."

to make it a better mousetrap, but this shows that an intelligent mind must have been at work with a clear purpose. It is another thing altogether to imagine a purely natural process making such a complex modification to an organism. And to use the biological example, what would explain the addition of a new "motor system" to the bacteria to make the flagellum spin around, if it was already functioning without it? That is, what would cause such a change, and if it did somehow occur, why would the new intermediate forms survive over the simpler ones that already function? But this discussion may take us into an ocean of complicated scientific data.

In other words, I would not try to use the "irreducible complexity" argument to prove that a gradual process is *impossible,* because this puts an excessively heavy burden of proof on us. I prefer to use the concept of intelligent design to point to the difficulty of defending the process of *natural selection* as an explanation of these complex forms.

Second, if we use intelligent design as a scientific argument without stating our religious presuppositions, we weaken our case and may appear to be hiding something. It is best to admit our religious beliefs and at the same time challenge the evolutionists to admit the relationship between their theory and religious commitments. Whether they believe God guided an evolutionary process or whether they leave God completely out of the picture, their religious views (atheism or theism) influence their scientific outlook. No one can pretend to be neutral and objective about this.

In conclusion, our argument is more likely to be persuasive if we emphasize that complexity points to an intelligent creator, whether the complexity is absolutely "irreducible" or not. As Norman Geisler says, if you came into the kitchen and saw alphabet cereal letters on the table that spelled your name and address, would you think it was just an accident?[14]

4. Natural forces are amazingly tuned to permit life. Since the 1960s, secular scientists have spoken of the "anthropic principle," which is a way of referring to the fact that the values of fundamental constants, such as gravitational force, are perfectly set to allow for life. *Anthropic* comes from the Greek word *anthropos*, "man," and was used by Brandon Carter, an astrophysicist at Cambridge University, in a paper he presented in 1973 to celebrate the 500th birthday of Copernicus. In a recent special edition of *U. S. News & World Report*, Patrick Glynn writes that "the picture of the universe bequeathed to us by the most advanced 20th century science is closer in spirit to the vision presented in the Book of Genesis than anything offered by science since Copernicus."[15] He concludes:

> The barrier that modern science appeared to erect to faith has fallen. Of course, the anthropic principle tells us nothing about the Person of God or the existence of an afterlife. But it does offer as strong an indication as reason and science alone could be expected to provide that God exists.[16]

Nancy Pearcey explains it as follows:

> Imagine that you found a huge universe-creating machine, with thousands of dials, representing the gravitational constant, the strong nuclear force, the weak nuclear force, the electromagnetic force, the ratio of the mass of the proton and the electron, and many more. Each dial has hundreds of possible settings, and you can twirl them around at will—there is nothing that presets them to any particular

14. Interview by Nancy Pearcey in "Geisler's Rebuttal: An Appeal to Common Sense," *Bible-Science Newsletter*, March, 1985, quoted by Nancy Pearcey, *Total Truth*, 193.

15. Patrick Glynn, "God: The Evidence; Why Some Scientists are Now Making the Case for a Creator," *U. S. News & World Report*, Special Edition, *Mysteries of the Faith: Secrets of Christianity*, 2007, 74.

16. Patrick Glynn, "God: The Evidence," 75.

> value. What you discover is that each of the thousands of dials just happens to be set to exactly the right value for life to exist. Even the slightest tweak of one of the cosmic knobs would produce a universe where life was impossible.[17]

5. Some of the evidence for evolution is weak and sparse at best and deceitful at worst. Imaginative conclusions often are drawn from one tooth or a part of a skull or some other bone fragment.[18] The famous fake "Piltdown Man" was fabricated from part of a skull and a jawbone, found in England. Since the skull had human characteristics and the jaw was supposedly ape-like, this was hailed as a specimen of early man. However, scientists later showed that the skull portion was from a modern human and the jaw from a modern orangutan. The teeth had been filed down, and the bones and teeth were chemically treated to give the appearance of being ancient.[19] Nancy Pearcey points out two other commonly cited cases of supposed evidence for evolution that have been falsified. One is the case of the peppered moths. Supposedly, when the industrial revolution in England caused smoke to darken the trunks of trees where these moths would perch, the dark-colored moths survived because they blended in, whereas the light-colored moths were more easily seen and therefore were eaten by the birds. This has been used as evidence of natural selection. However, recent studies have shown that peppered moths do not perch on tree trunks at all and that the photographs were falsified by gluing dead moths onto the trees! The second case is Ernst Haeckel's drawings of embryos. He tried to show the similarities between the embryos of humans, rabbits, calves, hogs, chickens, tortoises, salamanders, and fish in

17. Nancy Pearcey, *Total Truth*, 189.

18. Don Batten, "Not Another Ape-Man" http://www.answersingenesis.org/creation/v18/i3/apeman.asp (Nov. 9, 2007).

19. Nathan Aviezer, *Fossils and Faith: Understanding Torah and Science* (Jersey City, NJ: KTAV Publishing House, 2001), 185. See also A. J. Monty White, "The Piltdown Man Fraud," http://www.answersingenesis.org/docs2003/1124piltdown.asp (Nov. 9, 2007).

their early stages. Haeckel modified the sketches to exaggerate the similarities. Although more than a hundred years ago his colleagues accused him of this deceit, his drawings continued to be used in textbooks.[20]

6. One of the biggest challenges we face in harmonizing the Bible with science is the apparent age of the earth. The consensus of contemporary scientists is that the earth is 4.5 billion years old. At first, this would seem to contradict the creation account and a strict reading of the genealogies in Scripture. There are two basic positions among evangelicals—"young earth" and "old earth."[21]

"Young earth" proponents believe God created things with apparent age and that the earth is only a few thousand years old (some say 6,000,[22] others anywhere between 10,000 and 20,000[23]). Think about the moment God made Adam and Eve. Suppose you arrived one minute later. They may have appeared to be twenty years old, when actually they were only one minute old. God made them with age. How about the trees? They may have been made in one second, but if you had cut one down and counted the rings, you would have thought the tree was hundreds of years old. This reasoning could be applied to the rest of creation. The "young earth" view harmonizes well with the concept of irreducible complexity, since it asserts that all things were created about the same time. It would mean that all things, even very complex organisms, functioned properly from the very moment of their creation. In

20. Nancy Pearcey, *Total Truth*, 163–65.

21. See Grudem, *Systematic Theology*, 289–309, for a clear analysis of the different positions. See also the report of the Presbyterian Church in America, "Report of the Creation Study Committee," 2000. http://www.reasons.org/resources/apologetics/pca_creation_study_committee_report.shtml (Dec. 1, 2000).

22. See the "Answers in Genesis" web site: http://www.answersingenesis.org/ (Dec. 1, 2007).

23. Grudem, *Systematic Theology*, 290.

fact, since all of creation is so interdependent, it is easy to imagine that God may have created all things about the same time.

Some object to this view, saying it would be dishonest on God's part to leave evidence that "deceives" us about the age of the earth, especially fossils that appear to be millions of years old. Those who defend this view answer that dating procedures are not reliable. Dating methods are based on the fact that some elements "decay" and transform into other elements over time. For example, uranium becomes lead, carbon becomes nitrogen, and potassium becomes argon. Each element has a certain rate for going through the process of decay. Scientists project the age of a fossil or other object by calculating the portion of the materials that have been transformed—that have decayed. Those who question the accuracy of these procedures argue there may be unknown factors in the history of the object that produce erroneous conclusions about its age.[24]

There are several versions of the "old earth" position among evangelicals. 1) The "day-age" view is an interpretation of the "days" of the creation account in Genesis chapter one as long periods of time. Proponents of this position believe God created each species supernaturally but in stages that lasted millions of years.[25] They argue that the word "day" is not always used in the Bible to refer to a literal twenty-four-hour day. (See, for example, Genesis 2:4, ". . . in the *day* that the Lord made earth and heaven," referring to the whole creation process as a "day".) They also hold (as do other "old earth" scholars and many "young earth" scholars, too, for that matter) that the genealogies of Scripture sometimes are not meant to provide a complete list or a complete chronology. (For example, in Matthew 1:8–9 only Uzziah

24. Mike Riddle, "Does Radiometric Dating Prove the Earth is Old?" http://www.answersingenesis.org/articles/nab/does-radiometric-dating-prove (Dec. 1, 2007).

25. See, for example, Robert C. Newman, "Progressive Creationism ('Old Earth Creationism')," in *Three Views on Creation and Evolution*, ed. J. P. Moreland and John Mark Reynolds (Grand Rapids: Zondervan, 1999), 105–33.

is between Joram and Jotham, but we know there were several generations between them, according to 1 Chronicles 3:10-12.[26]) Scholars such as Antonio Cruz object to this theory because it means animals were dying—and leaving fossils—before the fall. Cruz believes death entered creation after the fall as a punishment for sin (Rom. 5:12). A possible answer to this objection is that plants and animals experienced death before the fall as part of a natural process but that death for man started after the fall as a punishment for sin.

2) The "gap theory." Others scholars, for example, Antonio Cruz, believe that first God made the material world, then there was a long period of time—a "gap" of millions of years, and then God created plants, animals, and man.[27] There are other versions of the "gap theory," including one that proposes that plant and animal forms existed for millions of years (leaving fossils), then a great cataclysm took place, and then God reconstituted things during the six days of Genesis one.[28] They would translate Genesis 1:2 as "the earth *became* without form and void."[29]

3) The "literary framework" view. Meredith Kline proposed that the creation account in Genesis one does not pretend to be a chronological one. Instead, he argues, it is a "framework"—a literary device—that teaches about God's creative activity. He shows that the first three days define realms, and days four to six describe what fills these realms. According to this view, the Genesis account highlights man as the pinnacle of creation and shows

26. See Grudem, *Systematic Theology*, 290–91.

27. Antonio Cruz, *La ciencia ¿encuentra a Dios?* (Barcelona: CLIE, 2004), 179. See also Bruce K. Waltke, *Genesis: A Commentary* (Grand Rapids: Zondervan, 2001).

28. Don Batten, " 'Soft' Gap Sophistry" http://www.answersingenesis.org/creation/v26/i3/softgap.asp (Nov. 9, 2007). See defenders of the theory, such as Waltke, *Genesis*, and Arthur Custance, *Without Form and Void* (Brookville, Canada: Arthur C. Custance, 1970). See Custance's book online at: http://www.custance.org/Library/WFANDV/index.html (Nov. 9, 2007).

29. See Grudem, *Systematic Theology*, 287. He refers to *The New Scofield Reference Bible* (Oxford: Oxford University Press, 1967) and its notes to Gen. 1:2.

God resting on the seventh day—preparing us for the call to worship him on the sabbath day. Negatively stated, the purpose of the Genesis creation account is not, Kline argues, to depict the order or length of the creation process. A supporting argument for this view is that there seems to be a discrepancy in the creation accounts of Genesis one and two between the sequence of creation events. In the first account, man is created *after* the plants and animals. In the second account, man appears to be created *before* the plants and animals. (See Genesis 2:5, "Now no shrub of the field was yet in the earth, and no plant of the field had yet sprouted, for the Lord God had not sent rain upon the earth; and there was no man to cultivate the ground."[30]) One possible reply is that Genesis two is focused only on the garden of Eden and that initially there were no plants there to be cultivated.

It is best to avoid adopting a dogmatic position on these issues at this point.[31] For apologetic purposes, it is not necessary to make a final decision but only to show the non-believer that there are several ways to harmonize the teaching of the Bible with the apparent age of the earth. The bottom line is that the scientific evidence does not disprove divine creation by any means.

7. Time also is a problem for evolutionists. According to the second law of thermodynamics, things tend to run down. That is, energy always spreads out. For example, if you heat a small portion of a long metal rod with a blow torch, within a few minutes the heat will be distributed throughout the length of the rod. In time, the rod itself cools off as the heat spreads into the air. In a similar way, the sun and the stars are continually losing their heat. This law suggests that matter has not always existed. If it

30. Grudem, *Systematic Theology*, 300–302, for an explanation of this view and sources of authors who support it.

31. To find resources and authors who support the "young earth" theory, see the web site, "Answers in Genesis" referred to above. To find resources and authors who support the "old earth" theory, see the web site "Reasons to Believe": http://www.reasons.org/resources/apologetics/index.shtml#young_earth_vs_old_earth (Dec. 3, 2007).

had, why would the universe not have "run down" by now? That is, why would the sun and stars not already have cooled down, for example?

The "big bang" theory may seem to answer this problem. According to the big bang theory, the universe began to expand at a certain point in time, billions of years ago. Before that, everything was densely concentrated in an extremely small point.[32] However, this theory is plagued with problems. How did the big bang occur? How did the first matter originate? This reminds me of the joke about the scientist who challenged God, saying that he could create a human being. God told him to go ahead and prove it. When the scientist bent over to pick up some dirt, God said, "Wait! Get your own dirt!" Some would say that matter has always existed and that the universe continually experiences recurring big bangs, collapsing (the "big crunch") at the end of each period. But scientists are hesitant to defend this theory.[33]

Expose his presuppositions. The non-Christian may assume science is objective and neutral. He may assume evolution is a proven fact. He may assume everything is material. At the heart of the matter, he is assuming he can decide what the truth is.

Navigate through his inconsistencies. We need to show our friend that if he takes God out of the picture, he is left with serious problems when he tries to construct a consistent system of truth. Given his presuppositions, his thoughts are nothing more than chemical reactions; they have no more meaning or significance than the "tick tock" of a clock or the bile that is secreted from his liver. The non-Christian cannot make himself out to be the

32. See Werner Gitt, "What About the Big Bang?," http://www.answersingenesis.org/creation/v20/i3/big_bang.asp (Nov. 13, 2007), and "Big Bang," http://en.wikipedia.org/wiki/Big_Bang (Nov. 13, 2007).

33. David Pearlman, "The Big Crunch," *Chronicle Science Editor*, Sept. 23, 2002. See also http://www.whyevolution.com/crunch.html (Nov. 14, 2007).

judge of truth without ending up with total uncertainty or total inconsistency.

Direct him to Christ. The real problem is not scientific, but moral and spiritual. The non-Christian resists recognizing God as creator and Lord and will look for any explanation to avoid him. The non-Christian's thinking has become distorted, and this leaves him with a dark and empty universe. His system reduces him to an insignificant spot of paint on an impersonal and mechanistic canvas. He needs to come to Christ for forgiveness and to have a personal relationship with his creator.

Question #5: How can a good God condemn people?

Einstein's problem with Christianity was that it would be unfair for God to punish people for what he caused them to do. Einstein had a distorted, fatalistic view of God's providence. He said, "In giving out punishments and rewards, he [God] would to a certain extent be passing judgment on himself."[34]

The "Losing My Religion" web site uses this issue like a knife to stick in our side. They say God is like a father who tells his son to love him or he will put him in the oven and bake him![35]

These are misunderstandings of Christianity and offensive distortions of God the Father. But to be honest, do we not all struggle with this issue at times? Is there really a hell, and is it really a place of eternal fire and suffering? Why would God create people who would end up this way?

34. Albert Einstein, *The World As I See It* (New York: Citadel Press, 1995), 27–29, quoted by Charles Colson in *How Now Shall We Live?* (Wheaton, IL: Tyndale, 1999), 207.

35. I participated for a while in a forum of the web site "Losing My Religion," basically giving them the bulk of the arguments of this chapter. It produced a series of reactions that seemed mostly to blast away at false notions of Christianity, rather than trying to answer me seriously. I challenged one critic to explain on what basis he decided if something was true, but he avoided the question.

Since this question is closely related to the broader question of the problem of evil and free will, our answers will be fairly brief. There will be a longer discussion of this issue in the next question.

Demonstrate interest. Remember we cannot jump into a subject like this without developing a degree of trust and respect. One thing we need to be extremely sensitive about as we discuss this question is that our non-Christian friend possibly is thinking about someone he loves who is not a believer or perhaps a family member who has died. This is not merely a theoretical question. I have been appalled at the harsh and insensitive way some Christians talk about hell.

Explain your faith. The Bible clearly teaches that not all people will be saved, that the saved will spend eternity in God's presence, and that the unsaved will be banished from his presence (e.g., Matt. 5:22–30; Luke 16:19–29; Rev. 20:12–15). Just as we do not know exactly what heaven will be like, neither do we know exactly what hell is like. These two realms transcend our comprehension. To depict hell, biblical language uses concepts such as "fire" (Rev. 19:20; 20:10; 20:14–15), "darkness" (Matt. 8:12; Rev. 16.10), "weeping" and "gnashing of teeth" (Matt. 8:12; 13:50), "destruction" (2 Peter 3:7), and a place to be "tormented day and night forever" (Rev. 20:10). If we took some of these terms too literally, they would seem contradictory. For example, fire gives light, so how could hell be literally both fire and darkness at the same time? If people are tormented forever, how could they literally be "destroyed"? Nevertheless, hell clearly is a horrible, everlasting experience, far from the presence of God.

Furnish answers. How could God do this?

1. First, we need to begin with another perspective: No one deserves salvation. No one is innocent (Rom. 1–3). God would be just to condemn all people. Once when Charles Spurgeon preached on Romans 9:13 ("Jacob I loved, but Esau I hated."), a lady at the church door told him she had a hard time understanding the verse. Spurgeon asked her what part was difficult, and she answered it was hard to believe God could hate Esau. Spurgeon replied, "That is not my difficulty, madam. My trouble is to understand how God could love Jacob!"[36]

2. Second, to be just, God must punish sin. His character does not permit him simply to overlook it. Sometimes, we focus exclusively on the fact that God does not save everyone, that some people are eternally punished. But would it not be unjust and reprehensible if God did not eventually punish Satan? We instinctively desire justice and vindication. If God saved everyone, surely we would complain that he saved frightfully evil people like Hitler, Stalin, Nero, and Caligula! The Scriptures tell of the punishment of Satan and his followers with great rejoicing (Rev. 19).

3. It is important to emphasize the truth that anyone who desires to be saved by Christ will not be turned away. Revelation 22:17 gives an open invitation, "Whoever is thirsty, let him come. Whoever wishes [*'o thelon*, "he who desires"], let him take the free gift of the water of life." Jesus says in Matthew 11:28, "Come to me, all who are weary and heavy-laden, and I will give you rest." This is not to say that human will is the ultimate factor in deciding who will be saved. Only God decides that. But from the human perspective, no one who really wants to be saved will be lost. Jesus combines both of these concepts in John 6:37: "All that the Father gives me will come to Me, and whoever comes to me I will never drive away" (NIV). Hell is for those who do not desire to be in the presence of God, who are not willing to repent of

36. Quoted by William R. Newell, *Romans, Verse-By-Verse* (Grand Rapids: Kregel, 2004), 364.

their rebellion and sin, and who refuse to ask for God's merciful forgiveness. In his novel *The Great Divorce*, C. S. Lewis describes people who had the opportunity to get on the bus going to heaven but preferred not to. One asked for the right to enter heaven because he had been so good. When he saw that a murderer was going to heaven, he became angry. In the end, he preferred condemnation in hell rather than going to heaven with a criminal.[37] Another man asked for guarantees before accepting the offer to go to heaven. He asked for the opportunity to use his talents and for an environment where he would have freedom to investigate things intellectually. When he learned those in heaven did not need his talents or intellectual research, he lost interest in going. He preferred to live where he could experience self-fulfillment.[38] The Marquis de Sade preferred hell over heaven, where "boring creatures presented themselves as models of virtue."[39] Lewis said, "the doors of hell are locked from the inside."[40]

4. This helps, but it does not completely resolve the problem, because we still ask why God does not save everyone. Why does God not exercise his sovereign power for just a moment and make everyone believe so that all will be saved? However we understand free will, predestination, and providence, we cannot escape from the fact that not everyone is saved, and that God does not change this.

The free-will argument is a valid *part* of the answer but only from the *human*, temporal perspective. There also is a *divine*, eternal perspective. It is as if we can look at events through a microscope, in time (human perspective), or look at them through a telescope, from eternity (divine perspective). Charles Spurgeon speaks of the sovereignty of God and the responsibility of man as

37. C. S. Lewis, *The Great Divorce* (San Francisco: Harper Collins, 2000), 25–31.

38. Lewis, *The Great Divorce*, 39–44.

39. Marquis de Sade, Afterword to *120 Days of Sodom, The Complete Marquis de Sade*, trans. Paul J. Gillette (Los Angeles: Holloway House, 2005), 301.

40. C. S. Lewis, *The Problem of Pain* (San Francisco: HarperOne, 2001), 127.

"two lines that are so nearly parallel, that the human mind which pursues them farthest will never discover that they converge, but they do converge, and they will meet somewhere in eternity, close to the throne of God, whence all truth doth spring." He says, "I do not believe that they can ever be welded into one upon any earthly anvil, but they certainly shall be one in eternity."[41]

Before continuing, we should clarify what we mean by "free will." We should avoid thinking of our will as totally free from any restraints or as only apparent, not real. Libertarians hold the former view—that man's will is free from any restraints, natural or divine.[42] The scholastic theologians of Islam represent the second view, since they assert that God continually creates and recreates the atoms of everything, including man's mind, in order to control everything, while giving man only the impression of free will.[43] In this book, I am using *free will* to mean "freedom to act according to our own desires," as John Frame defines it.[44] I agree with Frame that Scripture ascribes this capacity to all humans. Douglas Wilson compares human freedom to an arm that reaches into a treasure chest: "The will is simply the arm that God has given us each to reach into the chest in order to bring out the contents of the heart."[45] Wayne Grudem clearly summarizes the biblical teaching regarding free will:

> Thus, when we ask whether we have "free will," it is important to be clear as to what is meant by the phrase. Scripture nowhere says that we are "free" in the sense of being outside of God's control or

41. C. H. Spurgeon, *Autobiography, Volume 1: The Early Years* (Edinburgh: Banner of Truth, 1973), 174.

42. John Frame, "Determinism, Chance, and Freedom," in W. C. Campbell-Jack, Gavin J. McGrath, and C. Stephen Evans, eds., *New Dictionary of Christian Apologetics* (Downers Grove, IL: InterVarsity Press, 2006), s.v.

43. J. N. D. Anderson, *The World's Religions* (Grand Rapids: Eerdmans, 1968), 74.

44. Frame, "Determinism, Chance, and Freedom," s.v.

45. Douglas J. Wilson, *Back to the Basics*, ed. David G. Hagopian (Phillipsburg, NJ: P&R Publishing, 1996), 20.

> of being able to make decisions that are not caused by anything. (This is the sense in which many people seem to assume we must be free; . . .) Nor does it say we are "free" in the sense of being able to do right on our own apart from God's power. But we are nonetheless free in the greatest sense that any creature of God could be free—we make *willing* choices, choices that have *real effects*. We are aware of no restraints on our will from God when we make decisions. We must insist that we have the power of willing choice; otherwise we will fall into the error of fatalism or determinism and thus conclude that our choices do not matter, or that we cannot really make willing choices. On the other hand, the kind of freedom that is demanded by those who deny God's providential control of things, a freedom to be outside of God's sustaining and controlling activity, would be impossible if Jesus Christ is indeed "continually carrying along things by his word of power" (Heb. 1:3, author's translation). If this is true, then to be outside of that providential control would simply be not to exist. An absolute "freedom," totally free of God's control, is simply not possible in a world providentially sustained and directed by God himself.[46]

Now, returning to the "divine perspective" of our topic, Romans 9 is the key passage in the Bible that addresses the question why everyone is not saved. Take time to read this chapter carefully. Paul begins the chapter by expressing grief that not all Jews will be saved, despite the fact they have received many spiritual blessings (Rom. 9:1–5). Is this because God's plan has failed?

What is Paul's answer? Does he say the failure of all to be saved is due solely or primarily to human free will? No. He explains that the principle of divine, sovereign election is demonstrated throughout the Old Testament. According to Paul, it is important that we understand our salvation depends on one thing alone—God's merciful, sovereign choice.

46. Wayne Grudem, *Systematic Theology* (Leicester, England: InterVarsity Press, and Grand Rapids: Zondervan, 2000), 331. See also John Frame, "Determinism, Chance, and Freedom," s.v.

> It [God's choice] does not, therefore, depend on man's desire or effort, but on God's mercy. (Rom. 9:16 NIV)

Paul insists we *should not judge God.*

> One of you will say to me: "Then why does God still blame us? For who resists his will?" But who are you, O man, to talk back to God? "Shall what is formed say to him who formed it, 'Why did you make me like this?' " Does not the potter have the right to make out of the same lump of clay some pottery for noble purposes and some for common use? (Rom. 9:19–21 NIV)

Paul presents some answers in the form of rhetorical questions.

> What if God, choosing to show his wrath and make his power known, bore with great patience the objects of his wrath—prepared for destruction? What if he did this to make the riches of his glory known to the objects of his mercy, whom he prepared in advance for glory—even us, whom he also called, not only from the Jews but also from the Gentiles? (Rom. 9:22–24 NIV)

The plan of salvation demonstrates God's wrath, power, patience, and the riches of his glory. This is not the same argument as the philosophical one that evil must exist so that good also can exist. Evil is not an ontological necessity. In the end, whether we like it or not, the answer to the question "How can a good God condemn people?" is that *God does everything for his own glory.*

Notice that Paul does not sense a need to excuse God for his sovereign decisions, as we often try to do. He simply explains that we need to change our perspective. We are the clay, and God is the potter. God has a right to do whatever he wants with us.

The teachings of this chapter of Scripture can be difficult to chew on, much less to swallow, even for Christians, and in many cases it is not prudent to discuss these issues with non-Christians.

However, among Christians we cannot pretend to finish our discussion without reference to this passage that speaks directly to the question posed above. I believe the purpose of Romans 9 is more to help believers than to provide explanations for non-Christians. As the Westminster Confession of Faith says:

> The doctrine of this high mystery of predestination is to be handled with special prudence and care, that men, attending the will of God revealed in His Word, and yielding obedience thereunto, may, from the certainty of their effectual vocation, be assured of their eternal election. So shall this doctrine afford matter of praise, reverence, and admiration of God; and of humility, diligence, and abundant consolation to all that sincerely obey the Gospel.[47]

In the end, we must believe that God knows more than we do and that *he will do what is right, even though we do not understand all his actions.* Although God does not explain all his ways to us, he gives us clear, sufficient, authoritative revelation to know how we should live.

> The secret things belong to the LORD our God, but the things revealed belong to us and to our children forever, that we may follow all the words of this law. (Deut. 29:29 NIV)

How can we be happy in heaven, knowing that hell exists? John Frame puts things in perspective when he speaks of the moment when we will see God face to face: "We will see a face of such supreme trustworthiness that all of our complaints will disappear."[48]

Expose his presuppositions. Ask the non-Christian to state his basis for making ethical judgments. Why is one thing good

47. WCF, 3.8. See http://www.reformed.org/documents/wcf_with_proofs/ (March 20, 2006).

48. John M. Frame, *Apologetics to the Glory of God* (Phillipsburg, NJ: P&R Publishing, 1994), 189.

and another bad? On what basis would he judge God to have done something wrong? Determine his standards for making ethical judgments. If he is consistent and honest, he will admit he has appointed himself as the judge of what is true and false and of what is right and wrong—of epistemology and of ethics. As such, he has elevated himself, a creature, above God, the creator.

Navigate through his inconsistencies. If the non-Christian makes himself the judge of right and wrong, would he permit me to do the same thing? He would probably say yes. However, in that case there would be two people making these important decisions. What if I think it is correct to hit him in the nose? How could our friend try to convince me that it is wrong to do so? He might appeal to some universal notion of right and wrong, but where does that come from? If such universal notions exist, then he no longer is the judge.

If he denies absolute morals completely, how can he criticize God for doing something wrong? On what basis would he make a moral judgment?

Direct him to Christ. This delicate topic can be turned around so that it becomes a great opportunity to share the gospel. Instead of focusing on other people, challenge your friend to think about himself. Does he have assurance of salvation? Would he like to? He does not need to solve all the problems and answer all his questions, but he can be sure that he has eternal life by giving his heart and life to Jesus Christ. He must flee to the cross for forgiveness and the beginning of a new life.

Group Exercises

1. Using the question about evolution, have two students practice an apologetic dialogue using the steps of the

"DEFEND" approach. One of them can play the role of someone who believes in evolution. The other plays the role of a Christian sharing his faith. Afterwards, talk about how to improve the defense of the faith.

2. Using the question about hell, have two students practice an apologetic dialogue using the steps of the "DEFEND" approach. One of them can play the role of someone who rejects Christianity because of the idea of hell. The other plays the role of a Christian sharing his faith. Afterwards, talk about how to improve the defense of the faith.

REVIEW QUESTIONS

1. Explain the problem of fossil evidence that speaks against the theory of evolution.
2. Explain the problem of the fossil layers that make us question the theory of evolution.
3. Explain the argument of "irreducible complexity" and how we can use it to argue against the traditional theory of evolution.
4. Explain the "anthropic principle."
5. Give an example of false evidence used to prove the theory of evolution.
6. Explain four possible ways of harmonizing the apparent old age of the earth with the biblical creation account.
7. Explain why the laws of thermodynamics give evidence against the theory that matter has always existed.
8. What is wrong with the perspective of the person who questions how God could send people to hell?
9. Why must God punish sin?
10. What does the Bible teach about those who come to Christ seeking salvation?
11. How does the author define "free will" in this chapter?

12. Mention some of the lessons we learn from Romans 9 regarding why God does not save everyone.
13. In the end, what must we believe about God to help us deal with the question of hell?
14. Why is it inconsistent to judge God because of hell when one does not believe in ethical absolutes?

Questions for Reflection

1. What do you think about the theory of evolution? Has this been an obstacle to your faith in God and the Bible?
2. Which of the arguments presented in this chapter help you most to answer the question about evolution? Why?
3. Which of the theories about harmonizing the Bible with the apparent old age of the earth seems to be the most convincing to you? Why?
4. Which answer helps you most regarding the question of hell? Explain why.

11

The Question of the Problem of Evil

Question #6: If God is both good and all-powerful, why does he allow evil and suffering?

I cannot think of a question that gnaws more at people, including Christians, than why God allows evil and suffering. This is known as the problem of evil, and it is more than a philosophical question; it is personal and painful. I wondered why my father died when I was seventeen. We ask why God allows tsunamis, hurricanes, and earthquakes. Why are children starving in Africa? If God is both all-loving and all-powerful, why does he permit or cause such things? The problem of evil is our most difficult apologetic challenge.

The problem of evil is why existentialist Albert Camus (1913–60) "lost his faith." Howard Mumma, pastor of the American Church in Paris, developed a friendship with Camus and has written about some of the fascinating dialogues they had. In one of those conversations, the philosopher confessed that he found the universe "absurd."

> The silence of the universe has led me to conclude that the world is without meaning. This silence betokens the evils of war, of poverty, and of the suffering of the innocent. I have been immersed in this suffering and poverty since the rise of Fascism and Hitler's Nazism. So, what do you do? For me, the only response was to commit suicide, intellectual or physical suicide, to embrace Nihilism and go on surviving in a world without meaning. . . . While I always trusted the universe and humanity in the abstract, my experience made me begin to lose faith in its meaning in the practice. Something is dreadfully wrong. I am a disillusioned and exhausted man. I have lost faith, lost hope, ever since the rise of Hitler. Is it any wonder that, at my age, I am looking for something to believe in? . . . To lose one's life is only a little thing. But, to lose the meaning of life, to see our reasoning disappear, is unbearable. It is impossible to live a life without meaning.[1]

What can we say to someone like Camus?

Demonstrate interest. We must be sensitive to the painful experiences people have had and not look at the question of evil in a cold, abstract manner. Many people have suffered painful tragedies they can barely talk about. However, if you gain the confidence of a friend, usually he will appreciate the fact that he can talk with you about his deepest struggles. Frequently, his pain is the result of the loss of a child or some other family member. Or his pain may be due to a divorce or sickness. Let the person talk and explain how his pain and suffering has affected his faith in God. Try to understand and empathize with him. It is beyond our responsibility to satisfy completely the doubts of non-Christians. Neither can we provide total comfort for the tragedies they have endured. However, we can show them that we care.

Explain your faith. Be willing to share your own pains and

1. Howard Mumma, *Albert Camus and the Minister* (Brewster, MA: Paraclete Press, 2000), 13–14.

to be honest about your struggles with questions like the ones with which the non-Christian is struggling. However, do not leave your friend without hope. Explain that despite the fact that you do not have all the answers, you still believe in God and trust him that he is doing what is best.

Furnish answers. I believe our best answers to the problem of evil are related to man's free will and to God's plan to totally eliminate evil and suffering. But these points need to be explained carefully.

1) Man caused the problem. First, we need to explain that God made everything good, in fact *very* good, and that suffering comes as a result of the fall, which was caused by human sin.

> God saw all that he had made, and behold, it was very good. (Gen. 1:31)

God did not *create* evil, and he is not *guilty* of evil. Man's own decision in the fall introduced corruption into the world (Gen. 3:6–10). The word *fall* is almost too weak to describe what happened in that instant. It was like an atomic bomb that blew everything to pieces. Genesis 3:7–19 describes the consequences of sin—man hid from God and was afraid of him. Man is ashamed of himself. People fight among themselves. They suffer pain, and they find work frustrating. Death is inevitable. In a word, sin brought *conflict* to every dimension of human existence—conflict between man and God, between man and his neighbor, between man and nature, and between man and his own heart. Evil is like a sickness in creation; it is not part of creation per se.

2) God gave man freedom to choose, to make decisions. Why did God make man with the freedom to obey or disobey?

It is dangerous to speculate about God's purposes when the Bible does not reveal them clearly (Deut. 29:29). However, there is enough teaching in the Bible about God's nature to permit us to suppose that he did not want the love and obedience of man in a forced way but in a voluntary way, from the heart. The story of Job suggests this. When Satan approached God, he insulted him by saying that Job served him because of the benefits he received from God. This displeased the Lord, and he allowed Satan to make Job suffer in order to test him (Job 1). We conclude that God desires love and loyalty that come from the heart. Furthermore, if there are not two options—to obey or disobey, to love or not love, then such "love" and "obedience" do not mean a lot. God wants more than obligatory obedience. He wants our hearts.

3) God always does what is best, and he considered this the best plan. I would like to extrapolate on this and walk through some of the big events in history, trying to discern why God's plan was the best. Keep in mind that we are on sacred ground. We are speculating about God's thoughts, and the human mind is too limited to comprehend his thoughts. Therefore, my suggestions are only tentative.

> "For My thoughts are not your thoughts, nor are your ways My ways," declares the Lord. "For as the heavens are higher than the earth, so are My ways higher than your ways and My thoughts than your thoughts." (Isa. 55:8–9)

Notice I am not saying it was *impossible* for God to create a world in which there was free will and yet in which man would not sin. Rather, I am saying we have biblical evidence that God did not *want* to create such a world.

Neither am I saying that it is only *logically possible* that an all-powerful and perfectly good God would allow evil, as Alvin Plantinga argues. Plantinga, a brilliant contemporary Christian philosopher, distinguishes between explaining *why* God allows evil (an argument called a "theodicy") and a more theoretical "defense" of the *logical possibility* that God would allow evil for a good reason. Plantinga argues it is possible that man could not be free without eventually doing something morally wrong. Therefore, it also is possible that God had to allow evil in order for man to be free.[2] Plantinga believes that a "theodicy goes beyond what is required."[3] However, I would like to "go beyond" logical possibilities; I am saying the Bible actually warrants a kind of "theodicy," an explanation of why God allowed evil. The Bible indicates that God wanted man to be free and to serve him from the heart, as shown in the first chapter of Job.

In the recently popular movie *Bruce Almighty*, a man becomes angry with God for supposedly not doing a good job of taking care of him. God comes to him in the figure of a man and turns the city over to him for a while. Soon, Bruce realizes it is not easy to run things. By trying to answer everyone's prayers, he ends up messing things up. For example, he allows everyone to win the lottery, so each person wins only 25 cents. I would like us to do something similar for a moment—reverently and seriously. In order to try and see things from God's perspective, let us ask ourselves how we think God might have done things differently. If we are dialoguing with a non-Christian, let him express what he thinks God should have done, then show him the problems that would occur with this plan.

First, consider the creation of man. *Why did God not create man incapable of sin?* Could God have created man in a way that

2. Alvin Plantinga, *The Analytical Theist: An Alvin Plantinga Reader* (Grand Rapids: Eerdmans, 1998), 22–25.

3. Plantinga, *The Analytical Theist*, 25.

he would not sin? Hypothetically, yes, but apparently God did not *want* to. Why? Consider what such a man would have been like. He would be no different from a machine or a dumb animal; he would have no capacity to reason and to make moral choices. As C. S. Lewis suggested, God could have made our brains in such a way that they refused to work when we start to have an evil thought, but this is not freedom.[4] As we have said before, Scripture suggests that God wanted man to obey him out of love and loyalty, not because obedience was unavoidable.

Now let's take this idea a little further. Someone might ask if God could not originally have made man with free will and the *strength of character* that would make it *morally impossible* for him to sin. Let me explain.

I read a dialogue from the web site "Losing My Religion" that went something like the following. Someone asked, "Will there be free will in heaven?" A Christian answered, "Yes." Someone asked the Christian how he knew he would not sin and fall from heaven, just as Satan fell. No one answered this question.

However, the Bible teaches that in heaven we will be at another level of sanctification, so that our character will be made like Jesus. In Romans 8:17–18 and 28–30, Paul teaches that God's plan for us is to make us like his Son and that the last stage of the process of salvation is that we will be "glorified" with him. This is our guarantee that we will not sin and fall from heaven. We will not sin any more than Jesus would sin. We will not go back to the same state of Adam and Eve in the garden of Eden, but we will be in a condition better than theirs, made like Christ. Revelation 21:1–4 indicates that in the new heaven and new earth, there will be no tears, no pain, and no death, that "the old order of things has passed away" (NIV).

4. Lewis, *The Problem of Pain*, 33.

Jonathan Edwards made the distinction between "natural" freedom and "moral" freedom. On the one hand, a good person who is chained in a dungeon and wants to bow down to the king has "moral freedom" but not "natural freedom." On the other hand, an evil man who is *not* chained but does not *want* to bow down to the king has natural freedom but not moral freedom. That is, his character will not allow him to do what is right.[5] His will is free because it is not forced or compelled from without. However, his will is determined by his own moral inclination—in this case, an evil inclination (assuming the king is good). For Edwards, natural freedom means we are free to act in accordance with our desires, and moral freedom means we are able to do good, despite the barrier of our sinful condition. God gives us this moral freedom by his grace (John 8:32–36; Rom. 6:7, 18–23; 8:2).

Before the fall, man had natural freedom and moral freedom. After the fall, he has natural freedom but not moral freedom. When he becomes a Christian, he again has both natural freedom and moral freedom. However, he still struggles with sin and temptation. In heaven, again we will have both natural freedom and moral freedom, but the struggle will be over. We will not fall away or sin, any more than Jesus would sin or do anything that contradicted his own character. Our nature will be sanctified in a way that we share something of Christ's glory (Col. 3:4).

Augustine explained the four stages of man's relation to sin in the following way: (a) Before the fall, man was able to sin, and able not to sin (*posse peccare, posse non peccare*). (b) After the fall, man was *not* able *not* to sin (*non posse non peccare*). (c) When one becomes a Christian, he is able not to sin again (*posse non peccare*). And (d) in heaven, he will be unable to sin (*non*

5. See the discussion of Edwards's position about the freedom of the will in James Montgomery Boice, *Foundations of the Christian Faith* (Downers Grove, IL: InterVarsity Press, 1986), 211–16.

posse peccare). But Augustine clarifies that "this will not thereby restrict his free will." We will still be free in the sense of being able to decide according to our desires, but we will be "unable to sin" in the sense that we will not be able to do anything contrary to our new glorified nature. Our new nature will never desire to sin. As Augustine puts it, our soul will "be forever unable to will iniquity."[6]

If we agree with this, someone might ask if God could not originally have made man the way he will make Christians to be for eternity, that is, with free will and such *strength of character that he would not be able to desire sin*. Again, the answer is hypothetically, yes, but apparently God did not *want* to create man in this way. Why not? Because God had a plan of *salvation*, and salvation was to be a *process*, not something simply handed out to man at creation.

Have you ever wondered why we are not immediately sanctified when we become Christians? Although the following answer to this question involves some speculation, I believe the Bible provides hints that help us.

According to the Scriptures, we are to learn to fight against sin. We are told to put on the "full armor of God" and to "stand against the schemes of the devil" and that "our struggle is not against flesh and blood, but against . . . the spiritual forces of wickedness" (Eph. 6:11–12). We also are encouraged to "lay aside every encumbrance and the sin which so easily entangles us, and let us run with endurance the race that is set before us." In this race, we should fix our eyes on Jesus, "the author and perfecter of our faith, who for the joy set before Him, endured the cross" (Heb. 12:1–3). We are also told to accept the discipline of our heavenly Father in our process of spiritual growth (Heb. 12:5–11). "For whom the Lord loves He disciplines" (Heb. 12:6).

6. Augustine, *Enchiridion*, 27.105, *Confessions and Enchiridion*, 403.

These passages suggest that we learn important lessons through our experience of struggling with sin. Therefore, I believe a Christian gains something through this process that he would not gain if sanctification were granted immediately at conversion.

Furthermore, man is to be identified with Jesus in the struggle against sin and Satan. If we are to be like Christ, we must participate in this painful battle.

Theologians usually emphasize the fact that Jesus had to identify himself with man in order to take our place on the cross (Heb. 2:14–17). But sometimes we forget that the opposite also is true: Man is supposed to be like Jesus. Which plan came first? Obviously, God did not decide first that Jesus would be like man, since the eternal Son of God always has existed, and man was created in time. Jesus is the model for man, not man for Jesus.

One aspect of Jesus' character is to be the *Savior*. This was *always* an essential part of his character. His character did not suddenly change at some point in eternity; he is "the same yesterday and today and forever" (Heb. 13:8). I admire soldiers who are willing to risk their lives for a good cause. I admire the heroes in movies such as *Braveheart* and *Gladiator* who stand up against the enemy. But Jesus is our true "hero." Jesus threw himself into the coliseum of life, as it were, and fought with the enemy until the victory was won. Of course, Jesus was loving and gentle (Matt. 11:29; 12:19–20), and he willingly offered himself as a sin offering in our place, like a lamb led to the slaughter (Isa. 53:7; Acts 8:32). However, we should not forget that he also is a great warrior. From the very beginning, in Genesis 3:15, we are told that he would "crush the head" of the enemy. And at the very end, we see Jesus as the victorious warrior riding on a white horse. His eyes are like "blazing fire" (Rev. 19:12), a sharp sword comes out of his mouth (19:15), and he throws the enemy into a lake of fire (19:20).

Therefore, man also must be a spiritual "warrior." We must struggle against sin and Satan. Of course, man cannot be the redeemer, because we are not God, and we have been corrupted by sin. The point is that we must go through the process of struggle and growth if we are to become like Jesus. God could not simply have created us pure and left it at that.

Mysteriously, even Jesus had to "learn obedience." The Bible says, "Although he was a son, he learned obedience from what he suffered" (Heb. 5:8). This does not mean Jesus sinned but that he had to "grow in wisdom and stature" (Luke 2:52) as a human. Therefore, if Jesus had to go through a growth process, man should, too. Paul stated that Jesus' sufferings "flow over into our lives" (2 Cor. 1:5 NIV), thus pointing to the Christian's identity with Christ in our struggle of growing to be like him.

Second, think about the fall of man. After man rebelled against his creator, was it necessary for God to carry out the punishment so that creation was cursed and man corrupted? A non-Christian might think that God could have passed over this incident. However, because God is perfectly holy and therefore must punish sin, not to do so would be to violate his holy character, especially his *justice* (Ex. 20:4–6; 34:5–7; Num. 14:18; Rom. 3:25–26). God is holy, and because of who he is, he had to punish sin and separate sin from himself. God is not free to act out of character; to do so would be to sin. For example, God cannot lie (Heb. 6:18; cf. Num. 23:19; Titus 1:2). Similarly, God cannot leave sin unpunished.

Someone may think God should have destroyed everything immediately and ended it all. But this would have violated both his mercy and his plan for man to establish his kingdom on earth. No one would have been saved—not Adam or Eve or all the others who were born during the following millennia. God carried out justice—a justice that ultimately resulted in the incarnation, crucifixion, and resurrection of his Son in our place that we might be saved (Rom. 3:21–26).

Third, consider the victory of Jesus. Why did God not put an end to evil after Jesus conquered sin, Satan, and death through his crucifixion and resurrection? Why does Jesus not return now and establish the final form of his eternal kingdom? Scripture provides a clear answer to this question. We are told that God is waiting until the gospel is preached to the whole world (Matt. 24:14), waiting for the full number of his elect to be saved (Rom. 11:25–26), that he is patiently waiting for more people to repent and believe.

> The Lord is not slow about His promise, as some count slowness, but is patient toward you, not wishing for any to perish but for all to come to repentance. (2 Peter 3:9 NASB)

If a non-Christian challenges us with this question, we can assure him he would not really want God to put an end to all evil right now, because that would leave him with no opportunity for salvation!

Fourth, look at the creation of the spirit world. Someone might push us back another step and ask why God allowed Satan to fall or why God created him in the first place if he knew he was going to fall. Scripture indicates that Satan was an angel who rebelled and fell, along with a large group of rebellious angels (Isa. 14:12; Matt. 25:41; Jude 9; Rev. 12:9). These fallen angels most likely are to be identified with the "demons" mentioned infrequently in the Old Testament and New Testament epistles (Deut. 32:17; Ps. 106: 36–37; 1 Cor. 10:20–21; 1 Tim. 4:1; James 2:19; cf. Eph. 6:12) but frequently in the Gospels (e.g., Luke 4:33, 35; 7:33; 8:2 passim). Although our answers are basically the same as we have given regarding man, we must realize that the Bible does not say a great deal about the origin and fall of Satan.

God's character was the same before creation, and therefore we must conclude that he did not want the spirits to worship him in a forced, inevitable, or mechanical way.

In summary, we have looked briefly at key moments in history, and we can understand (in our severely incomplete way) why God's way has always been the best. In the plan of redemption, he has made known his "manifold wisdom" according to his "eternal purpose" in Christ (Eph. 3:10–11).

4) God brings forth good from evil and uses evil to accomplish his purposes. It is absolutely crucial to keep in mind that for Christians, God uses all that happens to us—good and bad things—to conform us to the image of Christ. Romans 8 explains this clearly. Paul shows that God's purpose for us is that we become like his Son Jesus Christ. He does not promise material prosperity or relief from suffering but spiritual blessing. All of our experiences help us grow spiritually.

> And we know that God causes all things to work together for good to those who love God, to those who are called according to His purpose. For those whom He foreknew, He also predestined to become conformed to the image of His Son, so that He would be the firstborn among many brethren; and these whom He predestined, He also called; and these whom He called, He also justified; and these whom He justified, He also glorified. (Rom. 8:28–30)

Paul's argument is that if God gave his own Son for us, there is no limit to what he will do for us!

> What then shall we say to these things? If God is for us, who is against us? He who did not spare His own Son, but delivered Him over for us all, how will He not also with Him freely give us all things? (Rom. 8:31–32)

It is not fair to complain to God about evil in the world, when he has kept nothing back in his plan to conquer evil, not even his own Son. Paul concludes the eighth chapter of Romans by stating emphatically and poetically that no creature and no thing can separate us from God's love in Jesus Christ.

God does not always explain the specific purposes behind any particular suffering. We must trust that our sufferings have a good purpose in God's divine plan for us. This is the lesson we learn from the book of Job. Job was a righteous man, but God allowed Satan to afflict him in order to test his faithfulness. Job lost his possessions, his family, and his health. Job's three friends tried to convince him that he suffered these tragedies because he had done something especially bad. However, Job knew this was not the case, and he questioned why he was suffering. He wanted the Lord to explain why he, an innocent man, was suffering. If we analyze it a little, we can understand why God did not want to tell Job the reason he was suffering—it was a test. Imagine that God had told Job, "Be patient! I'm trying to prove to Satan that you serve me because you love me, not because I have blessed you with prosperity!" It would have made things easier for Job, but it would have invalidated the test.

At the end of the book (Job 38–41), the Lord appears to Job, but he does not answer Job's question in the manner Job wished. Instead, God queries Job about his sovereign power in creation. Where were you when I laid the foundations of the world? (Job 38:4). Do you know where light comes from? (Job 38:19). Have you seen the ostrich, so stupid that she hides her eggs in the sand, but when she runs, not even the horse can keep up with her? (Job 39:13–18). What was God trying to teach Job by asking these questions? He was reorienting Job by reminding him that he was a creature and God was the creator, in a manner reminiscent of

Paul's argument in Romans 9:19–21. There are many things we do not understand. Why, then, should we be surprised that we do not understand the divine purposes behind our personal sufferings? Job needed to accept the fact that the sovereign creator was good and just, even though he did not understand God's purposes. The existence of suffering does not disprove the fact that God is all-powerful (omnipotent) and all-good (omnibenevolent) at the same time.

The cross of Christ is the best example of this. Although Satan and the people who crucified Jesus meant to destroy him, God purposed this to happen in order to save us (Acts 2:23–24; 4:27–28). Jesus' crucifixion is the most horrible and most wonderful thing that has ever happened. As Augustine said, God would not permit any evil unless he can bring good out of it.[7]

This principle can be applied to all life and history, not merely to the spiritual blessings Christians experience. God has a wonderful purpose for history—the establishment of a perfect kingdom of righteousness, peace, and joy (Rom. 14:17; Rev. 21–22). I like the popular illustration of the tapestry. When we view it from below with all the threads hanging loose, we cannot appreciate the beauty of the artwork. When we see it from above, we can appreciate its beauty and intricate design. Similarly, God sees history from above, and he is guiding the process to create an amazingly beautiful result, according to his perfect design.

5) Events may have multiple actors. Not only is God sovereignly involved in them, but we may be involved, other people may be involved, and even Satan. We may be responsible for some of our own suffering. If I were to get drunk, I certainly should not blame God for my headache the next morning! On the other hand, sometimes other people cause our suffering, as in the case of Joseph when his brothers sold him as a slave (Gen.

7. Augustine, *Enchiridion*, 3, *Confessions and Enchiridion*, 342.

37:18–36). Also, although we should avoid attributing too much power to Satan, we know he is constantly fighting to destroy God's purposes. When Peter tried to discourage Jesus from going to Jerusalem where he would die, Jesus said to him, "Get behind me, Satan!" (Matt. 16:23). 1 Peter 5:8 says Satan is

> prowling around like a roaring lion looking for someone to devour.

Paul says:

> For our struggle is not against flesh and blood, but against the rulers, against the authorities, against the powers of this dark world and against the spiritual forces of evil in the heavenly realms. (Eph. 6:12)

Each of these possible actors may have a distinct intention. The Lord always has a good purpose in everything, and Satan always has an evil purpose. We and other people have a mixture of motives, both good and bad.

Therefore, when we ask, "Who caused this suffering?" we must be careful. Sometimes, we give an insensitive answer and simply attribute it to God. Others may leave God out of the picture and simply blame Satan. The Bible provides a more complex answer.

Someone might ask, "If there is a mixture of good intentions and evil intentions in every event, how then should we react to suffering? Should I be happy or sad?" The story of Joseph in Genesis illustrates how we should react to suffering, taking into account both the negative and the positive causes, as well as the nature of sin and the sovereignty of God. Joseph's brothers had betrayed him, selling him as a slave. Nevertheless, God used Joseph in Egypt to store up wheat in order to save lives during the famine. When Joseph revealed his identity to his brothers, he neither dismissed their sin nor forgot God's sovereign purpose. He said,

> You intended to harm me, but God intended it for good to accomplish what is now being done, the saving of many lives. (Gen. 50:20 NIV)

Some interpret the verse "Give thanks *in* all circumstances" (1 Thess. 5:18), as though it said "Give thanks *for* all circumstances." However, there is a difference. This verse encourages us to be thankful for what God will do through our suffering. At the same time, it permits us to recognize that suffering also is a result of the fall. Just as we experience a mixture of emotions in many circumstances of life, we also can have a mixture of reactions to suffering. For example, when our children went off to the university, my wife and I were sad because we were going to miss them, but we were happy because they were beginning a new stage in their lives and because they had the privilege of studying. In the same way, we can follow Joseph's example of seeing evil as evil, while rejoicing in the fact that God will bring good out of it.

When young Joni Eareckson dove into shallow water in the Chesapeake Bay one July afternoon in 1967, she hit her head on a rock and was paralyzed from her neck to her toes.[8] Obviously, she would like to be healed, and she has had no reservations about saying that she has been disappointed many times while expecting God to heal her. But she also has learned to accept her condition and to recognize that the Lord has used it for many positive purposes.[9]

Jesus is the best example of how we should face suffering. Although Jesus did not look forward to his death, he "endured the cross" in anticipation of the "joy set before Him" (Heb. 12:2).

8. Joni Eareckson Tada, *Joni, an Unforgettable Story* (Grand Rapids: Zondervan, 2001), 13–14.

9. Joni Eareckson Tada, *A Step Further* (Grand Rapids: Zondervan, 1980), 115–46.

We, too, can be encouraged by the promise that one day "He will wipe away every tear from their eyes; and there will no longer be any death; there will no longer be any mourning, or crying, or pain" (Rev. 21:4).

6) Sickness and natural disasters have secondary causes and are the result of the fall. In a way, this is to say there may be still another "actor" in some events, not a person, but the consequences the fall brought to the creation. While maintaining a biblical view of the sovereignty of God, we should avoid an extreme Islamic fatalistic perspective.

The Bible teaches that God is the *ultimate* cause of all that happens in his creation but not always the *direct* cause. Theologians make a distinction between God's direct providence and his use of "secondary causes" or "means." Weather, for example, normally follows the "means" of the physical patterns and processes God established at creation. The same can be said about the way our physical bodies function and about the natural laws related to our health.

> God, in His ordinary providence, makes use of means, yet is free to work without, above, and against them, at His pleasure. (WCF, 5.3).

Without denying God's complete sovereign control of all things, the Bible also teaches that God set many things into motion to follow the patterns he gave them. God speaks to Job about the "laws of the heavens" (Job 38:33 NIV). For example, God placed the planets in their orbits, established the law of gravity, the characteristics of plant and animal growth, and the patterns of weather.

> When I consider your heavens,
> the work of your fingers,
> the moon and the stars,
> which you have *set in place*. (Ps. 8:3 NIV)

According to Proverbs 8, God greatly *enjoyed* making things, and his creative wisdom is evident everywhere in his planned and orderly universe. This is why scientists marvel at the wonder of nature, and this is why most things are normally predictable. Note that the speaker in the following passage is the personification of "wisdom," who is identified with God.

> I was there when he *set the heavens in place*, when he marked out the horizon on the face of the deep, when he established the clouds above and fixed securely the fountains of the deep, when he gave the sea its boundary so the waters would not overstep his command, and when he marked out the foundations of the earth. Then I was the craftsman at his side. I was filled with delight day after day, rejoicing always in his presence, rejoicing in his whole world and delighting in mankind. (Prov. 8:27–31 NIV)

This is neither deism nor fatalism, because our God is a personal, loving God who guides history to a positive end. Also, sometimes God interrupts "natural laws"; he intervenes whenever he wants to and changes the normal patterns. He can stop time, calm storms, hold back oceans, and send fire to burn entire cities. Normally, however, he allows things to follow their "natural" courses. If a man walks off the roof of a ten-story building, we would attribute his fall to gravity, rather than imagining God grabbed him and pulled him to the earth.

The problem is that due to sin and God's curse on creation, the proper functioning of these created natural patterns has been corrupted. Now creation is in conflict with itself, causing disasters and sickness. Paul explains that the creation is "groaning" as it waits to be renewed.

> For I consider that the sufferings of this present time are not worthy to be compared with the glory that is to be revealed to us. For the anxious longing of the creation waits eagerly for the revealing of the sons of God. For the creation was subjected to futility, not willingly,

> but because of Him who subjected it, in hope that the creation itself also will be set free from its slavery to corruption into the freedom of the glory of the children of God. For we know that the whole creation groans and suffers the pains of childbirth together until now. (Rom. 8:18–22)

Therefore, we need to be careful about explaining natural disasters and sickness. When Hurricane Katrina hit New Orleans, Christians speculated about God's reasons for allowing or causing this terrible event. Some suggested this was God's punishment on a sinful city that celebrates *Mardi Gras*. But it is not our place to make such judgments. Why would God punish this city and not others? Is there not enough sin in any city to deserve a hurricane? Are we going to say God is punishing Mexico and Chile with earthquakes? Are we supposed to conclude that God is *blessing* Muslim or Buddhist countries when they are *not* suffering such tragedies or when their economies prosper? Is the poverty in Africa God's punishment for something? Where do we stop with these judgments?

The same applies to sickness. Sometimes we look for a particular sin as the cause of our infirmities. How many women have felt they are being punished when they lose a child?[10] But as mentioned above, we should not assume we know the specific reasons God has for allowing a certain suffering. When the disciples asked Jesus who had sinned, the blind man or his parents, Jesus answered, "Neither

10. Sometimes people refer to the fact that David's baby died as a punishment for his sin with Bathsheba (2 Sam. 12:15–23) and conclude they also are being punished in a similar way. But we need to keep in mind that David was punished more severely because he was the king of Israel and his sin was going to "give occasion to the enemies of the Lord to blaspheme" (2 Sam. 12:14). Also, while the Lord still punishes sin and disciplines his children (Acts 5:1–5; Heb. 12:6–7), there is a greater manifestation of grace in the New Testament age (John 1:16–17; Heb. 4:16; 8:6; 10:19–22). John Calvin said that in the Old Testament God more frequently used temporal means to show both his blessing and his wrath (*Institutes*, 2.11.3) and that now "the graces of the Spirit [are] more liberally bestowed than they had previously been" (*Institutes*, 2.11.14).

this man nor his parents sinned, but this happened so that the work of God might be displayed in his life" (John 9:3).

In summary, sickness and natural disasters are caused by the corrupting effects of the fall, and they have secondary causes. Of course, God is sovereign over all that happens, but we must include secondary causes in our understanding of God's relationship to events in his creation in order to avoid a distorted view. We may still ask why God does not *stop* hurricanes or send them out to sea so no one is hurt. And we may ask why God allows us to be sick. But at least now we have a more precise understanding of how these aspects of the creation operate, and we can talk about such events with a less simplistic perspective. Again, it is not our place to speculate about why God allowed any particular tragedy to occur.

7) Time is a complete package of interdependent moments. I believe the concept of time helps us accept the two-sided mystery of providence and freedom, as well as the problem of evil—maybe not *comprehend* it but *accept* it. Have you ever thought about the relativity of time? What if an astronomer happened to be watching a star just as it burned out? When did it really burn out? From his perspective on earth, it just occurred, but if the star is 400 light years away, then you also could say it happened 400 years ago. From the perspective of a star 400 light years away, what we are doing now will not "happen" for 400 years. When did the events occur there? It all depends on your vantage point.

Things get more complicated when we learn, thanks to Einstein, that time and speed and mass are all interdependent. When an astronaut leaves the earth going very fast, time slows down for him. According to the theory of relativity, Newton's laws, such as *distance = rate x time,* are practical but not *exact*.

Einstein said, "The past, present and future are only illusions, even if stubborn ones."[11] Scientists are now recognizing that time is a *package*. Paul Davies, an Australian physicist, says,

> The most straightforward conclusion is that both past and future are fixed. For this reason, physicists prefer to think of time as laid out in its entirety—a timescape, analogous to a landscape—with all past and future events located there together. It is a notion sometimes referred to as block time. Completely absent from this description of nature is anything that singles out a privileged special moment as the present or any process that would systematically turn future events into present, then past, events. In short, the time of the physicist does not pass or flow.[12]

This makes a lot of sense, especially when we include God in the picture. He is the only one who understands time and space and who can see how it all fits together—past, present, and future. For man, time is relative, but God is the final reference point for everything. This gives new meaning to the verse we quoted above:

> But do not let this one fact escape your notice, beloved, that with the Lord one day is like a thousand years, and a thousand years like one day. (2 Peter 3:8)

Have you ever read a science fiction book or seen a movie about going back in time? When people go back, they can change their decisions, but somehow events always result in the same future. They have to, or else the starting context of the movie would change and they would self-destruct! For example, in the movie *Back to the Future*, Marty McFly, the young man portrayed by Michael J. Fox, goes back in time and watches his parents fall in love. If something changes to keep them from falling in love, he will cease to exist!

11. Quoted in Paul Davies, "That Mysterious Flow," *Scientific American* (September, 2002), 41.

12. Davies, "That Mysterious Flow," 42.

This points to the profound truth that just as the whole material universe is interdependent, so, too, are all the moments of history. The solar system cannot hold together unless all the pieces function together properly with the right force of gravity. As Nancy Pearcey says, all the cosmic "dials" are set just perfectly for life.[13] Each atom is like a tiny universe in which each piece fits together perfectly. In a similar way, all time is interconnected, and only God sees the whole picture. You cannot remove any event without destroying the final outcome. Even the events that seem bad to us somehow are a necessary part of God's overall plan. The best example is the crucifixion of Christ. From one perspective, Christ's crucifixion was an evil event (Acts 2:23; 4:25–27). From another perspective, it was one of the essential events in God's plan of redemption (Acts 2:23; 4:28).

At the risk of being misunderstood, for God, watching history must be somewhat like watching a movie that goes back in time. He already knows how it will turn out. In fact, he is the one who made the movie!

When we live out the moments of history, we make plans and decisions, but we cannot change the ultimate course of events. I cannot think of a better way to express this than the pithy proverb: "The mind of man plans his way, but the Lord directs his steps" (Prov. 16:9). Thankfully, we do not have to understand this in order to live our lives for God's glory. We are only required to trust him, do what he says, and leave the consequences up to him.

8) God does all things for his own glory. We are not finished with our answer until we come back to God's glory as his final motive for all he does, as we mentioned in a previous section. When I was a young boy, I remember hearing at church that God did all things for his own glory. I also had memorized the first question of the Westminster Shorter Catechism:

13. Pearcey, *Total Truth*, 189.

> Question 1. What is the chief end of man? Answer: Man's chief end is to glorify God and to enjoy Him forever.

I remember asking my mother why it was right for God to do everything for his own glory but that it was wrong for me to do anything for my own glory. She thought a moment and simply said, "I guess because he is God." I still cannot think of a better answer.

When the disciples asked Jesus about the blind man, he explained that he had been born that way to show God's power.

> Jesus answered, "It is not this man's sin or his parents' sin that made him blind. This man was born blind so that God's power could be shown in him." (John 9:3 NCV)

When Lazarus died, Jesus said it was for God's glory.

> But when Jesus heard this, He said, "This sickness is not to end in death, but for the glory of God, so that the Son of God may be glorified by it." (John 11:4)

When the heavens are opened in the book of Revelation, we see the ultimate purpose of all creation.

> Worthy are You, our Lord and our God, to receive glory and honor and power; for You created all things, and because of Your will they existed, and were created. (Rev. 4:11)

Jesus' most intimate prayer in John 17 reveals the ultimate motive for all he does.

> Jesus spoke these things; and lifting up His eyes to heaven, He said, "Father, the hour has come; glorify Your Son, that the Son may glorify You, even as You gave Him authority over all flesh, that to all whom You have given Him, He may give eternal life. This is eternal life, that they may know You, the only true God, and Jesus Christ whom You have sent. I glorified You on the earth, having accom-

> plished the work which You have given Me to do. Now, Father, glorify Me together with Yourself, with the glory which I had with You before the world was." (John 17:1–5)

A key aspect of the way Jesus glorifies the Father is by accomplishing salvation. This was planned from all eternity. Peter says Jesus was "delivered over by the predetermined plan and foreknowledge of God" (Acts 2:23). Furthermore, his mission cannot be separated from his nature. He did not just become the kind of Lord who saves after the fall occurred. He is "the same, yesterday and today, and forever" (Heb.13:8). The fall and redemption occurred so that God would be fully glorified.

In summary, evil exists because God in his wisdom allows it. There is nothing evil in God's nature, and it is not evil to allow evil to exist. It is in perfect accord with God's character to allow evil to exist for a good purpose. He chose to give free will to man, to permit a struggle between good and evil, to triumph as Savior, and to establish his eternal kingdom of righteousness, peace, and joy. He has everything under control, and his plan is perfect.

Expose his presuppositions. There are many erroneous assumptions made by non-Christians when they challenge us with the problem of evil. For example, Einstein understood the Christian view of God's providence to be more like fatalism. Thus man's free will is not taken into account.[14] Others assume evil actually is part of the creation.

But there are deeper presuppositions we might not normally consider. For example, the non-Christian assumes he has a right to judge God. He also assumes we should be able to understand everything. He thinks that if Christians cannot give a completely satisfactory answer to just one question, then our whole belief system is invalidated. However, within our worldview we have

14. Colson, *How Now Shall We Live?*, 207.

no problem recognizing that we do not have completely satisfactory answers for everything. We can offer good answers, but as finite creatures we can never see the complete picture. The partial answers we have given leave me satisfied, and if they are not quite in focus, then God has even better answers!

Navigate through his inconsistencies. We cannot adopt the non-Christian belief system and accept its postulates. However, we can reason with the non-Christian and show him that if we assume his presuppositions are true, this leads to disastrous contradictions. For example, if he holds to a monistic view of the world, he loses the right to make a moral judgment about God or anybody else, because his worldview does not support moral absolutes. In fact, monism invalidates his own thoughts in general.

Furthermore, we can challenge the non-Christian to explain the existence of evil according to his own scheme. For example, if he thinks evolution is true, where did evil come from? How did things turn against themselves in this natural process? If he thinks that Hegel is right about dialectical idealism, how could the one Absolute Mind turn against itself? It would be like a plant strangling itself! Dualism postulates that good and evil have always existed in parallel. But dualism erases the distinction between good and evil. If there is no God, and if these two tendencies—good and evil—are eternal, what makes one tendency better than the other? That is why Taoism pictures the black and the white within the same circle; if they are both eternal, then they are really one.

What is the conclusion? As the song says,

> Don't you know the devil is in me and God she is too
> my Yin hits my Yang But what the heck ya gonna do
> I choose a rocky ass path but that's how I like it
> life's a bowl of punch go ahead and spike it.[15]

If there are no ethical absolutes, how can non-Christians say God is doing something "wrong" or even that "evil" exists? No worldview other than Christianity can come close to explaining the problem of evil, and certainly no other system offers a solution to the problem of evil.

At some point in our conversation about the problem of evil, we should bring up the "problem of good." Whereas non-Christians challenge us to explain the existence of evil within our scheme, we can challenge them to explain the presence of good in their scheme. In other words, if everything just happens to exist by chance or as a result of an impersonal process, then where does love come from or joy?

Direct him to Christ. All theology comes back to Christ. The real explanation of evil must focus on him. He is the solution to the problem of evil. God conquers evil by turning it on himself in his Son.

One of the best sermons I have heard was at an Urbana InterVarsity Conference. Dr. Edmund Clowney, the late president of Westminster Theological Seminary, spoke about human suffering and despair.[16] He led us through the history of suffering and existentialist anxiety, and after every point he groaned, "Why?" By the time he was nearing the end of the sermon, we were ready to weep as we sat on the edge of our seats, waiting for him to answer the question, "Why?" Then he gently turned us to

15. 311, "Plain," http://www.najical.com/311/03ahydro.htm.
16. Edmund P. Clowney, "Jesus Christ and the Lostness of Man," 1973.

Jesus. He said, "Take your *whys* to Jesus, leave them at the foot of the cross, and listen to him ask 'why?' 'My God, my God, *why* have you forsaken me?' Jesus understands our struggles and has suffered in our place to relieve our pain. Let him ask the question for you." Believe me, if I had not been a Christian, I would have become one at that moment!

One of my favorite passages from C. S. Lewis's *Chronicles of Narnia* is the scene where Jill encounters Aslan the lion at the edge of the stream. She needs water, but the lion frightens her.

> "Are you not thirsty?" said the Lion.
>
> "I'm dying of thirst," said Jill.
>
> "Then drink," said the Lion.
>
> "May I—could I—would you mind going away while I do?" said Jill.
>
> The Lion answered this only by a look and a very low growl. And as Jill gazed at its motionless bulk, she realized that she might as well have asked the whole mountain to move aside for her convenience. The delicious rippling noise of the stream was driving her nearly frantic.
>
> "Will you promise not to—do anything to me, if I do come?" said Jill.
>
> "I make no promise," said the Lion.
>
> Jill was so thirsty now that, without noticing it, she had come a step nearer.
>
> "Do you eat girls?" she said.
>
> "I have swallowed up girls and boys, women and men, kings and emperors, cities and realms," said the Lion. It didn't say this as if it were boasting, nor as if it were sorry, nor as if it were angry. It just said it.
>
> "I daren't come and drink," said Jill.
>
> "Then you will die of thirst," said the Lion.
>
> "Oh dear!" said Jill, coming another step nearer. "I suppose I must go and look for another stream then."
>
> "There is no other stream," said the Lion.[17]

17. C. S. Lewis, *The Silver Chair* (New York: Harper Collins, 1953), 16–17.

God is sovereign, and he is not obligated to do things the way we prefer. Neither does he promise to answer all our questions. However, there is no other place to go for eternal life. There is no other God, and without him, we will die. His power and absolute control frighten us, but we know that we can trust him.

Group Exercise

Using the question about the problem of evil, have two students practice an apologetic dialogue using the steps of the "DEFEND" approach. One of them can play the role of someone who rejects Christianity because of the problem of evil. The other plays the role of a Christian sharing his faith. Talk about how to improve the defense of the faith.

Review Questions

1. According to the author, why did God not create man incapable of sin?
2. Explain the distinction that Jonathan Edwards makes between "natural liberty" and "moral liberty."
3. Explain Augustine's distinction of the four stages of man's relation to sin.
4. According to the author, why did God not create man with such strength of character that he would not be able to desire sin?
5. According to the author, why are we not immediately sanctified when we become Christians?
6. In what way is Jesus our "hero"?
7. In what way should we be spiritual "warriors"?
8. Why did God not destroy everything after the fall?
9. Why did God not put an end to all evil after Jesus won the victory in his death and resurrection?

10. Why did God allow Satan to fall?
11. What does Romans 8:18–30 teach us about God's dealing with evil?
12. Why is it not fair to complain to God about evil?
13. What does the book of Job teach us about understanding God's purposes in our suffering?
14. In what sense may events have "multiple actors," and how does this help us deal with the problem of suffering?
15. According to the author, how should we respond to suffering?
16. How should we explain sickness and natural disasters?
17. How does the Christian concept of time help us accept the mystery of God's providence and the freedom of man, as well as the problem of evil?
18. What is our final answer to the problem of evil? What is God's motive for everything he does?
19. According Dr. Edmund Clowney's sermon, what should we do with our questions regarding why God permits evil?
20. What does the story of Jill and Aslan the Lion, by C. S. Lewis, teach us about accepting some things we may not understand?

Questions for Reflection

1. Has the "problem of evil" been a source of doubt in your life? How have you dealt with it?
2. Has anything in this chapter helped you especially to deal with the problem of evil in your own mind or helped you learn to answer non-Christians? Explain how.
3. Do you feel you have taken your unanswered questions to the cross and left them with Christ?

Personal Postscript

As I make the last modifications to this manuscript, I am sitting in the room of a Korean guest house in Almaty, Kazakhstan, looking out at old grey buildings, an old red and white industrial smoke stack, and a new luxury hotel, which reflects the changes occurring here. I have just finished teaching some church leaders a course on the contents of this book. At lunch one day, one of the pastors asked me what experience I had in using apologetics. In my mind I thought of saying, "Not much! Not nearly enough!" I cannot help but feel a bit uneasy writing on this subject when I have not practiced more evangelism than I have. But I thought I should give him an answer that at least explains my profound interest in the subject. First, I believe my own doubts and spiritual pilgrimage have helped me understand others who are struggling. Second, I do have some years of pastoral and evangelistic experience. During my seminary years, I spent two summers at the Boardwalk Chapel in Wildwood, New Jersey, doing intensive evangelism. I was an associate pastor for two years in Silver Spring, Maryland. Then I was a missionary for twenty-one years in Chile, both teaching and planting churches. I have not done nearly enough, but I am not totally inexperienced. My hope is that others will benefit from reading this book and become more effective in defending the gospel.

BIBLIOGRAPHY

Anderson, J. N. D. *The World's Religions*. Grand Rapids: Eerdmans, 1968.

Anselm. *Proslogium; Monologium: An Appendix in Behalf of the Fool by Gaunilon; Cur Deus Homo*. Translated by Sidney Norton Deane. Chicago: The Open Court Publishing Co., 1903.

Aquinas, Thomas. Edited by Ralph McInerny. *Thomas Aquinas: Selected Writings*. London: Penguin Books, 1998.

Augustine. *Confessions and Enchridion*. Philadelphia: Westminster Press, 1955.

Bahnsen, Greg. *Van Til's Apologetic*. Phillipsburg, NJ: P&R Publishing, 1998.

Blank, Rodolfo. *Teología y misión en América Latina* [*Theology and Mission in Latin America*]. St. Louis, MO: Concordia, 1996.

Bonino, José Míguez. *Doing Theology in a Revolutionary Situation*. Philadelphia: Fortress, 1975, 1986.

———. "New Trends in Theology," *Duke Divinity School Review* 42 (Fall, 1997).

Borchert, Donald M., ed. *Encyclopedia of Philosophy*. 2nd ed. 10 vols. Detroit: Thomson Gale, 2006.

Brown, Colin. *Philosophy and the Christian Faith*. Downers Grove, IL: Inter-Varsity Press, 1969.

Calvin, John. *Institutes of the Christian Religion*. 2 vols. Edited by John T. McNeill. Translated by Ford Lewis Battles. Philadelphia: The Westminster Press, 1967.

Chesterton, G. K. *The Everlasting Man*. San Francisco: Ignatius Press, 1993.

———. *Saint Thomas Aquinas: "The Dumb Ox."* New York: Image Books, 1956.

Clark, Gordon. *Thales to Dewey*. Boston: Houghton Mifflin Co., 1957.

Colson, Charles and Nancy Pearcey. *How Now Shall We Live?* Wheaton, IL: Tyndale, 1999.

Copleston, Frederick. *A History of Philosophy*. 9 vols. Garden City, NY: Doubleday, 1962.

Cowan, Steven, ed. *Five Views on Apologetics.* Grand Rapids: Zondervan, 2000. Includes articles by Stanley N. Gundry, William Lane Craig, Paul D. Feinberg, Kelly James Clark, John Frame, and Gary Habermas.

Cruz, Antonio. *¿La Ciencia Encuentra a Dios?* [Does Science Find God?] Barcelona: CLIE, 2004.

———. *El cristiano en la aldea global.* Barcelona: CLIE, 2004.

———. *Darwin no mató a Dios.* Miami: Vida, 2005.

———. *Postmodernidad.* Barcelona: CLIE, 1996.

———. *Sociología: una desmitificación.* Barcelona: CLIE, 2001.

Darwin, Charles. *The Origin of Species by Means of Natural Selection.* Boston: Adamant Media Corporation, 2000.

Durant, Will. *The Story of Philosophy.* New York: Simon and Schuster, 2005.

Empiricus, Sextus. *Outlines of Scepticism.* Edited by Julia Annas and Jonathan Barnes. Cambridge: Cambridge University Press, 2000.

Frame, John. *Apologetics to the Glory of God: An Introduction.* Phillipsburg, NJ: P&R Publishing, 1994.

———. *Cornelius Van Til: An Analysis of His Thought.* Phillipsburg, NJ: P&R Publishing, 1995.

———. *The Doctrine of the Knowledge of God.* Phillipsburg, NJ: P&R Publishing, 1987.

Geisler, Norman. *Baker Encyclopedia of Christian Apologetics.* Grand Rapids: Baker Books, 1999.

———. *Christian Apologetics.* Grand Rapids: Baker Book House, 1976.

Geisler, Norman and Ron Brooks. *When Skeptics Ask.* Grand Rapids: Baker Books, 1990.

Giannini, Humberto. *Esbozo para una Historia de la Filosofía.* [*Outline of a History of Philosophy*] Santiago, Chile: Talleres Vera y Giannini, 1981.

Gish, Duane. *Evolution: The Challenge of the Fossil Record.* San Diego: Master Books Pub., 1985. (Later updated version: *The Fossils Still Say No!* Institute For Creation Research, 1996.) Spanish version: *Creación, evolución, y el registro fósil.* Barcelona: CLIE, 1979.

Graham, Gordon. *Eight Theories of Ethics.* London: Routledge, 2004.

Grudem, Wayne. *Systematic Theology.* Leicester, England: InterVarsity Press and Grand Rapids: Zondervan, 2000.

Groothuis, Douglas R. *Truth Decay.* Downers Grove: IL: InterVarsity Press, 2000.

———. *Unmasking the New Age.* Downers Grove, IL: InterVarsity Press, 1986.

Hegel, G. W. F. *The Phenomenology of Mind*. Translated by J. B. Baillie. London: Swan Sonnenshein and Co., 1910. Republished by Routledge, 2004.

Hume, David. *An Enquiry Concerning Human Understanding: A Critical Edition*. Edited by Tom L. Beauchamp. Oxford: Oxford University Press, 1999.

Hutchins, Robert Maynard, ed. *Great Books of the Western World*. 54 vols. Chicago: Encyclopaedia Britannica, Inc., 1952.

Jones, Peter. *The Gnostic Empire Strikes Back: An Old Heresy for the New Age*. Phillipsburg, NJ: P&R Publishing, 1992.

———. *Stolen Identity: The Conspiracy to Reinvent Jesus*. Colorado Springs: David C. Cook, 2006.

Kant, Immanuel. *Critique of Pure Reason*. Translated by J. M. D. Meiklejohn. New York: Prometheus Books, 1990.

Kierkegaard, Søren. *A Kierkegaard Anthology*. Edited by Robert Bretall. New York: Random House, 1946.

Kreeft, Peter and Ronald K. Tacelli. *Handbook of Christian Apologetics*. Downers Grove: IL: InterVarsity Press, 1994.

Lavine, T. Z. *From Socrates to Sartre: The Philosophic Quest*. New York: Bantam Books, 1984.

Lewis, C. S. *The Great Divorce*. San Francisco: Harper Collins, 2000 (original copyright, 1946).

———. *Mere Christianity*. New York: HarperCollins, 2001 (original copyright, 1952).

———. *Miracles*. Grand Rapids: Zondervan, 1968.

———. *The Problem of Pain*. New York: Simon & Schuster. 1996.

———. *The Silver Chair*. New York: Harper Collins, 1953.

———. *Surprised by Joy*. Harcourt Brace and Company, 1955.

Little, Paul. *Know Why You Believe*. Downers Grove, IL: InterVarsity Press, 2000.

MacArthur, John. *The Truth War: Fighting for Certainty in an Age of Deception*. Nashville: Thomas Nelson, 2007.

Marías, Julián. *History of Philosophy*. Translated by Stanley Appelbaum and C. Clarence. Mineola, NY: Dover Publications, 1967.

McDowell, Josh. *Evidence that Demands a Verdict*. San Bernardino, CA: Here's Life Publishers, Inc., 1979.

———. *More Evidence that Demands a Verdict*. San Bernardino, CA: Here's Life Publishers, Inc., 1981.

———. *New Evidence that Demands a Verdict*. Nashville: Thomas Nelson, 1999.

McDowell, Josh and Don Stewart. *Answers to Tough Questions Skeptics Ask About the Christian Faith*. San Bernardino, CA: Here's Life Publishers, Inc., 1983.

Miller, Elliot. *A Crash Course on the New Age Movement*. Grand Rapids: Baker, 1989.

Moreland, J. P. and John Mark Reynolds, eds. *Three Views on Creation and Evolution*. Grand Rapids: Zondervan, 1999.

Morris, Henry M. *Science and the Bible*. Chicago: Moody Press, 1986.

Morris, Henry and John Whitcomb. *The Genesis Flood*. Phillipsburg, NJ: P&R Publishing, 1989.

Mumma, Howard. *Albert Camus and the Minister*. Brewster, MA: Paraclete Press, 2000.

Nietzsche, Friedrich. *The Gay Science*. Cambridge: Cambridge University Press, 2001.

Packer, J. I. *God Has Spoken: Revelation and the Bible*. 3rd ed. Grand Rapids: Baker, 1993.

———. *Fundamentalism and the Word of God*. Leicester: Inter-Varsity Fellowship, 1958.

Pearcey, Nancy. *Total Truth: Liberating Christianity from its Cultural Captivity*. Wheaton, IL: Crossway, 2005.

Pinnock, Clark. *Set Forth Your Case*. Phillipsburg, NJ: P&R Publishing, 1967.

Placher, William C. *Readings in the History of Christian Theology, Volume 1, From its Beginnings to the Eve of the Reformation*. Philadelphia: Westminster Press, 1988.

Plantinga, Alvin. *The Analytical Theist: An Alvin Plantinga Reader*. Grand Rapids: Eerdmans, 1998.

———. *God, Freedom, and Evil*. Grand Rapids: Eerdmans, 1977.

———. *God and Other Minds: A Study of the Rational Justification of Belief in God*. Cornell University Press, 1990.

Pratt, Richard. *Every Thought Captive: A Study Manual for the Defense of Christian Truth*. Phillipsburg, NJ: P&R Publishing, 1979.

Raymond, Robert. *A New Systematic Theology of the Christian Faith*. Nashville: Thomas Nelson Publishers, 1998.

Rookmaaker, H. R. *Modern Art and the Death of a Culture*. Downers Grove, IL: InterVarsity Press, 1970.

Rushdoony, Rousas. *By What Standard*. Philadelphia: Presbyterian and Reformed, 1965.

Sade, Marquis de. *The Complete Marquis de Sade.* Translated by Paul J. Gillette. Los Angeles: Holloway House, 2005.

———. *Justine, Philosophy in the Bedroom, and Other Writings.* Translated by Austryn Wainhouse and Richard Seaver. Jackson, TN: Grove Press, 1994.

Schaeffer, Francis. *Escape from Reason.* Wheaton, IL: InterVarsity Press: 1968.

———. *Francis A. Schaeffer Trilogy—The God Who Is There, Escape from Reason,* and *He Is There and He Is Not Silent*. Wheaton, IL: Crossway Books, 1990.

———. *The God Who Is There*. Downers Grove, IL: InterVarsity Press, 1968. New edition with preface by James Sire, 1998.

———. *He Is There and He Is Not Silent*. Wheaton, IL: Tyndale, 1980.

Sire, James. *A Little Primer on Humble Apologetics*. Downers Grove, IL: InterVarsity Press, 2006.

———. *The Universe Next Door: A Basic World View Catalogue.* Downers Grove, IL: InterVarsity Press, 1997.

———. *Why Should Anyone Believe Anything at All*? Downers Grove, IL: InterVarsity Press, 1994.

Sookhedeo, Patrick. *A Christian's Pocket Guide to Islam*. Fearn, Ross-Shire, Scotland: Christian Focus Publications, 2001.

Sproul, R. C. *Defending Your Faith: An Introduction to Apologetics.* Wheaton, IL: Crossway, 2003.

Sproul, R. C., Arthur Lindsley, and John Gerstner. *Classical Apologetics: A Rational Defense of the Christian Faith and a Critique of Presuppositional Apologetics*. Grand Rapids: Zondervan, 1984.

Thilly, Frank and Ledger Wood. *A History of Philosophy*. New York: Henry Holt and Co., 1959.

Van Til, Cornelius. *Christian Apologetics*. Phillipsburg, NJ: Presbyterian and Reformed Publishing, 1976.

———. *The Defense of the Faith*. Phillipsburg, NJ: Presbyterian and Reformed Publishing, 1979.

Woodbridge, John, ed. *Great Leaders of the Christian Church*. Chicago: Moody Press, 1988.

Yancey, Philip. *Soul Survivor: How My Faith Survived the Church*. New York: Doubleday, 2001.

Zacharias, Ravi. *Can Man Live Without God*? Nashville: W. Publishing Group, 1994.

Index of Scripture

Index of Personal Names

Index of Subjects

Recommended Resources for Exploring Apologists and Apologetics

Asterisks indicate books that are especially recommended.

Philosophy

Borchert, Donald M., ed. *Encyclopedia of Philosophy*. 2nd ed. 10 vols. Detroit: Thomson Gale, 2006.

* Brown, Colin. *Philosophy and the Christian Faith*. Downers Grove, IL: InterVarsity Press, 1969. Analysis of Western philosophy from a Christian perspective.

Copleston, Frederick. *A History of Philosophy*. 9 vols. Garden City, NY: Doubleday, 1962. Considered by many to be the best and most complete review of philosophy. The author is Roman Catholic.

Durant, Will. *The Story of Philosophy*. New York: Simon and Schuster, 2005. Easy to understand.

Hutchins, Robert Maynard, ed. *Great Books of the Western World*. 54 vols. Chicago: Encyclopaedia Britannica, Inc., 1952.

Lavine, T. Z. *From Socrates to Sartre: The Philosophic Quest*. New York: Bantam Books, 1984.

Marías, Julián. *History of Philosophy*. Translated by Stanley Appelbaum and C. Clarence. Mineola, NY: Dover Publications, 1967. Serious, complete survey by a key Spanish thinker.

Thilly, Frank and Ledger Wood. *A History of Philosophy*. New York: Henry Holt and Co., 1959. Very complete, serious study.

World Relions

* Anderson, J. N. D. *The World's Religions.* Grand Rapids: Eerdmans, 1968. A Christian perspective.

Bowker, John. *World Religions: The Great Faiths Explored and Explained.* New York: Dorling Kindersley Publishing, 2006.

Smith, Huston. *The World's Religions: Our Great Wisdom Traditions.* New York: Harper Collins, 1991.

Sookhedeo, Patrick. *A Christian's Pocket Guide to Islam.* Fearn, Ross-Shire, Scotland: Christian Focus Publications, 2001.

Science

* "Answers in Genesis" web site: http://www.answersingenesis.org/ Conservative Christian, young earth perspective.

Gish, Duane. *Evolution: The Challenge of the Fossil Record.* San Diego: Master Books Pub., 1985. Later updated version: *The Fossils Still Say No!* Institute For Creation Research, 1996.

McGrath, Alister E. *The Science of God: An Introduction to Scientific Theology.* London: T&T Clark, 2004. Contemporary, evangelical "natural theology" by a well-known Oxford professor.

———. *A Scientific Theology: Nature.* London: T&T Clark, 2001.

———. *A Scientific Theology: Reality.* London: T&T Clark, 2002.

———. *A Scientific Theology: Theory.* London: T&T Clark, 2003.

Moreland, J. P. and John Mark Reynolds, eds. *Three Views on Creation and Evolution.* Grand Rapids: Zondervan, 1999.

Morris, Henry M. *Science and the Bible.* Chicago: Moody Press, 1986.

Morris, Henry and John Whitcomb. *The Genesis Flood.* Phillipsburg, NJ: P&R Publishing, 1989.

* "Reasons to Believe" web site: http://www.reasons.org/ Conservative Christian, old earth perspective.

Contemporary Culture

* Colson, Charles and Nancy Pearcey. *How Now Shall We Live?* Wheaton, IL: Tyndale, 1999. Challenge to develop a Christian worldview.

Guinness, Os. *Prophetic Untimeliness: A Challenge to the Idol of Relevance.* Grand Rapids: Baker, 2003.

Myers, Kenneth A. *All God's Children and Blue Suede Shoes.* Wheaton, IL: Crossway Books, 1989.

* Pearcey, Nancy. *Total Truth: Liberating Christianity from its Cultural Captivity.* Wheaton, IL: Crossway, 2005.

* Romanowski, William D. *Eyes Wide Open: Looking for God in Popular Culture.* Grand Rapids: Brazos Press/Baker, 2001.

* Rookmaaker, H. R. *Modern Art and the Death of a Culture.* Downers Grove, IL: InterVarsity Press, 1970. Brilliant Christian analysis of modern art, relating it to what we now call postmodernism.

Veith, Gene Edward, Jr. *Postmodern Times: A Christian Guide to Contemporary Thought and Culture.* Wheaton, IL: Crossway Books, 1994. An overview of the postmodern worldview.

Systematic Theology

* Berkhof, Louis. *Systematic Theology.* Grand Rapids: Eerdmans, 1996. Solidly biblical, Reformed, clear, and concise.

* Boice, James Montgomery. *Foundations of the Christian Faith.* Downers Grove, IL: InterVarsity Press, 1986. Basic Christian doctrine for lay readers.

Calvin, John. *Institutes of the Christian Religion.* 2 vols. Edited by John T. McNeill. Translated by Ford Lewis Battles. Philadelphia: The Westminster Press, 1967.

Frame, John. *The Doctrine of God: A Theology of Lordship.* Phillipsburg, NJ: P&R Publishing, 2002.

*———. *The Doctrine of the Knowledge of God.* Phillipsburg, NJ: P&R Publishing, 1987.

* Grudem, Wayne. *Systematic Theology.* Leicester, England: InterVarsity Press and Grand Rapids: Zondervan, 2000. Biblical, clear, and practical. The perspective is Reformed, baptistic, and moderately charismatic.

Raymond, Robert. *A New Systematic Theology of the Christian Faith.* Nashville: Thomas Nelson Publishers, 1998. Up-to-date Reformed perspective.

Apologetics

* Bahnsen, Greg. *Van Til's Apologetic.* Phillipsburg, NJ: P&R Publishing, 1998.

Chesterton, G. K. *The Everlasting Man.* San Francisco: Ignatius Press, 1993.

———. *Saint Thomas Aquinas: "The Dumb Ox."* New York: Image Books, 1956.

Cowan, Steven, ed. *Five Views on Apologetics.* Grand Rapids: Zondervan, 2000. Includes articles by Stanley N. Gundry, William Lane Craig, Paul D. Feinberg, Kelly James Clark, John Frame, and Gary Habermas.

* Frame, John. *Apologetics to the Glory of God: An Introduction.* Phillipsburg, NJ: P&R Publishing, 1994.

———. *Cornelius Van Til: An Analysis of His Thought.* Phillipsburg, NJ: P&R Publishing, 1995.

Geisler, Norman. *Christian Apologetics.* Grand Rapids: Baker Book House, 1976.

———. *Baker Encyclopedia of Christian Apologetics.* Grand Rapids: Baker Books, 1999.

———. and Ron Brooks. *When Skeptics Ask.* Grand Rapids: Baker Books, 1990.

Groothuis, Douglas R. *Unmasking the New Age.* Downers Grove, IL: InterVarsity Press, 1986.

*———. *Truth Decay.* Downers Grove: IL: InterVarsity Press, 2000. Analysis of postmodernism.

Jones, Peter. *The Gnostic Empire Strikes Back: An Old Heresy for the New Age.* Phillipsburg, NJ: P&R Publishing, 1992. Solid reformed perspective.

———. *Stolen Identity: The Conspiracy to Reinvent Jesus.* Colorado Springs: David C. Cook, 2006.

Kreeft, Peter and Ronald K. Tacelli. *Handbook of Christian Apologetics.* Downers Grove: IL: InterVarsity Press, 1994.

Lewis, C. S. *The Great Divorce.* San Francisco: Harper Collins, 2000 (original copyright, 1946).

———. *Mere Christianity.* New York: HarperCollins, 2001 (original copyright, 1952).

*———. *Miracles.* Grand Rapids: Zondervan, 1968.

*———. *The Problem of Pain.* New York: Simon & Schuster. 1996.

———. *The Silver Chair.* New York: Harper Collins, 1953.

———. *Surprised by Joy.* Harcourt Brace and Company, 1955.

Little, Paul. *Know Why You Believe.* Downers Grove, IL: InterVarsity Press, 2000.

MacArthur, John. *The Truth War: Fighting for Certainty in an Age of Deception.* Nashville: Thomas Nelson, 2007.

McDowell, Josh. *Evidence that Demands a Verdict.* San Bernardino, CA: Here's Life Publishers, Inc., 1979.

———. *More Evidence that Demands a Verdict.* San Bernardino, CA: Here's Life Publishers, Inc., 1981.

———. *New Evidence that Demands a Verdict.* Nashville: Thomas Nelson, 1999.

McDowell, Josh and Don Stewart. *Answers to Tough Questions Skeptics Ask About the Christian Faith.* San Bernardino, CA: Here's Life Publishers, Inc., 1983.

Miller, Elliot. *A Crash Course on the New Age Movement.* Grand Rapids: Baker, 1989.

Packer, J. I. *God Has Spoken: Revelation and the Bible.* 3rd ed. Grand Rapids: Baker, 1993. One of the most popular contemporary Reformed theologians—clear and practical.

———. *Fundamentalism and the Word of God.* Leicester: Inter-Varsity Fellowship, 1958.

Plantinga, Alvin. *The Analytical Theist: An Alvin Plantinga Reader.* Grand Rapids: Eerdmans, 1998. One of the best-known contemporary Protestant philosophers.

———. *God, Freedom, and Evil.* Grand Rapids: Eerdmans, 1977.

———. *God and Other Minds: A Study of the Rational Justification of Belief in God.* Cornell University Press, 1990.

* Pratt, Richard. *Every Thought Captive: A Study Manual for the Defense of Christian Truth.* Phillipsburg, NJ: P&R Publishing, 1979. Clear, simple, and practical manual that applies a Van Tilian approach to apologetics.

Schaeffer, Francis. *Escape from Reason.* Wheaton, IL: InterVarsity Press: 1968.

———. *Francis A. Schaeffer Trilogy—The God Who Is There, Escape from Reason,* and *He Is There and He Is Not Silent.* Wheaton, IL: Crossway Books, 1990.

*———. *He Is There and He Is Not Silent.* Wheaton, IL: Tyndale, 1980.

*———. *The God Who Is There.* Downers Grove, IL: InterVarsity Press, 1968. New edition with preface by James Sire, 1998.

Sire, James. *A Little Primer on Humble Apologetics.* Downers Grove, IL: InterVarsity Press, 2006.

*———. *The Universe Next Door: A Basic World View Catalogue.* Downers Grove, IL: InterVarsity Press, 1997.

———. *Why Should Anyone Believe Anything at All?* Downers Grove, IL: InterVarsity Press, 1994.

Sproul, R. C., Arthur Lindsley, and John Gerstner. *Classical Apologetics: A Rational Defense of the Christian Faith and a Critique of Presuppositional Apologetics.* Grand Rapids: Zondervan, 1984.

Sproul, R. C. *Defending Your Faith: An Introduction to Apologetics*. Wheaton, IL: Crossway, 2003.

Van Til, Cornelius. *Christian Apologetics*. Phillipsburg, NJ: Presbyterian and Reformed Publishing, 1976.

*———. *The Defense of the Faith*. Phillipsburg, NJ: Presbyterian and Reformed Publishing, 1979.

Zacharias, Ravi. *Can Man Live Without God?* Nashville: W. Publishing Group, 1994.

History

* Gonzalez, Justo. *Church History: An Essential Guide*. Nashville: Abingdon Press, 1996.

———. *The Story of Christianity*. 3 vols. New York: Harper Collins, 1984.

Latourette, Kenneth S. *A History of Christianity*. 2 vols. New York: Harper Collins, 1975.

Placher, William C. *Readings in the History of Christian Theology*. 3 vols. Philadelphia: Westminster Press, 1988.

Woodbridge, John, ed. *Great Leaders of the Christian Church*. Chicago: Moody Press, 1988.